FREDERICKSBURG
1862

SPECIAL CAMPAIGN SERIES. No. 3

FREDERICKSBURG

A Study in War

BY

MAJOR G. W. REDWAY

LATE NORTHAMPTONSHIRE REGIMENT
(RESERVE OF OFFICERS)

WITH FIVE MAPS

The Naval & Military Press Ltd

Published by

The Naval & Military Press Ltd
Unit 5 Riverside, Brambleside
Bellbrook Industrial Estate
Uckfield, East Sussex
TN22 1QQ England

Tel: +44 (0)1825 749494

www.naval-military-press.com
www.nmarchive.com

Front cover illustration:

During the Battle of Fredericksburg (December 13th, 1862) a crisis occurred on the Union side. When the brigade of General John C. Robinson assaulted the Confederate position on Prospect Hill, a counter attack threatened the Union guns while the generals horse was killed, pinning him to the ground. In this moment of confusion, Colonel Charles H. T. Collis rode to the front of his 114th Pennsylvania Infantry, took the regiments colours, rallied its men and led another attack. This action not only saved the guns but also won Collis the Medal of Honour.

In reprinting in facsimile from the original, any imperfections are inevitably reproduced and the quality may fall short of modern type and cartographic standards.

PREFACE

IT must be a primary object with every soldier to know exactly how war is carried on : how strategy is influenced, in its conception by politics and in its execution by tactics ; how both strategy and tactics are affected by *terrain*, by the seasons, by railways, telegraphy and sea power : how armies have been raised and organized, trained and led in battle ; how supplied with weapons and other means of defence, with food and clothing, ammunition and shelter ; how the sick and wounded are cared for ; how the waste of war is repaired.

The study of these matters in peace time can only be pursued seriously when we illustrate the subject continually by examples drawn from history. It is not by remembering maxims, by explaining military phrases or discussing general principles, that a soldier learns his trade ; he must probe deeply the problems of war, examine them in every detail, and never be content to accept the *ipse dixit* of any historian, however eminent in his day and generation, while actual evidence is available.

The following pages will, it is hoped, enable the student, with a minimum of trouble and the least possible expenditure of time, to become thoroughly familiar with the essentials of campaigning, by participating as it were in certain events that happened some forty years ago on the continent of America, in the decade that saw the battles of Magenta, Solferino and Sadowa in central Europe.

The campaigns of the great Civil War are especially fitted for study by the English-speaking soldier for several reasons; there exists a full description of every pitched battle in all its phases, the march orders and reconnaissance reports are also available. The names of persons and places are already familiar to the student, and records are accessible at first hand without the intervention of a translator. There are but few gaps that need filling up by aid of the imagination, and we have not to take into account any difference of race, method of training or armament on the part of the combatants, as in the case of " foreign " wars. The American armies were similarly conditioned in all respects, even to the extent of being commanded by officers who had been trained in the same military academy; and the official records of both belligerents have been printed without fear or favour side by side in that monumental publication just completed and entitled " War of the Rebellion."

Moreover, the American Civil War was in a certain sense a Renaissance; new methods of warfare were adopted, the Nation in Arms was made manifest; and from this period in the history of tactics we trace the appearance of heavy guns in the field, the genesis of modern cavalry, the establishment of signal and ambulance corps, and the use of hasty entrenchments, of field telegraphy, and of balloon reconnaissance.

PREFACE

The present volume presents a striking contrast to the story of an European campaign with which this Series commenced ; in place of the methodical strategy and forcing tactics of the Germans we must describe the puzzled flounderings of the Federal leaders ; instead of a disunited defence of the French frontier which in six weeks resulted in the unconditional surrender of a large army, we shall narrate the brilliant manœuvres by which Lee and his lieutenants kept the invaders of Virginia at bay until the Union government was at its wits' end and the Confederate cause almost won. The writer's task has been to examine many hundreds of letters and reports, written in the field and now preserved in the archives of the War Department at Washington, and, with such skill as he can command, produce for the Special Campaign Series a record of war which shall contain the Truth the whole Truth and nothing but the Truth, so far as that is possible in inditing the class of narrative which we call History.

CONTENTS

CHAPTER I

INTRODUCTORY

CHAPTER II

AFTER SHARPSBURG—REST AND RECRUITMENT—GENERAL LEE IN THE SHENANDOAH VALLEY—GENERAL MCCLELLAN ALONG THE POTOMAC—THE LINES OF COMMUNICATION—STUART'S CAVALRY RAID—STATE OF THE ARMIES IN OCTOBER, 1862—FEDERAL INVASION OF VIRGINIA—MCCLELLAN'S FLANK MARCH—LEE'S MANŒUVRES—FEDERAL LINE OF OPERATIONS . . 13

CHAPTER III

BURNSIDE ASSUMES COMMAND—THE ARMY OF THE POTOMAC AT WARRENTON—A NEW PLAN OF CAMPAIGN—THE MARCH TO FALMOUTH—A MARITIME BASE—LEE'S DISPOSITIONS FOR DEFENCE—JACKSON MOVES TO PORT ROYAL 31

CHAPTER IV

CAVALRY RECONNAISSANCE 55

CHAPTER V

FREDERICKSBURG—LEE'S PREPARATIONS—RIVER RECONNAISSANCE—BURNSIDE'S PLAN FOR CROSSING—CONFEDERATE DEFICIENCIES 71

PAGE

CHAPTER VI

FEDERAL ARTILLERY DISPOSITIONS—LAYING THE PONTOON BRIDGES—CROSSING THE RAPPAHANNOCK . 91

CHAPTER VII

THE CONFEDERATES CONCENTRATE FOR BATTLE—FINAL DISPOSITIONS OF LONGSTREET AND JACKSON—CAVALRY RECONNAISSANCE 105

CHAPTER VIII

MOVEMENTS OF THE THREE GRAND DIVISIONS—REPORTS BY SUMNER, HOOKER AND FRANKLIN—TOPOGRAPHY OF THE BATTLEFIELD—BURNSIDE'S ATTACK ORDERS 119

CHAPTER IX

THE MORNING OF DECEMBER 13—FINAL DISPOSITIONS FOR BATTLE—TACTICAL POINTS—FRANKLIN'S INTERPRETATION OF ORDERS—COST OF AN "ARMED OBSERVATION." 137

CHAPTER X

THE AMERICAN SOLDIER: HIS SOCIAL STATUS AND PROFESSIONAL ABILITY—A VOICE FROM THE RANKS . 159

CHAPTER XI

THE BATTLE OF DECEMBER 13—THE LEFT ATTACK BY FRANKLIN—JACKSON'S DEFENCE OF THE CONFEDERATE RIGHT SECTION—THE RIGHT ATTACK BY SUMNER—LONGSTREET'S DEFENCE OF THE CONFEDERATE LEFT SECTION—GENERAL BURNSIDE'S FAILURE—GENERAL LEE'S DECISION . . . 187

CHAPTER XII

After the Battle—The Departments of an Army—The Federals on the Defensive—Burnside's Retreat—Cavalry Reconnaissance—Burnside's Last Effort—The "Mud" March—End of the Campaign 223

APPENDIX

A.—Railroad Communications (Washington to Richmond 259

B.—March Tables, September 26—November 9 . 269

C.—Federal Field Return, December 10 . . 271

D.—Confederate Field Return, December 10 . . 272

E.—Return of Federal Transport, December . 273

F.—Comparative Tables of Losses at Fredericksburg 274

G.—Signallers' Report, December . . . 283

H.—River Reconnaissance, Report . . . 286

I.—Cavalry Reconnaissance, Report . . . 289

J.—Note on "Howison's" 297

MAPS

[*In pocket at end of volume.*]

   I. STRATEGICAL MAP OF THE EASTERN THEATRE OF WAR

  II. VICINITY OF FREDERICKSBURG

 III. FREDERICKSBURG TOWN

   V. GENERAL FRANKLIN'S SKETCH-MAP

 IV. THE RIVER RAPPAHANNOCK . . . *Page* 256

CHAPTER I

Introductory

CHAPTER I

THE American Civil War began with the bombardment of Fort Sumter by the Confederates on April 12, 1861. Within a year 232 engagements took place, and before General Kirby Smith surrendered to the Federals on May 26, 1865, no fewer than 2,260 battles, sieges and skirmishes had been recorded. Of the various armed forces under various leaders, operating over a vast area in forty states and territories, which contributed to this amazing total of combats, the most important organizations were known as the Army of the Potomac and the Army of Northern Virginia.

These commands were continually occupied during the whole of four years in protecting their own or threatening the enemy's capital. Washington on the left or east bank of the Potomac and Richmond on the left or north bank of James River are about 120 miles apart; the Potomac River is the State-line between Virginia and Maryland, and the crossing of this natural barrier by one force or the other constituted at this period an act of invasion.

The policy of the Northern States was aggressive; that of the Southern States was purely defensive; and throughout the war, rival commanders shaped their strategy largely by political considerations: on the part of the North the attitude assumed was that of an established Government suppressing a rebellion; on the part of the South the war was regarded as a struggle for freedom, a righteous resistance to intolerable oppression. The capture of Richmond and the overthrow of the newly constituted and rival Government was the aim of the Federal president Abraham Lincoln; while, on the other hand, Jefferson Davis, ex-Secretary for War of the Federal Government, and now President of the Confederate States, expected by the action of his armies to justify his political existence as an independent ruler, to enlist fresh sympathizers among the Federals themselves, and to win official recognition as a " belligerent " by foreign Powers.

It is, however, remarkable that of all the Generals operating in the Eastern theatre of war, the chief of whom had been trained in the same military school at West Point and had fought side by side in Mexico, the really aggressive fighters were found at the head of the Confederate army whose Government was longing for peace, while the offensive strategy of the Federals was, for three years at least, directed by officers whose characteristics were caution, timidity and vacillation. The triumvirate at Washington consisted of the President (Lincoln), the General in-Chief (Halleck), and the Secretary for War (Stanton); and the Federal generals in the field were, until almost the close of the war, largely controlled by a body which resembled the old Aulic Council in Europe during the Seven Years War. It is safe to assert that if the material resources of the North had been at the disposal of Johnston and Lee and Jackson, or if McClellan and Pope and Burnside had encountered the economic difficulties of the Confederate leaders, the War of Secession would have quickly ended in favour of the South. The Federal Government, however, which had resolved to invade Virginia and capture Richmond, and possessed enormous resources in men and material, was served by some singularly feeble generals, while the Confederate Government which stood on the defensive and sought foreign aid as an unprotected, infant State, was upheld for four years by such a master of war as Robert Lee and his lieutenants Jackson and Longstreet and Stuart.

The two causes combined to keep alive hostilities until half a million lives and thousands of millions' worth of property had been fruitlessly expended : not an acre being added to the possessions of the one belligerent, not a single concession or political privilege being secured by the other. The Confederates fought against time, hoping for European intervention (the emperor Napoleon III. had been invited to seize Mexico) or a change in political opinion in the North (a strong peace party often asserted itself), but failing these interpositions the result was inevitable : it became a mere question of wealth and population. The South was poor, its population scant and scattered, the Northern States were many, were thickly populated and were rich ; military adventurers from Europe poured into Washington, and high bounties could be paid to recruits for the " Union " armies. It was a contest of agricultural districts against industrial districts, comparable on a gigantic scale to a duel to the death between "Wessex" and the Black Country. The Federals, moreover, possessed the command of the Sea, and prevented the Southern States receiving money, guns or men from Europe; while reserving all these advantages for themselves. Then, too, there were dissensions in the Southern camp. " State rights " had always been Davis's political cry when a member of Congress: it told against Davis when head of a new Government fighting for political existence. He could not coerce. The States would not stand Conscription. The Cotton States in particular had interests of their own, which were not served by a protracted war. "State" troops and the Confederate troops were raised by competing agents, just as the East India Company once recruited in opposition to the Crown. Finally, the Federals refused to exchange prisoners, so compelling the South to maintain 192,000 deserters and prisoners while their own troops wanted bread. Against all these disabilities and drawbacks Davis and Lee struggled successfully for four years, and then the Confederacy collapsed.

In the summer of 1862, Lee, as commander of the Army of Northern Virginia, met the Army of the Potomac under McClellan, then besieging Richmond from the East, and, in a series of pitched battles between June 26 and July 1, drove it back to the sea and compelled it to re-embark for Washington with a loss of over 15,000 men. Lee then turned to the North, and advanced against another Federal organization known as the Army of Virginia, commanded by Pope. He defeated this force at Cedar Mountain, near Culpeper, on August 9. Ten days later Lee drove the Federal cavalry from Brandy Station and Kelly's Ford, and skirmished with the main body along the Rappahannock. Finally, Lee met the Army of Virginia reinforced by the Army of the

Potomac and between August and September 1 he beat them at Groveton and Gainesville, at Bull Run and Chantilly, and drove the last Union soldier out of Virginia across the Potomac, to seek shelter behind the fortifications of Washington. The Federals were ten days removing their wounded, under a Flag of Truce.

The offensive strategy of the Federals had so far cost them dear. Between June 26 and September 1 a loss of 32,749 men (killed, wounded and missing) had been incurred by McClellan's Army of the Potomac and Pope's Army of Virginia, in attempts to beat the Confederates in the field and seize their capital by " double lines " of operations southward and westward. It was now determined to secure at least unity of command, and the two organizations were accordingly merged into one, and a new Army of the Potomac created, and placed under the sole command of General McClellan.

The campaign which had resulted so disastrously for the Federals had occupied only two months, and on September 3 the Confederate general wrote to President Davis to say that in his judgment the time was come for a forward movement, carrying the war into the enemy's country. The general, fearing perhaps that the President's reply would again prescribe purely defensive strategy, did not wait to receive it, but, in spite of serious difficulties in regard to supplies, crossed the Potomac into Maryland. Lee reached the town of Frederick, about forty-five miles north-west of Washington, on September 8, and then again wrote to Davis, pointing out that the Federal president, with the enemy at his gates, might now perhaps be disposed to listen to proposals from the Southern government for peace, on the basis of " the recognition of our independence." At the same time Lee addressed a local proclamation to the people of Maryland, inviting them to throw in their lot with the Southern States. "Our army," he says, "has come among you, and is prepared to assist you with the power of its arms in regaining the rights of which you have been despoiled;" and as though to give point to his arguments, on September 9 Lee issued orders to his corps commanders for immediate operations—operations which were to result in the capture by the Confederates of Harper's Ferry, with its garrison of 12,000 men and seventy-three heavy guns.

Meanwhile the new Army of the Potomac had been put in motion through Maryland to repel Lee's invasion. Leaving a considerable force for the defence of Washington, the Federals moved north and west on five parallel roads (his army would have occupied fifty miles if marched on a single road, as some of McClellan's critics had advised), and on September 13, four days after the Confederates had evacuated Frederick, the Army of the Potomac entered the town and found there (accidentally preserved as a wrapper for cigars) a copy of Lee's "March" Orders, in which he had outlined his new plan of campaign. With all his faults, McClellan was a competent soldier—he had represented the United States with the allied armies in the Crimea—and knew how to profit by such intelligence as fortune had placed at his disposal; and accordingly the Confederate corps under Longstreet experienced next day a reverse that decided Lee to retire immediately to Southern territory.

At noon on September 15, however, news reached him of the victory of Jackson's corps at Harper's Ferry, and, better still, of the march of Jackson northwards to unite with Longstreet. So, when two hours later the scouts of McClellan's advanced guard were observed watering their horses at Antietam creek, Lee suddenly resolved to give battle, and began forthwith to post his guns on the high ground between the creek and the town of Sharpsburg, having the Potomac (which here flowed southward) a few miles in his rear. During September 16 the preliminary movements for battle occupied both armies, and at dawn on September 17 the fighting began : some 35,000 Confederates were opposed to 62,000 Federals (who had another 25,000 in reserve), and at the end of the day the Army of the Potomac had lost nearly 13,000 men. Lee's army had however suffered hardly less severely, and on September 18, when news was brought to the Confederate leader that McClellan's losses were about to be made good by reinforcements, and that the Pennsylvania Militia were ready to swarm into Maryland from the north, he felt that these circumstances, coupled with increasing difficulties in regard to his own supplies and consequent depletion of his rank by straggling, demanded a retrograde movement, and the abandonment of that strategic counterstroke which had promised no less a result than the immediate termination of the war in favour of the Southern cause.

The same night Lee recrossed the Potomac into Southern territory, covering his retirement by a cavalry attack on the enemy's rear at Williamsport, and securing his passage (a single ford) by batteries of heavy guns.

CHAPTER II

After Sharpsburg—Rest and Recruitment—General Lee in the Shenandoah Valley—General McClellan along the Potomac—The Lines of Communication—Stuart's Cavalry Raid—State of the Armies in October, 1862—Federal Invasion of Virginia—McClellan's Flank March—Lee's Manœuvres — Federal Line of Operations.

CHAPTER II

THE battle of Sharpsburg was memorable for fierce fighting. The Federals left over 2,000 dead upon the field, and even the Confederates, who on that occasion relied on defensive tactics, were appalled at their own losses. Then Lee and McClellan appear to have realized simultaneously that a period of recuperation must precede any further effort on either side. Lee in the Shenandoah Valley, south of the Potomac, and McClellan on the northern bank of the river, accordingly spent several weeks in recruiting their strength. Lee, writing from his camp on the Opequon, west of Charlestown, on September 21, says that the efficiency of his army is "greatly paralyzed by the loss to its ranks of the numerous stragglers." He mentions four brigades which between them mustered only 820 men. It must remain one of the unsolved problems of war that the Washington authorities had detained, for the protection of the capital from the south, a large force which by operating on McClellan's left flank in September might have severed the Confederate communications with Richmond while Lee's army was held fast by McClellan north of the Potomac. On the day of the battle of Sharpsburg a reconnaissance on the railway from Alexandria to Bull Run showed that the bridge there could be made passable for trains in an hour. Evidently Lee's right and rear were then protected only by small cavalry detachments, as McClellan had surmised a week before, when, in an able memorandum, he had protested against an unnecessary dispersal of forces.

To mismanagement at Washington no doubt Lee's army owed its salvation at this critical period of the war. Time to recover was all that the Army of Northern Virginia now wanted, and time is what the Federals gave without stint. Longstreet's Corps and Lee's Headquarters after recrossing the Potomac had encamped close to the Martinsburg road, about six miles from Winchester. Jackson had isolated the 2nd Corps as usual, which rested at Bunker's Hill, six miles further north. Cavalry Headquarters were at Leetown, and Stuart's three brigades under Lee, Hampton and Munford, distributed between Shepherdstown, Hedgeville and Charlestown, covered the army. In Winchester were large hospitals filled with wounded, and various military establishments (some supplies of boots and shoes came up during Lord Wolseley's stay there), but few civilians or shops. Guards picketed all the roads, and the provost marshal's written permission to enter or leave the town was demanded. The railroad between Manassas Junction and Strasburg, and between Winchester and Harper's Ferry, had just been destroyed by Jackson. The Richmond railroad at Staunton was a four days' journey (92 miles) up the Shenandoah Valley turnpike—perhaps the only regularly metalled road in the entire State—and up and down this road, crossing two or three streams, tributaries of the Shenandoah, by fords knee deep—the bridges having been destroyed in the course of Jackson's summer operations—poured all the traffic that accumulates in rear of an army in the field. Every twenty miles the Commissariat department had established "posts" for the relief of wayworn travellers to and from the army, such as prisoners and escorts—the former well clothed in the regulation blue frock-coat and light-blue trousers of the Union forces, the latter riding along in every variety of coat or jacket, or even in their shirt-sleeves—parties of convalescents marching to rejoin the army, batches of sick and wounded—many of them shoeless—slowly toiling home to recuperate; and ambulance carts filled with crippled soldiers or returning empty for a fresh burden. In one of these carts Lord Wolseley travelled from Staunton to Winchester to visit Lee at this period, and it is from his vivid picture that our knowledge of the Confederate lines of communication with Richmond is derived.

Just at this time long trains of guns and ammunition wagons—the spoils of Harper's Ferry—were being sent to the rear. The Army of Northern Virginia had been largely supported by these involuntary contributions on the part of the Federals. Every alternate wagon and ambulance cart, we are told, bore upon it the letters U S; in every camp were found tents, carts, horses and guns similarly marked. Confederate regiments had been known to go into action with smooth-bore muskets and destitute of kit, and appear on parade the next day with a complete outfit—knapsacks, blankets and greatcoats—and armed with new Austrian rifles.

Winchester had been a Confederate depot when Lee was in Maryland, and his drafts from Richmond proceeded there via Luray and Front Royal, after resting and drawing rations at Culpeper. A journey on wheels southwards from Winchester to Staunton would be first broken at Middletown, a village thirteen miles distant: the next night would be spent between Woodstock and Mount Jackson: by the evening of the third day Harrisonburg would be reached: and the remainder of the journey, twenty-five miles to Staunton, would be covered on the fourth day. Thus through the Shenandoah Valley—the garden of Virginia it had been called—Lee's communication with the railroad and so with Richmond lay, and evidence of the fact was abundant in the fields, where only farms fenced with loose stones were distinguishable from common or waste lands, since the wooden posts and rail fences had served to kindle the bivouac fires of the Confederate army.

Staunton, like Winchester, had become a Confederate depot; the few shops open demanded war prices for their goods—Lord Wolseley paid half a sovereign for a shilling pocket knife, and searched in vain for a tea-pot or kettle —the best of its houses had been converted into military hospitals; in its only hotel "beds" were represented by sufficient floor space to lie down upon, but at the station a south-eastern train might be caught for the journey of eleven hours (120 miles) over the steep slopes and sharp curves of Blue Ridge and South West Mountains, bending northwards to Gordonsville junction, thence south-east to Hanover, and so to Richmond, the "base" on which Lee's army depended ultimately for its supplies and stores, recruits and munitions of war. In September, 1862, a large proportion of the passengers from Staunton to Richmond were the sick and wounded with their attendants, and soldiers from the army at Winchester going home for ten days' furlough.

This season of rest and refitment was spent by the Federals in the neighbourhood of Harper's Ferry, where the Shenandoah joins the Potomac. The Union army stretched along the big river from Williamsport to Berlin, and had its supplies sent out from Washington by three routes, viz., the Chesapeake and Ohio canal, which follows the course of the Potomac ; the Baltimore and Ohio railroad through Newmarket to Berlin ; and the Cumberland Valley railroad through Chambersburg to Hagerstown : all were excellent lines of supply for an army that had nearly 4,000 wagons moving between the railhead and the troops.

On September 15, President Lincoln, on receiving McClellan's report of the successful operations at South Mountain, had telegraphed : " Destroy the rebel army if possible." But ten days had now elapsed without any progress being made in this direction, further than to fight a drawn battle at Sharpsburg ; the rebel army had been allowed to retire without molestation into Southern territory ; and the Army of the Potomac, which President Lincoln hoped to find pursuing and dispersing the Confederates, was itself in a state of exhaustion and its leader in his most lethargic mood. Far from taking the offensive, McClellan a week later apparently found himself unable to protect the territory his army occupied, for Lee's cavalry division on October 9 crossed the Potomac at McCoy's Ford, moved north through Maryland and Pennsylvania, and camped at Chambersburg, a Federal depot without a garrison. The Confederate leader, General Stuart, there took as prisoners and paroled all the sick and wounded in the hospitals, seized 500 remounts, cut the telegraph wires, obstructed the railway communication with Washington, destroyed all the arms, ammunition, and clothing stored in the town, and a train of loaded cars on the railroad. The raiding expedition then circled to the east towards Gettysburg, and, leaving Frederick on its right after turning southwards, recrossed the Potomac near Sugar Loaf Mountain, camped at Leesburg, east of Blue Bridge, on the night of October 12, and returned through Snicker's Gap to camp at Berryville, near Winchester, on October 14. Stuart's cavalry had covered 126 miles and had remained fifty-six hours within the enemy's lines, eluding every one of the numerous Federal detachments which had been warned—always just too late—to intercept him, and assisting materially in the breaking down of the Union cavalry, which formed the subject of lengthy correspondence between Lincoln and McClellan.

The commotion which this Expedition caused, not only at army Headquarters, but at Washington, may be gathered from the circumstance that orders and correspondence on the subject fill fifty pages of the Official Records, and General McClellan next day received a letter from the President to remind him that by remaining on the defensive with the Potomac between himself and his enemy, he was hardly carrying out the plans of the Government. On October 6, the General-in-Chief at Washington had written: " The President directs that you cross the Potomac and give battle to the enemy or drive him south. Your army must move now while the roads are good. If you cross the river between the enemy and Washington, and cover the latter by your operation, you can be re-inforced with 30,000 men. If you move up the Valley of the Shenandoah, not more than 12,000 or 15,000 can be sent to you. . . . I am directed to add that the Secretary of War and the General-in-Chief fully concur with the President in these instructions." And now, after Stuart's raid, President Lincoln personally rebuked his general for what he termed his " over-cautiousness," pointed out that the fears McClellan had expressed in regard to subsistence were groundless, and finally read him a lecture on strategy. Lincoln's remarks were not without point. " Change positions with the enemy," he says, " and think you not he would break your communication with Richmond within the next twenty-four hours ? . . . It is all easy if our troops march as well as the enemy, and it is unmanly to say they cannot do it."

In this letter, dated October 13, Lincoln summed up the situation. A call for troops on July 2 had resulted in 421,465 men enlisted for three years being furnished by twenty-four States and Territories ; and another " call " on August 4 had added 87,588 militia (enlisted for nine months only) to the Union forces. The administrative departments were found equal to enlisting, organizing and equipping 80,000 men in less than a month, and yet nothing had been accomplished by the general in the field ; though, the Federal Government having undertaken the rôle of invader, it was incumbent on its Generals to attempt to imitate the great masters of offensive strategy, to seize and keep the initiative, and leave the enemy no breathing time. From this point of view McClellan must be judged like any other general who accepts command of an army of invasion. Stung perhaps by the accusation that his conduct was "unmanly" McClellan promised to make a move.

A glance at the map will show that though the Federals in crossing the Potomac and again invading Virginia were actually moving nearer to their base at Washington, fresh lines of supply would become necessary, that the old depots must be abandoned and their stores removed to Washington, to be reissued and forwarded to new depots in Northern Virginia. McClellan could not, as Lee had done to a large extent, live on the country, for the Confederates would of course remove all that they could not themselves consume. It is true that railways existed, but they had never been constructed for military purposes; they were single-line tracks, only suited to the moderate traffic of an agricultural district sparsely populated; and no doubt the task was an onerous one to supply an immense shifting population, like the Federal army, dispersed over many camping grounds, with its enormous daily requirements. The wagon roads, too, had not been constructed for the passage of thousands of army wagons, and it was common knowledge that only so long as the fine weather lasted could roads be relied upon for transport purposes.

One thing, however, was clear: unless the Federal organization and Northern energy proved equal to all these difficulties the war had better be ended there and then, by the simple process of marching back to Washington and disbanding the army. The determination to prosecute the war necessarily involved the overcoming of these formidable obstacles to success, and every officer accepting high command must be supposed to have weighed the responsibilities he thereby assumed, and to have expressed his belief in his ability to surmount difficulties which were obvious and irremediable. As an example of the demands made upon the Chief Quartermaster at the Base we may note that a single requisition on October 22 embraced : 5,000 forage caps, 7,500 blouses lined, 7,500 knit jackets, 15,000 infantry dress coats, 10,000 pairs infantry trousers, 10,000 flannel shirts, 10,000 pairs drawers, 2,000 pairs cavalry and artillery boots, 10,000 pairs bootees, 15,000 pairs stockings, 5,000 infantry overcoats and straps, 5,000 knapsacks, 5,000 haversacks, 5,000 canteens, 5,000 ponchos or gum blankets, 1,500 artillery and cavalry jackets, 5,000 shelter tents, 500 camp kettles, 1,000 mess pans, 5,000 axe slings, 100 Sibley tents, 500 common tents, besides an assortment of blank books, drums, bugles, etc. From Harrisburg alone 4,500,000 lbs. of corn and 390 tons of hay were forwarded between September 7 and November 3, and during the same period New York furnished 20,000 blankets and 10,000 shelter tents ; Washington supplied 10,000 horses, besides filling the regular requisitions for 500,000 rations, and 500 barrels of potatoes and onions at a time.

Nevertheless McClellan's continual complaint was of deficiency of supplies of all kinds, and while no doubt a want of administrative ability on the part of regimental officers caused prodigious waste, it seems that a lack of organization in the transport department often caused masses of supplies within reach to remain undistributed to the troops. Then discipline, at least the iron discipline that was to come two years later under Grant, was yet undreamt of ; and in September, 1862, a circular order was necessary to comment on " the frequent absence from their commands while in camp and from their columns on the march of superior officers." McClellan pointed out that the army " cannot be successful if the soldiers are one half skulking to the rear, while the brunt of battle is borne by the other half, and its officers inattentive to observe and correct the grossest evils which are daily occurring under their eyes." It is evident that the general in command of the Army of the Potomac at this period, whoever he might be, had need of tremendous force of character, of an indomitable will and of absolute authority, to accomplish the task he had been set.

Shoals of correspondence and orders remain to testify to McClellan's red tape methods of moving his army sixty miles, and it was not until November 2 that he was able to report to Washington: " The last division of this army is now crossing the river." A week later he reached Warrenton.

To investigate the causes of delay, to attempt to apportion the blame, would serve no good purpose. Whatever material disabilities McClellan laboured under were suffered in at least an equal degree by General Lee, and though greater demands are made on the energy of an army of invasion than upon one acting on the defensive, the balance should have been adjusted by that superiority in numbers and morale which an offensive attitude postulates and confers. The fact remains that though McClellan could write an excellent letter, frame admirable reports, plan a campaign on paper, and argue the point with his superiors at Washington—he kept up an acrimonious correspondence with Lincoln in regard to the breakdown of the cavalry—yet he was incapable of inspiring his army with that ardour for the chase which is indispensable for success in offensive operations ; and unfortunately for McClellan, at this period of the war the Federal Government was most impatient for great results, and so it happened that ere General McClellan had reorganized his army and set it afoot again — his cavalry worn out by six weeks of aimless reconnaissance—the Lincoln Cabinet had appointed his successor.

President Lincoln in his letter had outlined a plan of " going to Richmond on the inside track," keeping Lee in the valley for a while with Blue Ridge between the Confederates and the Union army. " The gaps would enable you to attack if you should wish. For a great part of the way you would be practically between the enemy and both Washington and Richmond, enabling us to spare you the greatest number of troops from here." Unfortunately Lincoln had reckoned without his host. Though McClellan was dilatory, that fault could certainly not be charged against Lee, and on October 30 Longstreet's Corps was already passing through Winchester *en route* for Front Royal, and the early days of November saw Lee busy with preparations to take the field again ; exchanged prisoners from Richmond came to rejoin their commands, the sick were sent back to Staunton, and supplies of flour, tobacco, blankets, clothing and shoes—" sufficient to clothe twenty men of each regiment in Jackson's Corps "—slowly arrived : Longstreet's march was continued on November 2 towards Culpeper, where Lee (who had been to Richmond) was to join him, while Jackson's command remained for the present in the Valley. On November 5, a cavalry force with a few guns, under Colonel Chambliss, was holding Warrenton and Brandy, and Longstreet was examining the fords on the Rapidan and Robertson rivers. Stuart, with a cavalry brigade (1,000 strong), and a horse artillery battery, had crossed Blue Ridge on October 30, determined to delay the Federal advance while the Confederate Army was changing its position. He was afterwards joined by Hampton's brigade, and keeping in front of the Federals, never losing contact, he skirmished with them daily and engaged his two brigades at Barber's Cross roads on November 5 ; and when at length McClellan reached Warrenton and its vicinity, Stuart's cavalry still interposed between the Confederates at Culpeper and the enemy.

McClellan's farewell order to the Army of the Potomac was issued on November 7, and is dated from Rectortown on the Manassas Gap railroad, to which place his Headquarters had been moved from Upperville on November 4. He had broken up the depot at Berlin as he turned his back on Maryland, leaving 600,000 rations at Harper's Ferry and a month's supplies at Frederick. Supplies now came out from the Base Depot at Alexandria on the Orange and Alexandria railroad as far as Manassas Junction (held by one division under Sickles), where the branch line joined the main line. The branch line was in poor running order beyond Gainesville (where Sigel's 11th Corps was posted), and so McClellan proposed to establish his advanced depot at Gainesville until the main line could be repaired between Manassas Junction and Rappahannock, for the Confederate cavalry had broken down many bridges and otherwise attempted to obstruct the Federal operations in this region, and the necessary repairs to the line could not be commenced until it was covered by the Federal advance.

McClellan had decided to concentrate about Warrenton. The Federal left wing under Burnside consisted of Willcox's Corps and the divisions of Whipple and Stoneman, and these units lay about Amissville, Waterloo and Jefferson, their front and flanks covered by the cavalry under Pleasonton and Bayard at Newby's Cross Roads and Rappahannock Station. McClellan had withdrawn Couch's Corps from Aldie's (Snicker's) Gap, leaving a post at Leesburg, where 500 sick and wounded lay in hospital, and he relied on the Washington forces to watch this region with cavalry as he advanced southwards. Franklin's Corps and Porter's 5th Corps lay at White Plains, not far from Rectortown, getting their supplies on the Manassas Gap railroad, but were under orders to move as follows: Porter's (afterwards Hooker's) 5th Corps to Cedar Run near Warrenton, marching by Georgetown and New Baltimore, and drawing supplies by road from Gainesville; Franklin's Corps to New Baltimore.

Army Headquarters was to move at once to Warrenton, where Reynolds' Corps then lay. Sickles had pushed forward a post as far as Warrenton Junction, and Sigel from Gainesville kept scouts moving further south, who on November 7 reported Confederate cavalry (15th Virginia) at Fredericksburg, and Longstreet with 25,000 men at Culpeper, but the scouts had not been able to locate Jackson's Corps.

McClellan had issued orders for the repair of the Richmond railroad between Aquia Creek and Fredericksburg, and the materials had been collected; only the army's advance, to give the necessary protection to the working parties, was waited for. A heavy snowstorm heralded the winter season. The supersession of McClellan on November 9 prevented the development of an interesting situation. The Federal leader's ultimate plan, so far as it can be gathered from his elaborate report written August 4, 1863, was " to place the army of the Potomac in position, either to adopt the Fredericksburg line of advance upon Richmond, or to be removed to the Peninsula, if, as I apprehended, it were found impossible to supply it by the Orange and Alexandria railroad beyond Culpeper." McClellan had planned to " separate the enemy's forces and beat them in detail, or compel him to fall back as far as Gordonsville in order to concentrate." But the enemy had anticipated his wishes, and had in fact already separated his forces (Longstreet was at Culpeper and Jackson in the Valley), and it only remained for McClellan to proceed to carry out his plan of beating the enemy in detail. Unfortunately no letters exist to show the Confederate view of the situation at this date, but it is hardly to be supposed that Lee was ignorant or careless of the Federal movements; and it is at least arguable that McClellan's " great battle " would have been fought a long march distant from his advanced depots, with Longstreet in his front and Jackson on his flank, and that the Federal 12th Corps at Harper's Ferry, with perhaps Sigel's 11th Corps and Sickle's division, would have been required only to cover the Federal retreat across the Potomac. This at least is clear. At Sharpsburg both Lee and McClellan had been beaten to a standstill, and though tactically the battle of Antietam was a drawn encounter, since the Federals could not pursue, McClellan had by his Maryland campaign gained a strategic advantage, inasmuch as he had defeated Lee's attempt at a counterstroke. Only the detention about Washington of 72,000 men under General Banks to protect the capital—which was threatened, if at all, at this time only by such small detachments of " rebels " as could be spared from the Richmond defences—prevented the indirect pursuit of the Confederates south of the Potomac, and the accomplishment of a turning movement similar in character to that which destroyed the Army of the Rhine in 1870.

After September 18 the Army of Northern Virginia was free from molestation, and General Lee, having then abandoned offensive operations, could recuperate on friendly soil, collect subsistence from the farmers round about him, and refit from Richmond by rail and road. Being under no obligation to move, Federal procrastination served him well. On the other hand, McClellan's mission was to follow, attack and destroy the enemy; but he was restricted, as we have seen, as to the means, and instead of receiving heavy reinforcements, he was now asked to make fresh detachments from his army.

It is at such a juncture that a general shows the stuff he is made of. McClellan should have answered Halleck's dispatch of October 6 in one of two ways: by resigning the command for reasons stated, or by proceeding at once to invade Virginia with such a force as he could at the moment equip and supply, throwing upon the Cabinet the onus of protecting his communications and sending necessary reinforcements, under penalty of seeing the Army of the Potomac surrender to the enemy. No middle course would have suggested itself in the circumstances to any self-respecting general. Napoleon on a similar occasion wrote to the Convention at Paris: " Better one bad general than two good ones—accept my resignation." And McClellan in dallying with the situation proved his weakness: he held on to the command, but he did not advance ; he wrote supplicatory letters to Washington and was answered with insult; and when insult even failed to move the tame spirit of the commander of the Union Army, the triumvirate at Washington perceived that they had fully taken his measure—that " the young Napoleon," as his admirers dubbed him, was a mere routine general. They then dismissed him.

CHAPTER III

BURNSIDE ASSUMES COMMAND—THE ARMY OF THE POTOMAC AT WARRENTON—A NEW PLAN OF CAMPAIGN—THE MARCH TO FALMOUTH—A MARITIME BASE—LEE'S DISPOSITIONS FOR DEFENCE—JACKSON MOVES TO PORT ROYAL.

CHAPTER III

WHEN General Burnside was ordered to take command of the Army of the Potomac he was furnished with a copy of President Lincoln's letter to McClellan, and informed that the General-in-Chief at Washington would confer with him personally on the plan of campaign. It was believed, no doubt, that Burnside would prove a willing instrument to carry out the President's strategical views, but again Mr. Lincoln had miscalculated. Burnside had his own ideas on strategy, and, being the responsible general, was not willing to set them aside. The result of the interview between the General-in-Chief Halleck and Burnside is on record in a letter from the latter dated Warrenton, November 9. The President assented to Burnside's plan a few days later by telegram, which closed as follows : " It will succeed if you move rapidly ; otherwise not."

The essence of the plan was a change in the line of operations, by which the army might avail itself of the sea as a line of supply, and establish a depot at a point on the Lower Potomac easily accessible from Washington and unassailable by the enemy. The same idea had prompted McClellan in the spring to advance on Richmond from the east, and two years later General Grant proved its value, when in 1864 the Federals and Confederates again faced each other along the Rappahannock in Northern Virginia. During the campaign which ended the war—in spite of heavy losses in the Wilderness and at Spottsylvania—Grant always moved by successive marches to his left, keeping his face towards Richmond, until at length, instead of having his back to Washington, he had his back to the sea. We must therefore give Burnside due credit for quickly realizing in November, 1862, that Mr. Lincoln's plan to follow Lee southwards, and so

"Drag at each remove a lengthening chain"

in the shape of a line of communications, was wholly unsuitable to the circumstances in which the Army of the Potomac was placed. President Lincoln's plan would certainly have enabled the starving Confederates to replenish their stores out of the enemy's abundance, and add to their transport many of the U.S. wagons on which Chief Quartermaster Ingalls now justly prided himself. Burnside's plan, on the other hand, by substituting for the Orange and Alexandria railroad as a line of supply the broad waters of the Potomac between Washington and Acquia Creek, would shift all anxiety in regard to future supplies from the Federals to the Confederates, whose predatory expeditions would receive a check.

The strategical merits of the plan, however, soon became obscured by unforeseen difficulties on points of detail. Even General Burnside had supposed it would be an easy task to establish wharves at Acquia Creek, to rapidly lay or repair roads between the Creek and the army near Falmouth, and to transport immediately the pontoons and bridging material needed for the crossing of the Rappahannock. Events were to prove what the modern soldier takes for granted, namely, that an army by giving up, voluntarily or otherwise, its accustomed channel of communication with its base, abandoning all the posts, depots and stores which had been carefully established and garrisoned for permanent use, and suddenly demanding of its commissariat and transport department a similar arrangement in another part of the theatre of operations, goes far towards rendering itself temporarily ineffective. So it proved in the case of the Federal army, and the narrative will show that nearly a month was to elapse before all was in readiness for the movement which resulted in the battle of Fredericksburg.

It is surprising to find that so much impatience was expressed at the time at delays which we see now to have been inevitable, and which should have been allowed for in planning operations of such a character. Indeed, the plan was held to have failed because Burnside did not succeed in " surprising " Lee, though how any Federal leader could hope to do so at this date is hard to see, and Lee's letter of November 25 (page 48) shows how closely the Federal movements had been watched and how sound were Lee's deductions from them.

We must, however, return to Burnside at Warrenton, where on November 14 the 1st, 2nd, and 5th Corps had concentrated. The 6th corps was six miles distant, at New Baltimore, the 9th Corps, with Stoneman's and Whipple's divisions, were quartered on both sides of the river in the neighbourhood of Waterloo, the 11th Corps at Gainesville, New Baltimore and the gaps of Bull

D

Run Mountains. Pleasonton's cavalry was at Jefferson and Amissville, between Warrenton and Culpeper, with its advanced squadrons on Hazel River, an affluent of the Rappahannock; Bayard's cavalry was at Rappahannock station and the neighbourhood, midway between Warrenton Junction and Culpeper. Slocum was still at Harper's Ferry and Fayetteville, watching, and being watched by, "Stonewall" Jackson. Ever since General McClellan's departure on November 7 the units of the Army of the Potomac had been resting in the positions he had assigned them.

Burnside began (November 14) by decentralizing his command; he divided the Army of the Potomac—at least that part of it which was to move on Fredericksburg—into three wings, calling them Grand Divisions, the right under General Sumner, the centre under General Hooker, and the left under General Franklin. Of these officers Hooker was perhaps the ablest. He was forty-three years of age—five years older than Burnside. Educated at West Point, he had served in the Mexican War and in the Adjutant-General's office at Washington. A colonel at twenty-nine, he had retired only three years before the war broke out, in order to become a railroad superintendent. He had commanded a division under McClellan in the Peninsula Campaign, and was destined to succeed Burnside in the command of the Army of the Potomac. Lack of political influence had probably so far stood in the way of his promotion. The Right Grand Division consisted of the 2nd and 9th Corps, 30,000 all ranks, and 90 guns; the Centre Grand Division consisted of the 3rd and 5th Corps, 40,000 all ranks, and 104 guns; the Left Grand Division consisted of the 1st and 6th Corps, 46,000 all ranks, and 118 guns. The Commanders of Grand Divisions were to correspond directly with Washington in reference to "all such things as resignations, leaves of absence, discharges, recruiting, Service, etc.," and so the "very massive and elaborate" Adjutant-General's office which McClellan had established at Army Headquarters was swept away, and Burnside contented himself with a General Staff, consisting of an Inspector (Gen. Seth Williams), an Adjutant-General (Col. Richmond) a Chief Quartermaster (Gen. Rufus Ingalls), and a Chief of Artillery (Gen. Hunt), and their subordinates—67 officers in all. He had a Signal Corps (150 all ranks), an Engineer Corps (1,300 all ranks), a Provost Guard (1,100 all ranks), and a personal escort of 7 officers and 148 men.

Four detachments from the army, Sigel's (11th) Corps at Fairfax Court House, Slocum's (12th) Corps at Harper's Ferry, Morell's command on the Upper Potomac, and Heintzelmann's force for the defences of Washington, together accounted for 3,500 officers and 76,000 men, who took no part in Burnside's offensive operations.

The Army of the Potomac, in fine, consisted of no fewer than 10,000 officers and 192,000 men, and its mission was to cover by its operations the Union capital, beat in the field an army of 78,000 "rebels," and, assisted by the Union fleet, capture Richmond about 60 miles distant. The general's plan was "to concentrate all the forces near this place [Warrenton] and impress upon the enemy a belief that we are to attack Culpeper or Gordonsville, and at the same time accumulate a four or five days' supply for the men and animals; then make a rapid move of the whole force to Fredericksburg with a view to a movement upon Richmond from that point." The Washington authorities were expected to assist the operations by immediately providing (on receipt of Burnside's letter dated November 9) at least thirty canal boats and barges full of commissary stores and forage, which were to be towed to the neighbourhood of Aquia Creek, and followed by further supplies sufficient to subsist the army for thirty days; also a pontoon train to span the Rappahannock with two tracks; also a quantity of beef cattle, and wagon trains filled with "small rations such as bread, salt, coffee, sugar, soap and candles;" also fresh horses and mules and ferry boats.

Burnside expected to find on reaching Fredericksburg in a few days sufficient to fill his wagons with twelve days' supplies, so that " a rapid movement can be made direct upon Richmond by way of such roads as are open to us." This ambitious programme was not destined to be carried out. His chief quartermaster Ingalls had proceeded to Washington on November 13, and thence three days later to Aquia and Belle Plain. "We found," he says, "the old wharf and entire depot a mass of ruins, and the interior of the country still in the hands of the enemy." Temporary landings at both places had to be erected (the wharves were constructed of barges and trestle work) to land supplies, which were then hauled in wagons to the army fifteen to twenty miles distant, until the railroad from Aquia to Falmouth was in working order. The labour involved may be estimated from the fact that "full allowance" of forage required the daily receipt, distribution and issue of some 800 tons of grain and hay; and, of course, in addition were subsistence for the troops, besides ordnance, hospital and quartermaster's stores generally.

Burnside, apparently confident that his arrival at Falmouth would coincide with the appearance of ample supplies and bridging equipment, issued orders for the march on November 16, his Head Quarters then being "near Catlett's." His cavalry had been driven in from Jefferson on the previous evening (November 14), and on November 16 his cavalry at Rappahannock Station was attacked by a detachment from the Fredericksburg garrison, which had crossed the river to reconnoitre. Bayard had pushed forward the 10th New York Cavalry to picket Richard's and United States Fords, but the latter post was surprised in broad daylight, being attacked from the rear and nearly surrounded. We read that " the party undertook to cut their way through the rebel lines to the rear. Five of the men succeeded in doing so and brought away seven horses. Captain Peck escaped into the woods." The 2nd New York Cavalry were at Morrisville, and its commander reported November 16 : " I have strengthened the pickets at Ellis', Barnett's and Kemper's Falls fords since the reinforcements have arrived, and have picketed the road leading to Falmouth with 1½ company, and picketed also the road leading in the direction of Catlett's Station. Captain Ordner has returned from his scout and found nothing, but learned that the river was fordable at a good many places which it would be impossible for us to guard." Pleasonton's and Averell's cavalry was to protect the rear of the army, while Bayard covered its advance.

Meanwhile Burnside had dispatched his advanced

guard towards Falmouth at daylight on November 15. Sumner's command, marching south-east to Warrenton Junction and Fayetteville, arrived at Falmouth on the night of November 17. But it was not allowed to march unmolested; Couch's (2nd) Corps got away in safety, but a brigade of Willcox's (9th) Corps was attacked by a Confederate force consisting of a cavalry regiment, two infantry regiments and three guns. The brigade commander reported:—"Shortly after daylight I broke up camp and took up line of march toward Fayetteville, following the 1st brigade of the Division. Shortly after my command had passed the bridge crossing the Rappahannock near the Springs, several shells from a battery planted by the enemy on the hills south of the river burst in the midst of the wagon train following my brigade. The fire from the enemy's battery was very severe, nearly every shell exploding in the train or batteries. During the action the cavalry of the enemy charged on the bridge, but were repulsed by a volley from two companies stationed there to hold it." The 9th Corps headquarters halted one mile beyond Warrenton Springs in the afternoon, when its divisions were thus distributed: 1st (Burns) on both sides of the pike at Sulphur Springs picketing in both directions; 2nd (Sturgis) near Fayetteville with one regiment on picket at Fox's Ford, the intersection of the roads from Sulphur Springs, Jefferson, Fayetteville and Bealeton; 3rd (Getty) along Great Run from Fox's Ford to within one mile of Sulphur Springs.

Franklin's command followed, marching twenty-three miles to Stafford Court House, where it encamped on the night of November 18. Hooker's command marched by

Bealeton, Warrenton Junction, Weaversville, Morrisville and Spotted Tavern, halting finally at Hartwood opposite the United States Ford, six miles from Falmouth, on November 19, on which date Burnside established his Headquarters at Falmouth village. The cavalry under Pleasonton and Bayard were quartered just beyond General Hooker at Deep Run, picketing all the fords of the Rappahannock; and Averell's cavalry was at Spotted Tavern, picketing the roads in the direction of Catlett's, Brentsville and Dumfries. The railroad stations east of Manassas Junction had been vacated, and their guards withdrawn to join Sickles, who was directed to fall back over Bull Run, and keep his division prepared to join Hooker's command at an hour's notice, by way of Wolf Run Shoals and Dumfries. Sigel's 11th Corps was ordered to move to Centreville, leaving small outposts at Gainesville, Thoroughfare Gap and Aldie.

Thus Burnside by November 19 had effected the desired change in his line of operations; and now, protected by unfordable rivers south and east, his right flank watched by cavalry, and with Sigel's corps in his rear connecting him with Washington, the Federal commander had leisure to look about him and concert his next move. In the first place he had to consider a suggestion from Hooker, that the Centre Grand Division should at once cross the Rappahannock, and march to Saxton's Junction with three days' rations. Hooker proposed to move south to Bowling Green, and obtain further supplies from Port Royal. What he would do with an isolated force of 40,000 men in the enemy's country, cut off from support by an unfordable river, his letter does not state, but the mere fact of his suggesting an independent movement and notifying the Secretary of War at Washington privately of his intention, is remarkable as illustrating the chief difficulty of a commander like Burnside, who " would not think of making an important movement of this army without full consultation with his generals." Burnside, who anticipated the Germans in their objection to employing large advanced guards, which are apt to take the initiative and bring on a general action for which the main body is unprepared, felt obliged, it seems, to occupy himself on November 20 with an attempt to conciliate his subordinate by an explanatory letter and a visit. Later on, the Grand Division commanders were " assembled to discuss and determine the place and method of crossing the river," and on that occasion Hooker (to use his own expression) *objected by his vote* to his commanding officer's plan, that a portion of the army should cross the river at Falmouth and a portion twelve miles below. We seem to have here all the elements of the thinly veiled mutiny that broke out two months later.

In the meantime Burnside sat idle before Fredericksburg, waiting a week for the pontoons which were to have been at Washington but were discovered to have been left at Harper's Ferry. Orders were sent astray, misunderstandings took place in the Engineer Corps; and finally a portion of the train was dispatched by water to Belle Plain, while the remainder started to make the journey from Washington to Falmouth by road. The overland train was beset by misfortune; " it had commenced raining before the train left Washington . . . the roads got worse . . . in many places the wagons could only be moved by the greatest exertions of the men, lifting them out while standing in deep water and mud . . . from daylight to near midnight on the 21st the train could be moved but about five miles." The officer in charge then abandoned the idea of proceeding by road, and determined to move eastward to the Potomac, there put the train into the water, tow it to Belle Plain, and let the animals go on by land. The stream called the Occoquan (280 feet across) was bridged, the train taken over, the bridge then dismantled and made up in rafts, and all the material loaded on the rafts and floated down to the Potomac, where a steamer was found, but " the water in the harbour at Belle Plain was too shallow for the steamer to enter, and the party was towed in by a small tug, reaching the wharf just before dark. . . . He commenced unloading the wagons, putting them together, and loading them with boats and with bridge material. At midnight the men were allowed to lie down for a little rest. At 4 o'clock the next morning, 25th, the work resumed, and at 10 a.m. the train started for Falmouth, arriving near general headquarters about 3 p.m." The railway to Falmouth was at this date still unfinished. The train sent by water had reached Falmouth on the morning of November 24. Thus on November 26 General Burnside was at length in possession of his bridging equipment, and the " rapid move " to Fredericksburg contemplated a fortnight ago might have commenced. Nevertheless the pontoons were not actually used until the morning of December 11 ; and before tracing the cause of another fortnight's delay in the operations, which had for their object the " surprise " of General Lee and the immediate capture of Richmond, we will turn to the Confederates and learn how their movements had been affected by the changes in the Federal camp

On November 1 the Confederate general moved his reserve artillery and ordnance train from the Valley of the Shenandoah, and on the evening of November 4 it encamped near Culpeper Court House, where it remained for a fortnight. It was commanded by General Pendleton, Chief of Artillery, who on November 14, when Burnside's movement was suspected, was ordered to detach Lane's battery of long-range guns to co-operate with the cavalry under General Stuart in the attack on Sumner near Warrenton Springs. McLaws' division marched at daylight on November 18 on Fredericksburg via Raccoon Ford and Chancellorsville, preceded by W. H. F. Lee's cavalry brigade and followed by Lane's battery of long-range guns. On November 19 the whole of the reserve artillery and ordnance train followed the main body of Longstreet's Corps, taking a circuitous route south-east for the sake of forage, and arrived at Fredericksburg on Sunday, November 23.

It will be remembered that the Federal advanced guard under Sumner had begun its march to Falmouth on November 15, and on the same day Lee wrote twice to Colonel Ball, who commanded the Fredericksburg garrison, promising reinforcements and stating "it is reported that the enemy is moving from Warrenton today, and it is probable that he is marching upon Fredericksburg." The day before, Lee had telegraphed to Colonel Ball, instructing him as to the demolition of the railroad between Fredericksburg and Aquia Creek. "The bridges and culverts must be thoroughly destroyed, the cross ties removed and piled with the rails placed across them, and, when the timber is sufficiently dry, fired ; the weight of the bars will thus cause them to bend, and prevent their being relaid."

The promised reinforcements (61st Virginia and Norfolk Light Artillery) proceeded to Fredericksburg on November 16 via Stevensburg, " crossing the Rapidan at Raccoon Ford till they intersected the Plank road from Orange Court House to Fredericksburg." The officer commanding the detachment was ordered, in the event of Fredericksburg being found in the hands of the enemy, to fall back through Spottsylvania Court House, and take position on the railroad where it crosses the North Anna River. " After crossing the Rapidan, Colonel Grover must send forward his staff officers to ascertain the best roads, prepare forage for his command, etc., at points where it will be needed. He will be careful on the march to permit no straggling, depredation upon the citizens, country, etc., and be careful to pay for all articles consumed by his command, or to give proper receipts for the same." Such are the careful directions given for the march of a small detachment by that able leader, Robert E. Lee. On the evening of November 17 he writes : " Our scouts north of the Rappahannock report that three brigades of the enemy were advancing upon Fredericksburg, and that their advance last night had reached the Spotted Tavern. A division of Longstreet's Corps will move at early dawn in the direction of Chesterfield, and the rest will follow if the report is confirmed." On November 18 Lee wrote no fewer than seven letters. The situation was being rapidly cleared up. He knows that "the enemy" reported yesterday is Sumner's Corps, and that its cavalry reached Falmouth at 3 p.m. and was baffled in its attempt to cross the river. Lee's cavalry under Stuart had that day forced a passage of the Rappahannock in face of the enemy's cavalry, had driven them back, and reported their retirement towards Bealeton, and the evacuation of Warrenton by the Federals. Accordingly a brigade of cavalry (less one regiment) is ordered to cross the Rapidan en route for Fredericksburg, to further reinforce the garrison there, and the regiment detached is to "picket the Rappahannock until further orders." Longstreet had on November 16 issued a General Order commencing: "The troops of this command will be held in readiness for battle upon a moment's notice;" and on this day Stuart ordered Hampton to go on a scout to Orleans. On the day that McLaws marched on Fredericksburg, Ransom's division (then at Madison Court House) was ordered to Hanover Junction via Orange Court House and the Anna river, but the instructions were varied a few hours later, so that Ransom advanced from Orange to Guiney's station, about fourteen miles south of Fredericksburg. On November 19, Generals Lee and Longstreet and Anderson's division all marched on Fredericksburg via Raccoon Ford. Before leaving, however, Lee forwarded to the War Office, Richmond, a list of persons and places, in the counties of Culpeper, Madison and Green, where wheat and pork, corn and hay were procurable, and Lee reserves his longest letter for his *alter ego* General Thomas J. Jackson, whom he fully informs of all movements, and the relations between these generals may be gathered from the following passage :—

"Unless you think it is advantageous for you to continue longer in the Valley, or can accomplish the retention and division of the enemy's forces by so doing, I think it would be advisable to put some of your divisions in motion across the mountains, and advance them at least as far as Sperryville or Madison Court House. I telegraphed you to this effect to-day."

Here is no formal order, no anxious inquiry, no elaboration of instructions ; only a suggestion and a word of counsel breathing the great calm that filled the mind of the Southern commander and inspired his subordinates at every crisis. The perfect understanding, the mutual confidence, the steady affection that subsisted between Jackson and Lee has hardly a parallel in military history. How weak a term is " co-operation " to describe the military partnership between these two men, differing so much in age and temper, and only alike in respect of their enthusiastic practice of religion and war ! " General Lee is a phenomenon. He is the only man whom I would be willing to follow blindfold," said Jackson ; and when six months later Jackson fell wounded at the battle of Chancellorsville, Lee struggling hard to suppress his emotion, declared that " any victory is dearly bought which deprives us of the services of General Jackson even for a short time," sending him the message : " I congratulate you upon the victory which is due to your skill and energy." Lee then turned to his staff, and aroused to fierceness by the injury done his lieutenant, announced : " These people shall be pressed immediately," and the price exacted of the Federals for the fatal wound inflicted by them on Lee's " right arm " duly figured in their casualty returns. Lee's anguish of spirit, when he learned that Jackson might die, was piteous to behold. He could not go to him: he sent him another message. " Give him my love, and tell him I wrestled in prayer for him last night as I never prayed, I believe, for myself." It is hard to read the story in detail with undimmed eyes, even at this distance of time.

There is a series of letters extant from Lee to Jackson, penned during the ten days ending November, 1862, which exhibits the development of Lee's ideas on the situation. Unfortunately not one single letter of Jackson's in reply has been preserved, nor can we trace any of Jackson's " march " orders for the period. He had written to Lee on November 17, and Lee's reply, from Culpeper camp (which was connected with Jackson by telegraph), is the letter we have quoted above. On November 19 Lee writes again before starting for Fredericksburg : " Your letter of the 18th has been received. It is certainly important to deceive the enemy as long as possible as to our position and intentions, provided it is rendered certain that a junction can be made before a battle, and this latter point we must always keep in view, as necessary to enable us to resist the large force now on the Rappahannock." On this date, it appears, Lee did not anticipate having to make a " determined stand " north of the North Anna, but was nevertheless moving to Fredericksburg " opposite to which place Sumner's corps has arrived." Stuart was then near Warrenton, counting the Federal troops as they passed through, and reporting daily to Lee, who knew even of Halleck's visit to Burnside. Jackson telegraphed to Lee at Fredericksburg on November 21, and Lee's reply (dated " Camp Fredericksburg, November 23 ") gives the result of Stuart's further investigations into the Federal plans. General Stuart had been a pupil of Lee's when the latter was Superintendent at West Point in 1852, and he was destined, like Jackson, to fall in battle ere the war closed, but he may be said to have revolutionized the ideas current at the period as to the employment of cavalry. General Burnside would doubtless have been amazed to hear that the Confederate cavalry leader had collected information from all points between Harper's Ferry and Centreville, and that hardly a single brigade of the Union army was unaccounted for. With Stuart's reports before him Lee writes to Jackson: "Under this view of things, if correct, I do not see at this distance what military effect can be produced by the continuance of your Corps in the Valley. If it were east of the Blue Ridge, either in Loudoun, Fauquier or Culpeper, its influence would be felt by the enemy, whose rear would be threatened, though they might feel safe with regard to their communications. Another advantage would be, provided you were at Culpeper, that you would be in railroad communication with several points, so that the transfer of your troops would be rendered certain, without regard to the state of the weather or the condition of the roads."

Jackson's letter of November 21 (presumably in answer to Lee's letter from Culpeper) did not reach Lee until the night of November 24, a circumstance which gives point to the Commanding General's previous injunctions: " I will advise you from time to time of the movements of the enemy and of mine as far as they can be discovered, and with as little delay as possible ; but you must make allowances for the inaccuracy of the first and the delay of the second, and predicate your movements so as to be on the safe side." How seldom in war is such wise counsel given and acted upon; how often do generals attempt to excuse their blunders by affirming that they were misled by informants, or that "orders" were delayed! Writing on November 25, Lee did not even know where his messenger would meet Jackson, but he addresses him at Madison on the assumption that the 2nd Corps would cross the mountains at Millan's Gap. "Should you think it advisable," he says, "to halt at Culpeper or to make any demonstration on the enemy's rear, I request you to do so." Concluding his letter, Lee shows how completely he had fathomed Burnside's mind :—

"General Burnside has thrown back from view the force he so ostentatiously displayed on his first arrival, but I believe his object has been to secure his camps and facilitate his attainment of supplies. . . . I anticipate no forward movement until the wharves on the Potomac are constructed and the railroad to the Rappahannock repaired. . . . His plan is to advance on Richmond from this base; and to delay him as long as practicable and throw him into the winter, I have determined to resist him from the beginning. Your corps may therefore be needed here." The expression "throw him into the winter" had a special significance in Virginia, the land of forest and stream; and to an army like Lee's, fighting for time, the approaching winter season was as good as a heavy reinforcement. The author of *The Nation in Arms* has pointed out that the different seasons of the year exercise as great an influence as *terrain* upon strategy and tactics. The difference in the length of days—twenty hours in summer and in winter only ten—rain or thaw, snow and cold, increased hunger, the need for warm food and shelter, all combine to restrict a general's plans or drain the strength of an army, by demanding double energy on the part of the commander and double exertion on the part of the troops. Napoleon once said that he had discovered a fifth element—*mud*, and the experience of the pontoon train on the road from Washington was a foretaste of what lay before the Army of the Potomac.

Letters between Jackson and Lee were continually " crossing " each other, and on the evening of November 25, Lee writes again to acknowledge receipt of one from Jackson dated " near Strasburg." Lee now adds to his former suggestions the following, always providing that Jackson, the man on the spot, concurs in the views formed at Fredericksburg :—

" I believe now, if you take a position at Culpeper Court House, throw forward your advance to Rappahannock Station, and cross the cavalry over the river, the enemy would hesitate long before making a forward movement. Should, however, the condition of your corps, the weather or other circumstances render this movement unadvisable, you can proceed by easy marches through Gordonsville or Orange Court House, to join me here."

Lee's suggestions had been made on the supposition that Jackson would cross Blue Ridge by Chester Gap or thereabouts, when his forward move on Warrenton or Culpeper would have enabled him to threaten the Federal rear without deviating from his course, but Jackson had already crossed far to the south of Chester Gap, and so

Lee, writing next day (November 26), desired Jackson to pursue the best route by easy marches to Fredericksburg, advising Headquarters of his approach, so that the march might be hastened if necessary. The enemy had been discovered " for the last day or two " constructing covers for his batteries, and Lee now surmised that Burnside would attempt to cross either at Fredericksburg or at some other point on the river, and so desired that the whole army should be united. Jackson was now at Madison Court House, and there Lee addressed another letter on November 27, directing the march of the 2nd Corps to a position south of Fredericksburg, on the Massaponax Creek, " in easy distance from the railroad by which your subsistence will have to be drawn." A postscript notes that Jackson's letter dated Winchester, November 20, had only just been received.

The last letter of the series is dated November 28 : " I recommend that you send forward a staff officer to select an encampment convenient to wood and water, and to collect forage for your animals upon their arrival." Lee now has reason to believe that the enemy will cross at some point below Fredericksburg, and since five gunboats had appeared off Port Royal, where the approaches to the river from the Federal side were good, Lee assumed that Burnside would cross thereabouts, at some bend which could be flanked by his gunboats. Lee was well aware that a good road existed on the Southern side from Port Royal to Bowling Green, which would give the invader easy access to the Richmond railroad, when once a crossing at Port Royal had been effected. These views Lee communicates to Jackson, to explain why it may become necessary for his corps to move to a point within reach of the Port Royal—Bowling Green road. Jackson had marched 120 miles in eight days, resting on two days, and on November 29 his four divisions were thus disposed: A. P. Hill at Yerby House, five miles from Longstreet's Corps; Taliaferro at Guiney's Station, nine miles from Longstreet's Corps; Ewell (Early) at Shenker's Nek, twelve miles south-east of Fredericksburg; D. H. Hill at Port Royal, six miles further down the river.

The Confederate cavalry were now distributed as follows: Hampton's (1st) brigade watched the upper fords of the Rappahannock; W. F. H. Lee's (3rd) brigade, with the horse artillery attached, was on the river down at Port Royal; Jones' (4th) brigade was detached for operations in the Shenandoah valley; and Fitz Hugh Lee's (2nd) brigade apparently formed the reserve at General Stuart's headquarters.

The Confederates were now protected from anything in the nature of a surprise attack, for the fords over the Rappahannock and Rapidan, at no time desirable communications for a large army, were in the winter season quite unreliable, and though it was possible for parties of cavalry to cross by choosing favourable opportunities and keeping the horses well separated, such enterprises as Sumner and Hooker had proposed on reaching Falmouth, in the absence of pontoons for the prompt advance of the main body, would have exposed their commands to capture or investment in positions where starvation awaited them. Burnside was undoubtedly right in his contention that the immediate supply of pontoons by which subsistence could be brought over the river from Aquia Creek was essential to his plan, and General Halleck's criticism in his Annual Report, to the effect that Burnside erred in not crossing the river by the upper fords, appears to be unsound (Halleck might rather have explained why the War Department neglected Burnside's suggestion that supplies should be sent up the Rappahannock as far as Port Royal, under convoy of light-draught gunboats), for while it is true that the ever-victorious and swiftly-moving armies of Napoleon contrived in some measure to make war support war, by living on the inhabitants of the country invaded, a host like the Federal army, requiring subsistence and forage for 150,000 men and 40,000 animals, would have fared badly in Northern Virignia cut off from Washington while Lee's army was still undefeated.

CHAPTER IV

Cavalry Reconnaissance.

CHAPTER IV

THE interest of the Fredericksburg campaign for a month preceding the great battle centres round the achievements of the cavalry. During the last week of November the horsemen on both sides were active, the Federals pushing their reconnaissances over Blue Ridge into the Shenandoah Valley, and the Confederates effecting another raid into Maryland from the Valley, and crossing the Rappahannock above and below Fredericksburg. On the night of November 24 a company of 35th Virginia Cavalry commenced a march of seventy miles, which the report calls a " Scout into Maryland." The official account of this raid within the enemy's lines for twenty-four hours, without the loss of a man or a horse, affords a view of the methods of the Confederate cavalry when utilized as the eyes and ears of the army. The lesson was not altogether lost upon Europe, as the exploits of the Uhlans in 1870 demonstrated. The commander reported : " Left my camp on the evening of the 24th instant 7 p.m. with forty-six men, proceeded direct to Conrad's Ferry, four miles below Leesburg, and sent an advance guard across the Potomac, who reported none of the enemy near. The main body then crossed and started direct for Poolesville ; when within two and a half miles from the town caught four of the enemy, who were guarding some stores—principally medical stores. They reported some sixteen of the enemy in the town guarding the stores left there. Arrived at the town about 6 a.m. and charged it; captured sixteen of the enemy, together with the telegraph operator, all of whom were paroled; captured stores of all kinds consisting of guns, tents, clothing, medicines, etc., all of which were destroyed with the exception of what the men could carry away on their horses. They remained in the town about three hours; sent scouts around the country in various directions. The company is from that immediate neighbourhood, and knew the country well. Some of the men were near Frederick City, and report about 200 cavalry in the town, together with some 200 convalescent infantry. The company re-crossed the river at White's Ferry without encountering any of the enemy's scouts." Such enterprises kept the Federal flanking detachments in a state of alarm. On the other hand, the Federal commander at Falmouth still remained ignorant of the movements of Jackson, though General Sigel did his best to furnish information, and at the end of November organized a reconnaissance, in which a brigade of infantry and a cavalry brigade took part, under the command of General Stahel. The report sent in to Burnside on November 30 by the O.C. 11th Corps (Sigel) considerably magnifies the achievements of this cumbrous reconnoitring party, which started from Chantilly and occupied Aldie with its infantry on the night of November 27. The next morning the cavalry advanced to Middleburg, White Plains, Salem, Rector town and Ashby's Gap, and reported all the country between Bull Run Mountain and Blue Ridge clear of the enemy. The commander had learned that "one part of Jackson's troops marched by way of the gap to Culpeper, but that his main force with those of the two Hills marched up the valley and were at Newmarket last Wednesday." (On this date, November 26, Jackson's corps was in fact at Madison Court House). General Stahel further reported: "There is a brigade under General Jones at Winchester."

Stahel's cavalry successfully encountered some of General Jones's cavalry, and brought in eighty cattle and eighty horses; his men "used only their swords—no firearms." He took forty prisoners and two colours, and believed he had killed and wounded fifty of the enemy (his own loss was fifteen); and the Confederate account admits that Major White's command suffered the penalty of surprise at Berryville.

White, however, reported his loss as two officers and thirteen men (fourteen prisoners, one wounded) and two wagons, and the other Confederate commander, Colonel Burks, whose camp was two miles from Berryville, reported his loss as seven prisoners and three wounded; we must therefore assume that Stahel encountered a third force of Confederates with results that justified him in reporting that he "achieved a complete victory over a strong force of the enemy's cavalry, routing them, breaking up their camps, taking their colours and many prisoners and commissary and ordnance stores." There exists, however, no evidence on the point, and we need to be always on our guard against a cavalry commander's propensity to magnify a skirmish until it assumes the dimensions of a pitched battle.

On this expedition Colonel Di Cesnola commanded the

Federal cavalry, and his method of working is detailed in his report: "The second day my brigade was in the order of march in the rear, and such it remained until we reached Snicker's Ferry. During that march, small camps found in the woods, and fires whose ashes were still warm, cautioned me that the enemy was, perhaps, not far distant, so I redoubled my vigilance, sending out on my rear scouts to the right and left, and arrested several civilians, whom I questioned. By threatening to send them under escort to Fairfax Court-House, I obtained some useful information as to the whereabouts of the enemy, their strength, and where last seen. Some had seen them that very morning. Being in the rear, I did not consider it necessary to communicate these facts, as Colonel Wyndham, in the advance, had doubtless possessed himself of the same information. In crossing the Shenandoah River, I took the main road, and continued to advance carefully, leaving at short distances small pickets, whose duty it was to keep communications open with the strong picket I had left at Snicker's Ferry, to be informed immediately if the enemy were to make his appearance at any point between the ferry and my command. Thinking that my chance for this time was not that of fighting, but only to act as a support, I detailed several small detachments, to act as flankers, and other small ones to scour the road and search all the houses within a mile on both flanks. Then escorts arrived, bringing me orders from you to take charge of prisoners and send them to the rear. I then detailed Lieutenant Wight to take charge of the prisoners, to take from them their papers, arms, and horses, if any, and gave him sufficient force to keep in check the prisoners, who were becoming every moment more numerous.

"With my command, which, by detachments, was decimated so much as to represent scarcely 100 men, I met you, who ordered me to take the town of Berryville by assault, and, with yourself at our head, we charged through the main street of Berryville, scattering in every direction whatever we met with. When arrived at the outskirts of the town, I formed line of battle, and then yourself took command of a portion of the 9th New York cavalry and charged toward the right side of the wood, and I, with the balance of my command, charged to the left, on the road which leads to Winchester. I met three squadrons of the enemy drawn up in line of battle, covering a large building containing commissary stores, as if awaiting my arrival. I did not give them [an opportunity] to see the difference in numbers, but charged upon them. They broke and ran, not liking our sabres. I pursued the enemy to within five miles of Winchester, but the horses gave way, and I was obliged to leave them behind, so when I returned to Berryville I had with me but one officer and nine men.

"When I charged on the left, I passed through a small camp, and discovered a large building containing commissary stores. I succeeded in capturing it, but the small force I had did not permit me to detail any more men from it, so I continued to charge on the flying squadrons. Seeing that the enemy did not want to have a hand-to-hand fight with us, and, having better horses than ours, I would not be able to capture them, I contented myself with firing at them, dismounting about a dozen of them, wounding some, and the balance keeping the open field. Halting my command, I immediately detached a squad of men, under Capt. B. J. Coffin, to take possession of the commissary stores. During the halt, to give my horses a short rest, orders came from yourself to re-form at once, as my rear was menaced.

"On the third day of the expedition, by the strategical march through Leesburg, instead of Aldie, my command arrived safely in camp at Chantilly."

A Confederate cavalry reconnaissance on November 27 in the neighbourhood of Falmouth, as reported by Gen. Wade Hampton, who commanded it, was deemed worthy of Lee's special commendation, and his detailed report may enlighten the modern cavalry leader on many points of practice: "I crossed the Rappahannock at Kelly's Mill, and proceeded, through Morrisville, across the country toward the White Ridge road. Before reaching this point I learned that a regiment of the enemy was stationed at the Yellow Chapel, eight miles from Falmouth, with their pickets extending to Deep Run, on the Marsh road, and on the White Ridge road in the direction of Warrenton. Finding that I could not reach them before night, I halted within two miles of the chapel, and moved off at 4 a.m. this morning. Striking through the woods between the two roads, I came out on the Marsh road half a mile from the chapel. A charge was immediately made, and my men dashed into the camp of the enemy before he could form. The other detachments followed in quick succession, and in a few moments we had captured every man who was at this camp. One squadron was here, and another was on picket on the two roads already mentioned. Having taken the reserve squadron, I sent the detachment from the Cobb Legion to take the pickets on the White Ridge road, which was successfully performed, as they returned in a short time with seventeen of the enemy—all who were on that road. Sending off the prisoners (about seventy in number), except four who were too severely wounded to be moved, I immediately turned up the Marsh road to sweep off the line of pickets there. This was soon done, as there were but twenty men, under a lieutenant, and I reached Deep Run about 8 a.m., having taken eighty-seven privates and non-commissioned officers, two captains, three lieutenants, two colours, about 100 horses, and the same number of carbines. Of the pickets on the two roads, but five, I think, escaped, and they succeeded in doing this by leaving their horses and fleeing to the woods.

"I am happy to say that there was no casualty on my side. A part of my plan was to have cut off the force at Richards' Ferry, but though I had got completely in their rear, I found my numbers so reduced by the necessary guards to the prisoners that I was forced reluctantly to abandon my design. The Sixth Regiment Regulars was on post there, and I had to leave them for another time."

Hampton is careful to state the exact number of men drawn from each unit who accompanied him; the total is 208. On turning to the Federal report on what General Hooker describes as "that disgraceful affair," Hampton's two weak squadrons appear as "a cavalry force of the enemy 700 or 800 strong." To the credit of the Federal leaders be it said, the officer in charge of the captured picket was "dismissed the service for disgraceful and unofficer-like conduct." It appears that " the instructions to the officer commanding the pickets had been to post his reserve at or near Hartwood, and to keep it entirely screened from observation; to picket all the roads approaching our army between the Rappahannock River and Poplar road, connecting on the left with the pickets of the Second Cavalry Brigade, and on the right with the pickets extending to Aquia Creek. The greatest vigilance and carefulness were enjoined upon him; patrols were frequently to examine the country in front, and his reserve was to stand to their horses from one hour before sunrise until one hour after, every morning.

" On the evening of the 26th instant, an officer was sent to visit the pickets, who remained with them until the morning of the 27th. He was directed to warn them of an expected demonstration on the part of our enemy; to direct the officer in command to keep his reserve constantly saddled and ready for action; to increase the vigilance of the patrols and pickets, and guard against the attack, which he must soon expect. He was told to expect the attack in the morning. It appears that the enemy avoided all pickets and roads, making their way through the woods directly to the reserve, which they first attacked and surprised; then, turning back, took the pickets in the Marsh road, recrossing the Rappahannock at Ellis' Ford."

Averell reconnoitred with two regiments to Grove Church, near Hartwood, on December 1: " Sending a party of one officer and twenty men from Hartwood Church, along the Marsh road, to the crossing of Deep Run, in order to attract the attention of the enemy to that point, I started with my main body up the Warrenton road toward Spotted Tavern. After going three miles, turned to the left, taking an obscure road, which led to the Marsh road near Grove Church. This by-road is about 3½ miles long. When about half way across, we came upon a scouting party of three men, well mounted, who were pursued at full speed by the advanced guard, the column following rapidly, expecting to come upon a camp of the enemy. The Marsh road was soon reached, at a point half a mile this side (east). One of the scouts was captured, and we pushed on at once to Grove Church and beyond, toward Morrisville, without hearing anything or discovering any traces of the enemy. There is no camp at Grove Church, and has not been recently. General Hampton encamped this side of there last Thursday night, but has since recrossed the Rappahannock. I was above Ellis' Ford, and one of my officers and some of my men, who had been there, described the crossing as deep and uncertain. Barnett's Ford, more commonly known, I think, as Skinner's, is also a bad crossing; but Kelly's, nine miles above, is said to be excellent.

"The prisoner states that there is nothing this side of the river, as far up as Kelly's Mill Ford, except small scouting parties like his. He says that there is an impression among the rebels that our army is about to cross the Rappahannock above Ellis' Ford. He belongs to a company of confidential scouts; knows all the generals of the rebels; is a sharp fellow, of some Mexican war experience. He says he was sent out to ascertain if our infantry were in motion in that direction. It is not improbable that General Hampton will take a look at us to-morrow morning. I shall wait to give him a chance, and then return to camp if the general has not further orders for me. This prisoner says that they have a system of signals, established by men on horseback, so that information is conveyed very rapidly. I shall organize something similar to that in this vicinity."

On the evening of the same day, some miles down the river, a detachment of Stuart's cavalry crossed the Rappahannock and captured a Federal picket. As usual, the report by the defeated commander (General Pleasonton in this instance) augments the enemy's strength (from 60 to 200) and diminishes his own losses (from forty-nine, including two officers, to " twenty at the outside ") and even finds comfort in the fact that the enemy "hastily returned to the other side of the river." The sketch printed on page 256 shows exactly how the affair was managed, and the Report is an instructive example of Stuart's methods of work at this period. A Federal mounted detachment of seventy-three officers and men had been sent to Leedstown, to prevent the enemy on the right bank of the river getting supplies from the inhabitants (rebel sympathizers), which they had been doing by means of a ferry at E. F. The O. C. detachment on the night of December 2 posted a sentry at A near a row of cedars ; a group of eight men in Leedstown ; another sentry at C (one-quarter mile from Leedstown) ; and at B (one-half mile from the town and thirty yards from the river) a piquet of thirty-eight men under the O. C. detachment. The remainder of the detachment formed another piquet at D (patrolling beyond G) under a lieutenant. The river was three-quarters of a mile wide and was patrolled by Federal gunboats, which however were often absent "coaling." On the opposite bank was a regiment of Stuart's cavalry with artillery, which undertook to disperse this force of Federals. The artillery, escorted by one squadron, took up a position to prevent the interference of the gunboats, and a detachment of ninety men was ordered to cross the river and capture the Federal piquets. Only sixty men crossed—in skiffs—but the enemy was surprised just before the setting of the moon, about 2.30 a.m. The sentries at A and C, the group in Leedstown and the piquet at B were all captured, together with their horses, though many of the latter were lost by the Confederates in re-crossing the river.

On November 28 the War Department at Washington telegraphed to General Slocum at Harper's Ferry: "What of the rebel forces? Anything about Jackson?" To which Slocum replied two days later: "Scouts report that Jackson has left the Valley,—that he passed through Strasburg last Wednesday (26th inst.), and is moving toward Staunton." As we have seen, Jackson was at this date guarding the river below Fredericksburg, but even so late as December 4 General Kelley, at Cumberland, in Maryland, reported: "Jackson is undoubtedly yet in the Valley."

Early in December General Geary, commanding 2nd division of Slocum's (12th) Corps, started with about 3,200 infantry, fifty cavalry and twelve guns, taking one day's rations in haversacks and five days' supplies in wagons, and marched by the Harper's Ferry and Winchester turnpike to Charlestown, at which point his advanced guard came in contact with the Confederate cavalry, and skirmished with them along the Berryville

F

road till dusk. He bivouacked for the night in line of battle, "felling trees as temporary barricades." Next day he reached Opequon Creek and "found the camp of General A. P. Hill's troops vacated three or four days previously." On December 4 he caused the evacuation of Winchester by the Confederate cavalry which had been holding the town, and " captured 118 rebel soldiers including four commissioned officers " [presumably sick in hospital] and " a quantity of flour the property of rebels." Having obtained what information was procurable Geary returned via Bunker's Hill and Smithfield, but " at Oakland about seventy-five cavalry fired upon and sought to harass my outposts." After bivouacking two nights in the woods and being caught in a severe snowstorm, the column rejoined at Bolivar Heights without a single casualty, and the Federal leaders were informed on December 8 that " General D. H. Hill left with his division about November 17, Jackson with his command about the 25th, and A. P. Hill from the 27th to the 29th of the same month . . . . The two Hills and Jackson were last reported as marching directly toward Fredericksburg and as within twenty miles of Lee's army." History, however, records that on November 29 Jackson's four divisions were stationed between Yerby House and Port Royal, five to eighteen miles south of Fredericksburg, and it is to be feared that General Geary was carefully misinformed by the people of Winchester, whose " great revulsion of sentiment in favour of the Union " he found so " highly gratifying."

Bayard's cavalry in camp near Brooke's Station on the evening of December 2 lost a picket post of fourteen men and the officer in charge of the post was " dishonourably dismissed;" an occurrence which shows that the Confederate cavalry was even then in rear of the Army of the Potomac on the Dumfries road.

The cavalry brigade of General W. H. F. Lee was at this period doing splendid service on the Lower Rappahannock, and on December 5 it undertook the curious duty of fighting Union gunboats. Four of these vessels, carrying twenty-one guns, were lying off Port Royal, and it was desired to drive them out of the river without drawing their fire upon the town. So General D. H. Hill planted his Whitworth gun in a position to open fire at a range of three miles, and Lee detailed Pelham, of the Horse Artillery, to take two rifled guns to a point where the gunboats—outranged—had tried to get shelter from the Whitworth gun: Pelham waited until they were within 300 yards, and then "opened with deadly effect." The Whitworth gun here mentioned had at Upperville driven entirely off the field a Yankee battery and a large force of cavalry and artillery at a distance of $3\frac{1}{2}$ miles, a feat which modern gunners could hardly excel; but then the Confederate Whitworth was in the hands of Captain Hardaway,—"the best practical artillerist I have seen in service," says D. H. Hill, whose account of the affair is here quoted.

The Federal cavalry was undoubtedly at this period completely outclassed, and its inferiority was admitted by its leaders. General Pleasonton, in a memorandum dated December 1, stated his belief that "the rebel cavalry owe their success to their organization, which permits great freedom and responsibility to its commanders," and he petitioned on behalf of the Federal mounted troops for a "Corps" organization. Pleasonton advocated a cavalry corps of two divisions with eight batteries of horse artillery; but the essential thing was, in his opinion, divorce of the cavalry from the infantry, the withdrawal of cavalry brigades from the commands of Generals Sumner, Hooker and Franklin, and the appointment of an independent General to command the whole of the cavalry, subject only to the commander-in-chief of the army. Unfortunately the Army of the Potomac possessed in 1862 no general fit to utilize a large force of mounted troops. Sheridan, who was destined to fill the post ultimately, was now, at the age of thirty-one, commanding a division in the Army of Ohio, and so for two years longer the Federal cavalry was to languish for want of a leader. The history of cavalry seems to prove that whenever an army throws up a Seidlitz, a Ziethen, a Murat or a Kellerman, the mobile arm has flourished. Stuart alone created the Confederate cavalry, and made it what it was in 1862, and his death and the coming of Sheridan immediately caused the 'balance of power,' in regard to cavalry, to pass over to the Federals. In the meantime the Federal horsemen lay under the stigma of being scarcely able to sit their horses when trotting, and Lord Wolseley tells the story of a Northern cavalry officer excusing the failure of his command in an enterprise against Confederate cavalry by saying: "What can we do? We can never catch them, for whilst we are opening the gates they are all over the fences." Their admirable leader, James E. B. Stuart, was eulogized by General Lee in few though memorable words: "*He never brought me a piece of false information.*"

CHAPTER V

FREDERICKSBURG—LEE'S PREPARATIONS—RIVER RECONNAISSANCE — BURNSIDE'S PLAN FOR CROSSING — CONFEDERATE DEFICIENCIES

CHAPTER V

FREDERICKSBURG before the war was a typical old Virginia town, redolent of the early colonial days of which we read in "The Virginians." Called after the Prince who, had death spared him, would have reigned over us as George III, and who perchance would have averted the Revolution, the town was situated between King George and Fairfax counties, and its very street-names were reminiscent of the Hanover dynasty and the mother country. Marye's Heights recalled the school-days of George Washington, the young Virginian who was agent for Lord Fairfax, owner of the adjoining county—Washington, who fought as a Colonial officer for the British against the French, and whose family coat, the famous Stars and Stripes, still endures alongside the Spencer brasses in the village church of Brington, in Northamptonshire. His mother's farm lay across the river in Stafford County and the " Mary Washington " monument yet stands in the town, where she had a house which is owned to-day by the Society for the Preservation of Virginia Antiquities. Round about the city were the mansions and estates of wealthy planters, who drank their wine in Fredericksburg taverns (reckoning their score in pounds sterling, not in dollars and cents), and drove their coach-and-four to Mulberry races. Standing in Commerce Street on market days before the railroad era would be seen scores of fine road-wagons, which had brought in the produce of the country between Fredericksburg and the Shenandoah Valley, journeying on the old Plank Roads. For more than a century Fredericksburg had been a flourishing town, and its riverside appanage, the so-called village of Falmouth, on the opposite bank of the Rappahannock, had boasted its local newspaper since 1786, had been a port for large vessels and a place where a merchant might build up a fortune. Unfortunately for its citizens, Fredericksburg was a strategic point: it stood, as President Davis had aptly said, " right in the wrong place," for it was on the direct line between Washington and Richmond, and so was periodically exposed to the ravages of war for four long years and its National Cemetery to-day preserves the memory of 15,000 American soldiers who fell in the vicinity. It was on April 27 that Fredericksburg first fell into the hands of the Federal military forces. The M.S. journal of an inhabitant thus records the event:—

" Fredericksburg is a captured town! The enemy took possession of the Stafford hills which command the town on Friday, the 18th, and their guns have frowned down upon us ever since. Fortunately for us, our troops were enabled to burn the bridges connecting our town with the Stafford shore, and thus saved us the presence of the Northern soldiers in our midst; but our relief from this annoyance will not be long, as they have brought boats to the wharf, and will of course be enabled to cross at their pleasure. It is painfully humiliating to feel oneself a captive but all sorrow for self is now lost in the deeper feeling of anxiety for our army, for our cause! We have lost everything, regained nothing; our army has fallen back before the superior forces of the enemy, until but a small strip of our dear Old Dominion is left to us. Our sons are all in the field, and we, who are now in the hands of the enemy, cannot even hear from them."

On July 23 the Federal authorities administered martial law by arresting four of the principal citizens and sending them north. The diarist remarks: "The recent orders of Secretary Stanton and General Pope make it appear that we are not to be treated with the least leniency hereafter. Our provost marshal has been changed because he was 'too kind to the rebels,' and they are now doing everything they can to persecute and annoy us. All the stores in town are closed to-day to prevent us from getting any supplies, and they have been sending their wagons around to everybody's farm in the neighbourhood, taking their hay and other products. I am afraid my poor brother will have nothing left for his winter supply."

The month of August brought a welcome change; General Lee's successes in the field had thrown the Federals on the defensive, and the last day of the month witnessed some exciting events, which are thus described in the Journal: "We saw clouds of smoke rising from the encampments on the opposite side of the river. We walked down several squares towards the bridges. Everything indicated an immediate departure; the guards were drawn up in line; the horses and wagons packed at headquarters; cavalry officers rode up and down giving orders; company after company of pickets were led into town from the different roads, and joined the regiment at the City Hall; ambulances with the sick moved slowly through the streets ; and as we stood watching we saw the officer who acted as provost marshal of the town ride by with his adjutant ; and in a few moments, as we stood watching, the command was given to march, and away went infantry down one street and cavalry down another to the bridge. It was very quietly done ; there was no music—no drum ; not a voice broke the air except the officers' 'Forward, march !' I felt glad to be relieved of the presence of the enemy, and to be freed from the restraints of their power ; glad to be once more within Southern lines, and to be brought into communication with our own dear people. But the great gladness was that the evacuation of Fredericksburg showed that they had been defeated up the country, and could no longer hold the line of the Rappahannock. And this gave us strong hope that Virginia might yet be free from the armies of the intruder. We had scarcely reached home when a thundering sound shook the house, and we knew it was the blowing up of the bridges. Several explosions followed, and soon the bright flames leaped along the sides and floors of the bridges and illuminated the whole scene within the bounds of the horizon ; the burning continued all night, and our slumbers were disturbed by frequent explosions of gunpowder placed under the two bridges . . . went out with his gun and joined the guard which it was deemed proper to organize for the protection of the town against any stragglers or unruly persons who might chance to be prowling about. The first thing I heard this morning was that my two servants [slaves], Martha and Susan, had returned and requested permission to engage in their usual work."

A few days later Confederate cavalry came to garrison the town, and Fredericksburg was *en fête*. The diary records the event as follows : " The sound of the bugle and the tramp of cavalry fell upon our ears, and very soon a troop of seven hundred horsemen appeared; they were our own 'greys.' We could have told it by their gallant bearing if it had not been revealed by their dress. The air was rent with shouts. As we came home the streets were filled with excited people, and everybody's face was lighted up with a glad smile." The diary continues : " Sept. 4.—Sent my portion of the soldiers' breakfast to Hazel Run by J—— and S——, who came back with a great account of the way the soldiers were feasted on hot rolls, beafsteak and coffee, and their enjoyment of the good things after so long an abstinence." Before the year was ended, however, the gentle diarist was to witness a scene of desolation, amid which Fredericksburg was conspicuous ; and the last state of the unhappy town was worse than the first, by reason of the peculiar attraction possessed by court house and churches, walls and windows, for the projectiles of one hundred heavy guns and fifty thousand rifles.

Coming events, says the proverb, cast their shadows before, and on November 10 a party of Federal cavalry dashed into the streets of Fredericksburg skirmished with a few Southern horsemen who held the post, and withdrew with what information they had gained after burning the bridges. This affair reflected little credit on either side. The burning of the bridges by Dahlgren's cavalry was disapproved by the Federal authorities as unnecessary, and Lee caused a Court of Inquiry to investigate the circumstances in which the garrison was surprised, with the result that neglect of duty on the part of the piquets was shown, but excused on the ground that the garrison consisted of raw troops lately sent from Richmond. A week later (November 16) the Confederate cavalry, now on the alert, reconnoitred in turn and warned Colonel Ball, the Commandant, of the approach of Sumner's corps on the Warrenton, Stafford Courthouse and Poplar roads. Ball telegraphed to Richmond for support, and was reinforced by four companies, which brought his force up to 520 men. His infantry were posted in the mill race and mill, opposite Falmouth, the cavalry in the upper part of the town, and a battery of four guns on a plateau half a mile above the town. On November 17 the Southern scouts again went out, but were driven back across the river by the Federal advanced cavalry, and four hours later the enemy's main body (Sumner's 1st and 2nd divisions) appeared on Stafford Heights and opened fire with twenty guns on the Confederate battery half a mile distant. On November 18 Colonel Ball received reinforcements from General Lee (about 500 men), who relieved the wearied infantry at the mill, and replaced the 4-gun battery. On November 19, at daybreak, W. H. F. Lee arrived with his cavalry, followed by Longstreet's 1st and 2nd Divisions, and on November 20 Lee himself was holding a conference with the Mayor of Fredericksburg at "Snowden," about a mile out of the town. The interview closed by the mayor saying: "Then, General Lee, I understand the people of the town must fear the worst." He replied: "Yes, they must fear the worst."

The day following, November 21, at 10 a.m., a flag of truce was sent across the river by the Federals and detained in a log hut by the bank, while the following letter was forwarded by Colonel Ball through the proper channels to General Lee. It was addressed by General Sumner to the Mayor and Common Council of Fredericksburg :—

"Under cover of the houses of your city, shots have been fired upon the troops of my command. Your mills and manufactories are furnishing provisions, and the material for clothing, for armed bodies in rebellion against the Government of the United States. Your railroads and other means of transportation are removing supplies to the depots of such troops. This condition of things must terminate; and by direction of Major-General Burnside, commanding this army, I accordingly demand the surrender of the city into my hands, as the representative of the Government of the United States, at or before five o'clock this afternoon Failing an affirmative reply to this demand by the time indicated, sixteen hours will be permitted to elapse for the removal from the city of women and children, the sick, wounded and aged; which period having elapsed, I shall proceed to shell the town. Upon obtaining possession of the town, every necessary means will be taken to preserve order, and secure the protective operation of the laws and policy of the United States Government." At seven o'clock in the evening the flag of truce was rowed back over the river with the Mayor's reply to the effect that Confederate troops were in the vicinity, who in the circumstances would not themselves occupy the town, but neither would they permit the Federal troops to do so.

Before nightfull on November 22, General Lee had with him at Fredericksburg two brigades of Stuart's cavalry, Pendleton's Reserve Artillery, and four divisions of Longstreet's Corps, and he had already expressed his determination to resist any attempt at crossing on the part of the enemy, " though the ground is favourable for him." Longstreet's 5th division was expected to arrive the next day. Hampton's brigade of cavalry now occupied the forks of the Rappahannock with headquarters at Stevensburg, and Jackson was desired to move out of the Valley and take up a position at Culpeper, " where he would be in railroad communication with several points, so that the transfer of his troops would be rendered certain without regard to the weather or the state of the roads." Already the troops at Fredericksburg had experienced three days of rain and cold. Stuart's reconnaissances north of the Rappahannock, and scouts sent towards Aquia Creek, had informed Lee of the position and strength of the enemy, of his difficulties in regard to transport and supplies, of the evacuation by the Federals of Fauquier and Loudon counties, of the Corps of Observation at Harper's Ferry, of the destruction of the railroad bridges from the Rappahannock to Bull Run, of the burning of military stores at Warrenton Junction and Manassas, and of the distribution of Sigel's Corps between Washington and Falmouth. And Lee pointed out to Jackson, in transmitting Stuart's reports, how the appearance of the 2nd Corps east of Blue Ridge (where it would find forage and subsistence) would threaten the Federal rear, adding that all supplies in Rappahannock, Culpeper, Madison and Greene, Upper Fauquier and Loudon ought to be collected and secured.

As regards the enemy's intentions, Lee writes : " I am apprehensive that while keeping a force in our front he may be transferring his troops to some other quarter." And his anxiety in this respect increased with every day that passed without action on the part of the Federals. Lee nevertheless lost no time in preparing for defence the position he had taken up to oppose the advance of the Federals. Of capital importance, of course, was the choice of artillery positions, and it will be instructive to quote fully from the report of the Chief of Artillery, General Pendleton, who had followed the 1st Corps and arrived with the reserve artillery and ordnance train on Sunday, November 23, and who next morning proceeded to the front to observe the dispositions of the enemy and examine the ground, with a view to the best positions for works and batteries.

"The enemy was conspicuously in force, and often within easy range, from above Falmouth to a point a mile or more below Fredericksburg. They had batteries in position, and were in a few places beginning earthworks. On our own line a few hurried works were in progress. Lane's battery was already well posted, on the heights overhanging the river bend above Falmouth, and forming our extreme left. Epaulements had been thrown up, but they needed much additional work. Lewis' and Grandy's batteries, recently called from Richmond, were also in position on the lower plateau, about half a mile to the right of Lane and nearer the town. These needed for their protection much additional labour." These observations and a general survey of the ground between the river above Falmouth and the Telegraph road occupied the entire day, the distance being considerable and the points of importance numerous.

The next day, November 25, after detailing Captain Ross to proceed with his battery to a point on the river three or four miles below (to be indicated by a member of the commanding general's staff) where gunboats might be attacked, General Pendleton again visited the front to study the ground "with reference alike to its own features and to the apparent designs of the enemy." Commanders of the reserve batteries accompanied him along the line, that they also might become familiar with routes and positions. On November 28, General Lee having requested that another rifle battery should be placed eight or ten miles lower down the river to assist in repelling gunboats, Pendleton took Milledge's battery of light rifles to a commanding bluff, just below Skinker's Mill. Here the battery was left, with one of General Stuart's, under charge of Major John Pelham, with whom, moving from point to point as gunboats threatened, it remained more than ten days. Next day saw the arrival of men and horses with two 30-pounder Parrott guns, which Lee had ordered up from Richmond, and measures were taken to have the guns tested, and to fit them in all respects for service.

On December 1, Pendleton again examined the whole line, to find good positions for these two large guns, facility of ingress and egress being important for them, as well as extensive command of the field. The points selected were reported to General Lee, and on his approval the sites were next day pointed out, working parties engaged, clearings commenced, etc. The work on the right and back of Mr. Howison's house was directed by General Cobb; that on the eminence farther to the left, and near the Telegraph road, was staked off and directed by Pendleton himself. This point, densely wooded when first chosen, became the most important, perhaps, in the entire locality, as the position affording the best view of all the field, and, therefore principally occupied by the commanding general and his staff during the battle. In such duties, and in designating the various batteries to occupy the assigned positions, General Pendleton was engaged till the evening of December 11. General Longstreet had upon his arrival at Fredericksburg, on November 19, assigned his troops to positions as follows : McLaws' division upon the heights immediately behind the city and south of the Telegraph road ; Anderson's division on McLaws' left, and occupying the heights as far north as Taylor's Hill ; Pickett's division on McLaws' right, and extending to the rear along the margin of a wood which skirts the watercourse called Deep Run ; Hood's division was moved a few miles south near Hamilton's Crossing on the railroad ; Ransom's division was held in reserve near the Corps headquarters. The Corps batteries were posted along the heights, pits being made for their protection. A portion of the reserve artillery was assigned to McLaws' division. Walton's "Washington" Artillery occupied the heights at Marye's Hill, and some of Alexander's reserve artillery occupied the other portion of Anderson's front, "extending to the Taylor house, on our left." The brigade batteries that were not assigned to positions on the heights were held in readiness to co-operate with their commands, or for any other temporary service. Longstreet established his picket line along the river bank, from Banks' Ford

G

to Talcott Battery, the most important portion of it being under the immediate orders of General McLaws. In addition to the natural strength of the position, ditches, stone fences, and road cuts were found along different portions of the line, and parts of McLaws' line were further strengthened by rifle trenches and abatis. Upon the approach of Jackson's Corps (December 12) Hood's division was marched back and closed in upon the right of Pickett, occupying the heights on the opposite side of Deep Run.

On November 22 General Sumner had, " through mistake," shelled a train leaving the town, and from that date the railroad terminus was fixed five miles nearer Richmond, out of range of the Federal batteries. A few days later Lee contemplated breaking up the railroad, as a means of retarding Burnside's advance, by compelling him to move with a large wagon train in the event of his establishing his army on the southern bank of the river, but after detailing a party of 400 men for the work the measure was abandoned in order to reassure the citizens, who had not yet learnt the lesson which the burning of Moscow teaches for all time. Lee's consideration for the inhabitants had already been exhibited by his resolution not to draw the enemy's fire upon the town by a military occupation. In the meantime Lee had employed an engineer officer to examine the banks and approaches to the river from the enemy's point of view, and to indicate favourable points of crossing. The engineer's report (printed in our Appendix) is worth studying, as an example of river-reconnaissance, and it is deeply to be regretted that the Coast Survey Charts mentioned are not available for reference, since existing maps do not show all the places mentioned in the Report.

Lee's foresight is remarkable, if we consider that Burnside afterwards stated that he had made preparations to cross the river at Skinker's Neck, about fourteen miles below Fredericksburg. " The ground at this point was favourable for crossing, but our preparations attracted the attention of the enemy, after which he made formidable arrangements to meet us at that place. The necessary orders, both written and verbal, had been given for the troops to be in readiness to move with the requisite amount of ammunition and supplies. . . . I should have endeavoured, in case of success, to have moved in the direction of Guiney's Station with a view of interrupting the enemy's communications, and forcing him to fight outside his entrenchments." In his telegram to Washington dated 2.20 a.m., November 25, Burnside states : " Enough pontoons have arrived to make one bridge, and we hope to have enough for two by daylight. I have selected two places of crossing which I will report by letter." The next day the commander of the gunboats writes an enigmatic note to Burnside : "Would it not be well to keep an eye on the present place of obstructions in the river ? Will you communicate with me on the river bank as far down as possible ? I expect to reach Port Royal to-morrow (November 27). You will judge when to start the supports against the sharpshooters." And on November 30 he writes again : " I recommended the crossing point to be at Port Royal or Mill Bank, on a bridge at each, as the most desirable points for joint operations. The points are clear and can be well covered by my vessels. The hills back from the water can be taken quietly by cavalry, followed by artillery, which will effectually cover the crossing, the gunboats forming the extreme right flank."

Everything had favoured the Federals during the week ending November 29. Lee's army was then divided, the bridging equipment was available, the gunboats ready to co-operate, the road from Port Royal to Bowling Green clear, and but one thing was apparently needed—the will to advance. But the fatal paralysis of energy that always overcame Burnside at the moment when action became necessary to carry out his fully matured plans now intervened, and the opportunity was lost, for Jackson was approaching, and Lee's prescience had already assigned the 2nd Corps a position from which it could make those "formidable arrangements" which, Burnside averred, put an end to the Federal enterprises below the Massaponax.

Notwithstanding the apparent advantages which accrued to the Confederates from the lethargy which again overcame the Army of the Potomac, at the begining of December, 1862, General Lee was feeling the strain of anxiety that always accompanies defensive operations. Holding a frontier 200 miles in length from Richmond to the Shenandoah Valley, the Confederates waited expectant of a heavy blow, but ignorant of where the blow might fall if delivered by an active and determined enemy. General Gustavus Smith was vigorously improving the defences of Richmond (impressing thousands of slaves for labour on the fortifications), anticipating a possible advance of the Federals south of James River. A battalion (3rd North Carolina) was holding the bridge over the North Anna, and emplacing guns on the south bank of that river, preparing for an enemy who might appear either from the Lower Rappahannock or the Lower Pamunkey. Jackson's Corps was distributed between Port Royal and the Massaponax. Longstreet's Corps held the bend of the river about Fredericksburg, and between him and the Valley (held by General W. E. Jones since Jackson's departure) there was nothing but a brigade of cavalry under General Wade Hampton. Jones still held Winchester, having sent back his trains to Strasburg on the approach of the Federals under General Geary from Harper's Ferry. Lee's dépôt at Staunton was held by a garrison of about 200 men; and in the general hospital there about 1,000 men lay sick, whose arms had " from the necessities of the service " been sent to another Confederate army in the southwest. " Weak in numbers at all points," as Lee had declared on November 28, the Confederates were also in want of arms (3,000 were needed for Jackson's Corps); a number of the cavalry were dismounted through their horses having been killed or worn out in the service, and between 2,000 and 3,000 men were still barefooted, their boots having been lost in the long marches over rough roads. Moreover, " I have felt," says Lee, " in every battle the advantages that the enemy possessed over us in their artillery . . . I am greatly in need of longer range smooth bore guns." Since the price of horses had become so high that the Confederate government was unable to procure remounts, the cavalry question was solved by transferring to an infantry unit any troopers without serviceable horses, and recruiting the mounted branch by allowing to join it such of the infantry as were fit for mounted service and could provide themselves with horses at their own expense. Lee was trying at this time to organize a corps of scouts and couriers, in order to relieve the cavalry from duty as orderlies to general and staff officers. Of shoes and blankets the War Department at Richmond had promised a supply, by impressment, even, if necessary,—manufacturers at Richmond were just then demanding £3 a pair for boots, and the raw hides of slaughtered cattle had been used for foot-coverings in Longstreet's Corps—but Lee is warned that " the first received may of necessity be applied to the urgent necessity of one of our Western armies." These western armies were clamorous for reinforcements, too, and Lee, expecting battle every day, was beset with applications for troops to strengthen other parts of the theatre of operations. Moreover, on December 8, the General had to tell the President that " unless the Richmond and Fredericksburg railroad is more energetically operated it will be impossible to supply this army with provisions, and oblige its retirement to Hanover Junction." The ordnance difficulty was partly overcome by recasting the bronze 6-pounder and 12-pounder howitzers to furnish the metal for some Napoleon guns (12-pr). which were much wanted. Lee remarked that nearly all the guns the army possessed had been captured from the enemy.

Hardly a day passed without one or other of these administrative worries demanding a letter from the Commanding General to President Davis, the Secretary of War (Seddon), the Chief of Ordnance, or the Inspector-General at Richmond, and in a " confidential " letter to the President on December 8 Lee reports " vast preparations for our suppression, and the expression of great confidence on the part of the North. Re-inforcements are still coming to General Burnside's army." This information he had obtained from a scout who had been absent several weeks visiting the Northern cities from Washington to New York, and who had just rejoined the Confederate army, travelling via Alexandria and Dumfries within the enemy's lines.

At this date, by a curious coincidence, General Burnside was perusing a remarkable document prepared by a Federal scout, which threw considerable light upon affairs in the South. A certain Joseph Snyder, described by General Sigel as " one of the best scouts in this corps," had allowed himself to be captured at the end of October and, while traversing as a prisoner of war the Confederate lines of communication from Winchester to Richmond, had diligently collected information bearing upon the enemy's garrisons, ordnance and fortifications, his morale and resources. Having spent a month in these investigations, he contrived, by what means we know not, to report at Sigel's headquarters on December 3, with an elaborate diary of his adventures and discoveries, which Sigel transmitted to Burnside, with a request that its author's name be kept secret, and the naïve remark " He is still a scout, and might be tried as a spy in case he was again made a prisoner."

CHAPTER VI

FEDERAL ARTILLERY DISPOSITIONS—LAYING THE PONTOON BRIDGES—CROSSING THE RAPPAHANNOCK.

CHAPTER VI

ON December 10 General Burnside commenced the operations which resulted in the battle of Fredericksburg three days later. He had ordered General Slocum to move from Harper's Ferry to Falmouth, intending to use his force to protect his communications when he advanced, and on December 8 he directed Slocum to march via Centreville, which was the shortest way, getting his supplies from some of the depots in Maryland, or from Washington or by the railroad.

Burnside's later views as to the place of crossing are stated in the following letter to the Chief of Staff at Washington, dated 11.30 p.m., December 9, the concluding sentence of which suggests the timidity of a subordinate official rather than the resolution of a commander:—

" All the orders have been issued to the several commanders of grand divisions and heads of departments for an attempt to cross the river on Thursday morning (December 11). The plans of the movement are somewhat modified by the movements of the enemy, who have been concentrating in large force opposite the point at which we originally intended to cross. I think now that the enemy will be more surprised by a crossing immediately in our front, than in any other part of the river. The commanders of grand divisions coincide with me in this opinion, and I have accordingly ordered the movement, which will enable us to keep the force well concentrated, at the same time covering our communications in the rear. I am convinced that a large force of the enemy is now concentrated in the vicinity of Port Royal, its left resting near Fredericksburg, which we hope to turn. We have an abundance of artillery, and have made very elaborate preparations to protect the crossings. The importance of the movement and the details of the plan seem to be well understood by the grand division commanders, and we hope to succeed. If the General-in-Chief desires it, I will send a minute statement by telegraph in cipher to-morrow morning. The movement is so important that I feel anxious to be fortified by his approval. Please answer."

At dusk on Wednesday, December 10, the four artillery commanders, Hays, Tompkins, Tyler and De Russy joined their batteries at the places of concentration, and conducted them into position, completing the movement an hour before midnight, without any noise by which Lee's outposts could learn what had taken place. For this occasion the whole of the guns, except one battery per division, had been attached to what in those days was called the Artillery Reserve, and this mass of 147 guns was divided into four commands, to each of which specific duties were assigned. The right division (forty guns under Colonel Hays) was posted north of Beck's Island and east of Falmouth, to clear the hills on the south side of the river and their slopes down as far as the town; to engage the Confederate batteries on the crests, and to sweep the plain from below the ford to the hills, and generally to aid the Federal assault on the right. All were rifled guns (six were 20-pounder Parrotts), and their emplacements extended from Falmouth dam to a deep long ravine about 500 yards below Falmouth. The right centre division (thirty-eight guns under Colonel Tompkins) was to protect the throwing of the bridges, cover the pontoons and workmen, and sweep the streets of Fredericksburg, so that no reinforcements could reach the Confederate advanced troops, which were suspected of being in the houses and behind cover opposite the bridges. The guns were those known as " light rifles " and light 12-pounders, and were emplaced from the ravine to near the point assigned for the middle bridge. The left centre division (twenty-seven guns under Colonel Tyler) was placed to prevent the Confederates reinforcing either flank from the other, except by a circuitous route in rear of the position, to sweep the valley of Hazel Run and control the railway bridge which crossed it. The guns were all rifled (seven were $4\frac{1}{2}$-inch siege guns, and eight were 20-pounder Parrotts), and they occupied the crest of the high ridge from near the middle bridge to a wooded ravine near the centre of the ridge. The left division (forty-two guns under Captain De Russy) was directed to cover the ground below the lower bridges, protect the workmen while throwing those bridges, and generally protect the left flank of the attack ; its light batteries were to be moved if necessary down the river to prevent the Confederates crossing the Massaponax Creek. The guns included eight Parrotts (20-pounders), and thirty-six 3-inch rifles, and they occupied the remainder of the crest of the high ridge, and the whole of the low ridge, terminating at Pollock's Mill. Tyler's and De Russey's batteries were to unite in keeping clear the plain in front of the lower bridge, and in covering the passage of the troops at that point. All batteries were ordered to select targets in the following order; 1st, Confederate works or guns opening fire on the Federals while massed near the bridges for crossing; 2nd, troops attempting to oppose the crossing; 3rd, troops advancing on the Federals while the latter were deploying on the southern bank; 4th, ground in front of the Federal advance. Commanders were however warned not to fire over the heads of their own troops after the deployment, except in case of absolute necessity.

The question of ammunition supply had caused the Chief of Artillery on December 4 to call attention to the fact that "in small skirmishes between 300 and 400 rounds per battery are often expended, the fire averaging 1 round per minute per gun; while in general engagements batteries have been known to expend all their ammunition in little over an hour and a half . . . in no case, except when firing canister at short ranges, should the fire exceed 1 round from each gun in two minutes, and that rate should only be reached at critical moments . . . twelve shots in an hour at an object over 1,000 yards distant, the time being spent in careful loading and pointing, will produce better results than fifty shots will ordinarily produce from the same gun in the same time." Artillery training had not much improved two years later, when an intelligent gunner in the Army of the Potomac described what he termed "the artillery humbug." Speaking of course of a field battery, he says:—

"Teams were hitched to the guns almost daily, and they were whirled over comparatively dry ground in a highly bewildering but exceedingly useless manner. Every enlisted man in the army knew that we were to fight in a rugged, wooded country, where the clearings were surrounded by heavy forests, and where deep shrub and timber-clad ravines hazed the air, and where practice and practice and still more practice in estimating distance was required, if we were to fire accurately and effectively. Did the artillery officers zealously practise us in estimating distance? Never, to my knowledge. They taught us how to change front to the right, to the rear, and on the several pieces that formed the battery . . . never while I was in the artillery camp did I see the guns unlimber for target practice. The dismounted or gun drill was useful, but this too was loaded down with memory-clogging detail."

The Chief of Artillery further hinted that the reckless expenditure of ammunition was sometimes prompted by a desire to leave the field quickly, and he ordered that in future both guns and gunners should remain in position throughout the action, and that " as soon as one caisson from each section has been emptied the empty caissons will be sent to the rear under charge of a non-commissioned officer, to replenish at the Ammunition train." The Federal batteries established along the Stafford Heights were placed in communication with the troops crossing, with General Headquarters, and with each other, by means of signal stations which were fixed near the headquarters of the artillery commanders—one upon a hill near Falmouth ; one upon the Corn Bluff southeast of the Phillips house ; another at the Lacy house ; a fourth station was fixed south of the Corn Bluff near De Russy's batteries.

General Burnside, having posted his heavy artillery to

command the southern bank of the Rappahannock for six miles, issued orders to his engineer units to the following effect :—

"Two bridges to be thrown at upper end of Fredericksburg, one at lower end, and two a mile below, making the distance between the extreme bridges nearly two miles. Each bridge to be covered by artillery and a regiment of infantry. Heads of bridge trains to arrive at bank of river at 3 a.m.; material to be unloaded and boats in the water by daylight, and bridges to be then finished in two or three hours, if not interrupted by the enemy."

On both sides of the river, in the vicinity of the bridges, the ground rises rapidly to a plateau 30 to 50 feet above the water. The river being sunk 30 feet below the plateau on both sides, the bridges would be covered from the Confederate artillery fire ; and the Federal artillery officers believed that they could at once silence any musketry fire from the town, or from the bank opposite the lower bridges. On the Federal bank the plateau runs back half a mile, and then the ground rises again 30 to 100 feet, forming a second plateau or ridge. This higher ground commands the town and the ground behind it westward ; and below the town the whole of the Confederate bank of the river for one or two miles was exposed to artillery fire from the ridge, which is known as Stafford Heights.

Since the operation of bridge-building in presence of an enemy is one with which few are familiar (technical reports seldom find their way into a general's dispatches) some account of the work done at Fredericksburg in 1862 will be instructive to students. According to the

Report of the O.C. Engineers at the lowest bridge, his battalion, with a train of thirty boats, arrived near the bank of the river about 3 a.m. On account of the difficulty of the approach, the train was obliged to unload 200 yards from the site of the bridge, and transport all the boats and material to the water by hand. This occasioned an unexpected delay of two hours. By 7 a.m. all the material was at the water's edge, and in spite of progress being retarded by ice in the river, at 10.30 a.m. the bridge was completed and the approaches half an hour later, when General Franklin was notified that all was ready for the passage of artillery and infantry.

Confederate skirmishers on the opposite bank had opened fire about 9 a.m., but were soon forced to retire by the Federal covering parties: only one man was wounded, and though at this time some engineers were at work on the approaches on the south shore, only two of this party were taken prisoners by the Confederates.

General Woodbury commanding the engineer brigade engaged in throwing the four upper bridges, reported to the following effect :—

Four bridge trains were taken to the banks of the river at 3 a.m., preparatory to the construction of two bridges at the rope ferry above the centre of the town, one bridge opposite the lower end of the town and one bridge about 1 mile below the town. All these bridges were commenced soon after 3 a.m., protected each by a regiment of infantry, placed under the cover of the adjacent low banks. The lower bridge was completed, all but the last bay, at 8. 15 a.m., when a Confederate volley wounded three engineers and caused for the time a suspension of the work; but the enemy, having no shelter, was soon dispersed by the Federal artillery. The bridge was finished at 9 a.m. The lower town bridge and one of the upper ones were about two-thirds built at 6 a.m., when the Confederate riflemen, under cover, opened fire upon the pontoniers and the infantry supports. Three officers and many privates were soon disabled. The Federal artillery in a dense fog tried in vain to silence this fire, and though the work was resumed several times during the morning, little progress was made. About 10 a.m. eighty volunteers were led to the scene of operations, one-half of them being placed under cover as a reserve. Before the remainder could touch the bridge several men were shot down, and the others then refused to work. When the fog cleared up soon after noon, the Federal guns became very effective, and so the fire of the enemy was greatly diminished. About 3 p.m. preparations were made for sending over men in pontoons, and after heavy cannonading by the batteries on Stafford Heights about 120 men crossed at the upper bridge in six pontoons, rowed each by three men. The infantry on reaching the opposite bank formed up and gallantly rushed the buildings occupied by Confederate sharpshooters and took some prisoners. Other parties rapidly followed, and the bridges were finished without further opposition. Soon afterwards 100 men crossed at the lower town bridge in four pontoons. Others followed, and the sharpshooters of the enemy who still remained were immediately captured. The bridge was soon afterward finished. Among the Confederate entrenchments was a loop-holed block-house, directly opposite the upper bridges, and only a few yards from their southern abutment. This little fort was found quite uninjured by artillery fire. In the neighbourhood was a rifle-pit behind a stone wall, some 200 feet long, and cellars enclosed by heavy walls, where the Confederate sharpshooters could load and fire in almost perfect safety.

The Chief of Artillery reported to the following effect with reference to the assistance rendered by his guns on December 11.

Soon after daylight, the upper and middle bridges being about half constructed, a heavy fire of musketry was opened upon them by the Confederates from the opposite bank, which drove the engineers from their work, notwithstanding the fire from their infantry supports. The Federal batteries were then opened, and they partially silenced the fire of the enemy. As the fog was dense and the Federal batteries at a distance—those on the bluff could not be used safely on the immediate banks of the river—six light 12-pounder batteries (thirty-six guns) were drawn from the divisions and posted on the banks (four near the upper and two near the middle bridges) to open a severe cannonade upon the cover which protected the Confederate sharpshooters. After the enemy's fire was thus silenced another attempt was made to throw the bridges; but Lee's skirmishers soon opened again, and a column of his infantry moved down the principal street toward the water. A Federal battery drove these back; but the sharpshooters again succeeded in stopping the work on the bridges, for it was impossible for the Federals to open with their artillery so long as the pontoniers were at work, and the enemy's cover was proof against the Federal infantry fire. All the batteries that could be brought to bear were now, by order of General Burnside, turned upon the town, and soon it was rendered untenable by any considerable force. Once more the fire of Confederate sharpshooters was beaten down by the Federal artillery; and the work of throwing the bridges was resumed by volunteers. Again, a few hundred Confederate sharpshooters, scattered among the cellars, in ditches, and behind stone walls, drove the engineers from the bridges. At length some one proposed to fill with infantry the bateaux (pontoons) not yet in their places in the bridges, make a dash to the opposite shore, and, while the troops should land and attack the enemy in his cover, to row the pontoons to their places and complete the bridges. It was now 2.30 p.m. The guns again opened fire, and by a furious cannonade completely suppressed the Confederate fire, when the boats at a given signal—cessation of fire—pushed across. The infantry (volunteers from the 7th Michigan and 89th New York) jumped out and dashed at the Confederates, driving them from cover and capturing over eighty prisoners. At the lower bridge less difficulty was experienced. Five batteries—two withdrawn from the divisions waiting to cross, and three from De Russy's command—were brought near the bridges, and soon drove off the Confederate sharpshooters, who endeavoured, however, to prevent the cutting down of the banks to form a practicable road for artillery.

The Federal troops now commenced crossing, and Lee's guns on the crests opposite the upper bridges opened fire, but " without doing any damage." During the night of December 10-11, between sunset and two in the morning, a corduroy road 1,000 feet long was laid at a point on the river about fourteen miles below town. "This ruse seems to have been very effective in deceiving the enemy," says the engineer officer in charge, but we find no record of the matter elsewhere. Besides the bridges above mentioned, one was built by the " regular " Sappers and Miners, and another was afterwards built a mile below the town, so that six bridges, each about 400 feet long, finally spanned the river.

The next day (Friday, December 12) was spent in completing the crossing. The Confederates occasionally fired upon the troops during the passage, Burnside's rifle batteries in position replying. The light 12-pounders, which had been drawn from the divisions the previous day to cover the construction of the bridges, rejoined their respective commands as they crossed.

At the upper bridges there crossed with Summer's grand division ten batteries (fourteen rifles and forty-two 12-pounders), and with Butterfield's Corps and Whipple's division (Stoneman's Corps) nine batteries (twenty-six light rifles and twenty-two light 12-pounders), so that in all nineteen batteries (104 guns) were established in the town in readiness for battle. The greater number of these guns however could not be used, and were left in the streets of Fredericksburg (a portion was eventually ordered back over the river); and one statement is to the effect that only seven batteries were wholly or partially engaged in connexion with the Right Attack. On the left seventeen batteries (forty-six light rifles and forty light 12-pounders) crossed with Franklin's grand division; but to complete this number five batteries (twenty-four rifles) had been taken from De Russy's command and ordered to rejoin their divisions. Franklin was reinforced on the following day by Birney's and Sickle's divisions with five batteries (six rifles and twenty-four light 12-pounders), so that in all twenty-three batteries (116 guns) crossed the river at the lower bridge. The development of the attack on this flank was such that all these batteries were in position and all but one of them engaged, many of them very severely.

CHAPTER VII

THE CONFEDERATES CONCENTRATE FOR BATTLE—FINAL DISPOSITIONS OF LONGSTREET AND JACKSON—CAVALRY RECONNAISSANCE.

CHAPTER VII

ON December 9 the Confederates had occupied the streets of Fredericksburg with Barksdale's "Mississippi" brigade of four regiments, which had orders to defend the river crossings as far down as 440 yards below Deep Run, and to guard the city from a surprise attack. Above the town the river bank was picketed by two regiments. Below the town the 18th Mississippi encamped at Ferneyhough on the old Richmond (Bowling Green) Road. The pickets were doubled on the night of December 10, and about 2 a.m. (December 11) Barksdale warned his divisional commander, General McLaws, that the enemy was in movement. A few hours later he reported that the pontoon bridges were being commenced, and then the prearranged alarm signal was given. At 5 a.m. McLaws fired two guns, but Barksdale kept his men quiet and concealed until the bridges were so far advanced that the working parties had come within easy musket range, and then his sharpshooters, " posted in rifle pits, in the cellars of the houses along the banks, and from behind whatever offered concealment," opened fire with such effect that " nine separate and desperate attempts " to complete the bridges had to be abandoned. The Federals were thus kept at bay for twelve hours, but at 4.30 p.m. the last of the river bank positions became untenable through the Federal artillery fire, and Barksdale's men retired to Caroline Street. The Federals now crossed in boats: the bridges were completed, and a large force passed over the river. Street-fighting lasted until 7 p.m., and then Barksdale's force was withdrawn from the town. The Mississippi brigade had already lost in killed and wounded 169 men and 9 officers, and 62 were cut off in retreat and made prisoners. General Longstreet's account of the action is as follows:—

"The enemy held quiet possession of the Stafford Heights until 3 a.m. December 11, when our signal guns gave notice of his approach. The troops, being at their different camp-grounds, were formed immediately and marched to their positions along the line. Ransom's division was ordered to take a sheltered position in easy supporting distance of the batteries on the Marye Hill. Before the troops got to their positions McLaws' pickets (Barksdale's brigade) engaged the enemy at the river, and from time to time drove back different working parties engaged in laying the bridges. The enemy was compelled eventually to abandon his plan of laying his bridges, and began to throw his troops across the river in boats, under cover of the fire of his sharpshooters and one hundred and fifty odd pieces of artillery. At many points along the river bank our troops could get no protection from the artillery fire. This was particularly the case at the mouth of Deep Run, where the enemy succeeded in completing his bridge early in the afternoon. Later he succeeded in throwing large bodies of troops across at the city by using his boats. Barksdale, however, engaged him fiercely at every point, and with remarkable success. Soon after dark McLaws ordered Barksdale's brigade to retire. The general was so confident of his position that a second order was sent him before he would yield the field. His brigade was then relieved by that of General Cobb, which was placed by McLaws along the Telegraph Road in front of the Marye House, where a stone fence and cut along this road gave good protection against infantry. When Cobb's brigade got into position Ransom's division was withdrawn and placed in reserve. During the night the enemy finished his bridges and began to throw his troops across. The enemy's movements early on December 12 seemed to be directly against our right, but when the fog lifted columns were seen opposite Fredericksburg, the head of them crossing at the bridges opposite the city. Ransom's division was moved back to the Marye Hill. Featherston's brigade of Anderson's division (previously occupying this hill) was closed in upon the other brigades of Anderson. The entire day was occupied by the enemy in throwing his forces across the river and in deploying his columns. Our batteries were opened upon the masses of infantry whenever they were in certain range. Our fire invariably drew that of the enemy's batteries on the opposite heights, and they generally kept up the fire long after our batteries had ceased."

On December 12 General Lee completed his concentration for battle by calling in D. H. Hill's division, which had been sent to Port Royal on December 3 and now was encamped down the river eighteen to twenty-two miles below Fredericksburg. Hill got his orders just before sundown, and marched until Early's division was met, some three miles from Hamilton's Crossing.

Hill then waited till daylight and followed Early into position. Four companies of an artillery regiment (1st. Virginia) were brought in from Rappahannock Academy in Caroline county, where they had arrived on December 3, having started from Winchester (160 miles distant) on November 21, arriving in time to take part in the fight with the gunboats just below Port Royal on December 9. Taliaferro's division marched at daybreak on December 12 to the battlefield from its encampment near Guiney's Station. One of his brigades, consisting of five Virginia regiments and a battery, was hardly stronger than a British infantry battalion; only about 1,100 men were in the ranks, though its complement of officers (123) was excessive, and it is necessary always to remember how weak were the units in both armies compared with our own War Establishments.

In consequence of the movements on December 12 the Confederate right wing, composed of Jackson's (2nd) Corps and Stuart's Cavalry Division, was distributed as follows on the morning of December 13: 1st line, one division (A.P. Hill); 2nd line, two divisions (Early, Taliaferro); Reserve, one division (D. H. Hill). A. P. Hill's division was deployed in two lines near the edge of a wood, which partly concealed them; his right rested on the road leading from Hamilton's Crossing to the Port Royal road; his left extended nearly to Deep Run; the whole of this frontage was occupied by four brigades *less* two regiments, with intervals which were covered by the local reserve (two brigades). Upon "the eminence immediately to the right" (which is presumably the same "height on the extreme right of the crest" which Burnside proposed that Franklin should capture as a preliminary to more serious enterprises) Jackson had posted fourteen guns under Colonel Walker, supported by two regiments from A. P. Hill's division, and during the fight the fire of these batteries was crossed with the fire of other guns, one battery having marched sixteen miles since midnight to come into action. Further yet to the right and in front of the position the cavalry was massed under General Stuart, with Pelham's horse-battery on the Port Royal road (aided during the fight by sections from other batteries), and on the extreme right, beyond the Massaponax, was the long range Whitworth gun, in charge of that remarkable artillerist, Captain Hardaway. On the left of Jackson's line, near the Bernard Cabins, the batteries (twenty-one guns) of Captain Davidson had been posted; and on Davidson's right front, beyond the railroad, were Brockenbrough's (twelve) guns. Such was the distribution of Jackson's command, according to his own Report, which we must accept as correct, notwithstanding other and differing accounts which exist of his dispositions for defence at the battle of Fredericksburg. Certain arrangements that were peculiar to American armies were made on December 12, which are sufficiently disclosed by the following extract from the Provost Marshal's Report :—

" On December 11,—received an order to move toward Fredericksburg with two days' rations, cooked and placed in haversacks. December 12,—moved at dawn on the Fredericksburg road to Hamilton's Crossing, where I placed a guard for the purpose of arresting all stragglers. Also placed a guard, consisting of cavalry and infantry, along the whole line of the corps and in rear of the line of battle about half a mile, with instructions to arrest all men without proper passes on authorized business for their commands, to be brought to the guard placed on the railroad; there my surgeon was stationed to examine all men claiming to be sick without proper passes from their brigade or regimental surgeons. Numbers, however, were really sick and totally unfit for duty; they were without passes. When a sufficient number were collected together, I sent them under charge of cavalry to be delivered to the first major-general whose command was going into the fight, to place them in front and most exposed portion of his command. I am happy to state the number arrested and sent forward were comparatively few in consideration of the size of the army. During the 13th and 14th the number sent in under guard was only 526. Numbers were turned back, owing to their not having proper passes to return to the rear to cook, etc. I am most happy to state I had no occasion to carry into effect the order to shoot all stragglers who refused to go forward, or, if caught a second time, upon the evidence of two witnesses to shoot them. Had I occasion to carry it into effect, it certainly should have been executed to the very letter. During the 13th and 14th,—received and placed under guard 324 prisoners of war, which I sent to Richmond, by order of General Lee. Eleven of them were commissioned officers, and paroled by me; the balance I took names, regiments, brigades, and corps as far as possible, in obedience to your order. December 16,—received 109 prisoners of war, which I paroled and sent to Guiney's Depot, under command of Captain Upshaw, with instructions to have them forwarded by railroad to Richmond, if possible, which orders were carried into effect. During the same day I went through Drs. H. Black's and W. H. Whitehead's hospital, where I paroled 23 Federal prisoners. A considerable number of wounded prisoners were sent to Richmond. They do not appear in this statement, nor could I by any means ascertain the number."

The Provost Marshal opined that " the present system of provost guard if carried into effect will prevent all future straggling." The system was perhaps copied from the Federals, who were obliged even to the close of the war to picket the rear of their battle lines and prevent any soldier quitting the field unless he could show a wound.

The deliberation with which the battle of Fredericksburg was prepared must strike a modern soldier as savouring of a theatrical performance. The actors con their parts, the scenes are " set," and not until all is ready will the curtain go up. And if, as a preliminary on the stage, alarums and excursions precede the play, the simile is perfect: for in war it is the cavalry that keep up a pretence of hostilities, while the infantry and artillery are making ready for their dramatic appearance before a world-wide " audience." The Confederate cavalry leader, Hampton, crossed the Rappahannock on December 1 with three regiments and a battery on a reconnaissance, but returned the next day. Federal scouts reported the circumstance as follows on December 7 :—

" Left Hartwood Church after dark night before last, and travelled all night, all day yesterday, and last night ; on account of the storm, were compelled to go slowly. Went to Grove Church by Telegraph road ; thence to

Ellis' Ford. Saw camp fires on the other side. We passed for Texas Rangers, and were treated by the citizens very kindly. They told us that the left of our (the rebel) army was opposite Ellis' Ford; that there was nothing above, excepting Hampton's Legion, with a battery at Kelly's Ford. We then went by a wood road, about five miles, to Kelly's Ford. Saw about a company on the other bank on picket; appeared to be infantry. Could see camp fires beyond in the woods. Left the ford at daylight yesterday morning; came about ten miles, out to the Telegraph road, crossed it, and went north five or six miles, to a mill where a widow woman lives. General Hampton came over on Monday (December 1st) with three regiments and a battery, and camped near this mill; went back on Tuesday. We were told that there were some of our (the rebel) camps on this side of the Rappahannock. We came out on the ridge road and returned. The roads are very bad."

The Federal scouts who furnished this report belonged to Averell's 1st Cavalry Brigade. Averell had also sent out scouts on the Poplar road ten miles toward Warrenton Junction, and thence ten miles north toward Bristoe, who reported this country clear of the enemy. Averell, however, remarked: "The report of these last is not satisfactory. I shall keep out some good men." On the same date (December 7) another Federal cavalry leader, Pleasonton, reported the capture near Port Royal of a rebel officer, who was known to him as Chief of Artillery to a general then serving in another part of the theatre of war. "This shows," said Pleasonton, "the rebels have brought up troops from the southwest." He was, however, wrong in his inferences, for the officer in question had lately been transferred to Lee's staff. Pleasonton also noted that two Confederate deserters whom he had sent to headquarters had been released and furnished with passes to go to Westmoreland County, which is just outside the Federal lines. There is little doubt that espionage was a profitable trade in 1862, and that Burnside and Lee need have had few secrets from one another.

The next day (December 8) Pleasonton reports the capture by his pickets of two rebel officers, one a signal officer from Richmond, " in citizens' dress." And another cavalry leader, Bayard, writes from Stafford Court House to say : " I am camped 1½ miles from Dumfries. My rations are out to-morrow, and I have no forage tonight, and the terrible roads have thrown the shoes off of a number of my horses. There have been none of the enemy in that section of the country for some time, except a party of eight men who captured two of my cavalry stationed at Occoquan, who had straggled off to Greenwood Church without their arms . . . I think the brigade should refit . . . please reply soon, am waiting in telegraph office." It will hardly be rash to assume that the Confederates who captured the two stragglers obtained the information which gave Hampton another chance to distinguish himself, since two days later (December 10) he set out with 520 men " thinly clad and scantily fed," and at daylight on December 12 surprised the Federal garrison at Dumfries. He took fifty prisoners and the contents of twenty-four sutlers' wagons, and brought away also the telegraph operator with his instruments. He then marched forty miles to Morrisville, and there crossed the river with the spoils of war, without the loss of a man or a horse, and prepared to take part in the coming fight. On the same day, (December 12) the cavalry brigade under Jones in the Valley raided Poolesville in Maryland, destroying the enemy's stores and capturing 77 men and 43 horses. The Federals retaliated near Bunker's Hill, and took 13 " rebel " prisoners.

Although the battle of Fredericksburg, like other engagements that have proved unsuccessful, has often been described as a Reconnaissance in Force on the part of the attackers, it is remarkable that the bulk of the Union cavalry, acting under orders, or perhaps we should say doing nothing for want of an independent leader, remained for three days mere spectators of the operations. On December 11 Sumner's cavalry (two brigades and one battery under Pleasonton) had been massed in columns of squadrons behind the ridge which commanded the upper bridges; on December 12 two squadrons were sent across the river to reconnoitre, who reported the enemy's pickets strongly posted at the bridge over the canal, and were ordered to remain in observation. The remainder of the force stood fast on the left bank, detaching three regiments as follows: One to picket the river in the vicinity of King George Court House, and watch the country between the Potomac and the Rappahannock, so covering the left rear of the army; one to picket the fords above Falmouth, and the country in the direction of Hartwood on the army's right flank; one as escort to the batteries about Falmouth on December 13. Hooker's cavalry, under Averell, apparently acted in accordance with the following order:—

BRIG.-GEN. W. W. AVERELL,—

Move with your command to a position in rear of the corps of General Butterfield, which will be directly across the Rappahannock, with three days' rations and forage issued to your men, the residue to be in wagons. General Butterfield will be established in his new position, in readiness to cross the river at 9 a.m. to-morrow, and your command should be there at or before ten o'clock. No vehicles will cross until further orders, but the train should be compactly parked near you, ready to move at a moment's notice. All the avenues leading down to the Rappahannock are to be left open, and you will regard this in taking your new position.

On the day of the battle Averell received two orders from Army Headquarters, one directing him to detach a force to patrol towards Hartwood, covering the right flank of the army; another order, cancelling the former instructions because "Pleasonton with a heavy force will move in that direction," assigned to Averell the duty of crossing the Rappahannock at the United States Ford, if practicable, in order "to move up in rear of the enemy." It does not appear that any attempt was made to carry out these instructions on December 13.

Franklin's cavalry under Bayard crossed the river with the Left Grand Division on the morning of December 12, and beyond Franklin's statement—"General Bayard has just returned from a reconnaissance. He was fired upon by a large force, five or six companies of infantry, he says, about 500 yards from the railroad directly in front of here "—no record remains of its doings on the battlefield. Bayard himself was killed by a splinter of shell while at Franklin's head quarters waiting for orders.

CHAPTER VIII

MOVEMENTS OF THE THREE GRAND DIVISIONS—REPORTS BY SUMNER, HOOKER AND FRANKLIN—TOPOGRAPHY OF THE BATTLEFIELD—BURNSIDE'S ATTACK ORDERS.

CHAPTER VIII

ON December 9, nearly a month after he had assumed command of the Army of the Potomac, General Burnside had found everything in readiness for the movement preparatory to crossing the Rappahannock opposite Fredericksburg, and he accordingly issued from "Phillips House" the following "Memorandum Orders" at 5 a.m.

"The three commanders of Grand Divisions will report at these Headquarters at twelve o'clock to-day. In the meantime they will give the necessary orders to enable them to place their commands in position at daybreak on the morning of the 11th instant, at such points as may be indicated by *verbal instructions* from the general commanding, not to exceed eight miles from their present positions. The officers and men should be provided with three days' cooked rations. Forty rounds of ammunition must be carried in cartridge boxes, and twenty rounds in pockets. The ammunition wagons and batteries will be supplied with at least three days' forage. *Definite verbal instructions* will be given as to the disposition to be made of the other trains of the command. The chief of artillery will detail such batteries as may be necessary to protect the crossing of the river, and, if the crossing is successful, the batteries will join their proper columns; if necessary. *Definite verbal instructions* will be given as to the dispositions of the cavalry of the different Grand Divisions."

The plan of attack which General Burnside had in his mind on this date is not clearly laid down in any available document, but it may be roughly gathered from various notes that passed between him and his Grand Division commanders, e.g.—On December 10, in reply to a direct question by Franklin as to whether he should attack " without waiting for General Sumner to open," Burnside pencilled the following memorandum : " The intention is for you to cross as soon as the bridges are completed. If you deem it advisable you will attack as soon as you cross, without waiting for General Sumner. It would, of course, be preferable to make it simultaneous." The next day (December 11) Burnside issued another set of orders, in which it is Sumner who is to make the first move, by " taking the heights that command the Plank road and Telegraph road," employing his entire force for the purpose, and looking to Hooker and Franklin for the protection of his flanks. That is the substance of his Order to Sumner, written at 4.20 a.m. Half an hour later he writes an order to Hooker, directing him to be ready to support either Sumner or Franklin, or to pursue the enemy when dislodged. Yet more. Within an hour of first taking pen in hand Burnside has veered away from his original point and instructs Franklin, in the following terms : " After your command has crossed, you will move down the Old Richmond road in the direction of the railroad, being governed by circumstances as to the extent of your movements. An aide will be sent to you during your movements." Here is no hint to protect Sumner's left flank, his solicitude for which is apparent in his order to Sumner; in fact, Franklin is ordered to turn his back on the Right Grand Division and move some miles in the opposite direction. Since war began has ever a force of 60,000 men been ordered to be marched to a flank in face of the enemy with no other objective than to be " governed by circumstances," except on December 11, 1862 ? It will remain a subject for interesting speculation what would have happened if Franklin had been allowed to cross and march off under these orders. However, none of these instructions were carried into effect, for we find that a third set of orders reached the Grand Division commanders on the morning of December 13, after they had firmly established themselves upon the southern bank of the river.

It will be convenient at this point to follow the operation of crossing the Rappahannock, as detailed by the Grand Division commanders and their corps leaders.

Sumner's Right Grand Division.

Couch (2nd) Corps.—During the night of December 10 two regiments were ordered to protect the working parties throwing bridges opposite the city where the corps was to cross. At 8 a.m., December 11, the corps was massed under cover in rear of the bridges and held in readiness to cross. One brigade was attached to General Woodbury's Engineers. Three regiments crossed in pontoon boats, seized the buildings occupied by the enemy's sharpshooters, took many prisoners and entered the town. Bridges were completed at 4.30 p.m., and Howard's division crossed before dark and occupied the town. At sunrise, December 12, the remaining two divisions crossed, and were assigned positions in the streets of the town, parallel with the river. The 9th Corps was on our left. Scarcely an inhabitant was found in the city. The troops took tobacco, flour and other eatables. In rear of the town the ground is a broken plain, traversed about midway by a canal or ditch, running from right to left. Across this plain, some 600 yards from the outer edge of the town, commences the first rise of hills, on which the enemy had planted his batteries. Two roads cut the plain, nearly at right angles with the canal—the one, a plank road leading to Culpeper, to the right; the other to the left is the Telegraph Road leading to Richmond.

Willcox (9th) Corps.—December 11—one regiment covered the engineers on the central bridge near the old steamboat landing, from 2 a.m. to 4 p.m., and then crossed in boats (one officer and twenty-five men in each); one regiment crossed the bridge followed by Hawkins' brigade, and occupied the town that night. The remainder of the corps crossed on December 12, following the 2nd Corps. General Sumner's Report is to the same effect:—

"Howard's division crossed near the Lacy House, occupying at first the streets of the town nearest and parallel to the river. The upper portion of the town was held by the enemy, who opened effective fire upon the heads of Howard's columns as they showed themselves in the streets perpendicular to the Rappahannock. Howard made judicious dispositions, advanced, and after sharp fighting drove the enemy, so that at daylight on the morning of the 12th, in conjunction with Hawkin's brigade of the 9th Corps, he occupied the entire town of Fredericksburg. During this day the remainder of the 2nd and 9th Corps crossed the river. The 2nd Corps held the centre and right of the town, and the 9th Corps, reaching to the left, connected with Franklin's right. The enemy held the successive crests and wooded slopes which encircle the town, his infantry covered by breastworks and rifle-pits, his guns protected by earthworks, and mostly in embrasure, the general dispositions of his lines being such as to give front and enfilading fires on any troops who might debouch from the city with the intention of crossing the gradual slope which swells from the town to the crest. The enemy had also concentrated many guns on the bridges necessarily to be crossed by the troops after leaving the cover of the houses before reaching the open plain. The enemy was quiet during the day and night."

Hooker's Centre Grand Division

Butterfield (5th) Corps.—December 11—broke camp and marched to the bank of the river in the following order : 2nd division on the right by the Stafford road, 1st division on the left and to the left of the road from camp to Phillips House, 3rd division in the centre on a route to the right of that taken by 1st division. The artillery marched in rear of their divisions. The commands carried three days' cooked rations in haversacks, and forage for the animals with the batteries. The corps bivouacked on the night of December 11 and December 12 near the river bank, waiting orders to cross.

Stoneman (3rd) Corps.—On December 9 received

orders to be ready to move on night of December 10. Wagons packed and parked, and the corps prepared to march at an hour's notice any time after sundown December 10, with three days' rations for men and animals. December 11—the corps marched and occupied position assigned, and there bivouacked for the night. December 12—the corps moved towards the bridges and was held ready to cross at a moment's warning, in support of Right Grand Division. At 2 p.m., one division ordered to cross; the town however was so "packed and jammed" with troops that the division (Whipple's) had to bivouac at the foot of the three bridges. Shortly before sundown ordered to move with the remainder of the corps about $3\frac{1}{2}$ miles down the river, by the road, and place it at the foot of the two bridges there, and report to General Franklin (Left Grand Division); this movement completed by 10 p.m. The night was foggy and dark, the road muddy and rough. We avoided the river road, a shorter and better route, in order not to expose our movements to the enemy.

General Hooker's account of his movements between November 25 and December 12 is to the following effect:—

"Upon the arrival of the pontoons, which had been delayed, it was determined to cross the Rappahannock. Meanwhile the enemy had assembled in force and entrenched himself upon the opposite bank, in rear of the city of Fredericksburg. The Grand Division commanders were assembled to discuss and determine the place and method of crossing the river. It was proposed by the general commanding that a portion of the army should cross at Falmouth and a portion twelve miles below. To this I objected by my vote, and proposed a crossing above. It was finally determined by General Burnside to cross at Falmouth and twelve miles below. This plan was afterwards changed, and three bridges were thrown across the river at Fredericksburg, and two about four miles below. My orders were to hold my troops in hand, and in event of a successful crossing to spring upon the enemy's line of retreat with my whole force. My corps were moved to the three upper bridges to carry out the proposed plans, Stoneman's Corps in advance followed by Butterfield's Corps. The night previous to the attack (December 12) I was ordered to send two divisions (Sickles' and Birney's) of Stoneman's Corps to the bridges, four miles below, to support General Franklin.

Franklin's Left Grand Division

Smith (6th) Corps.—December 11—marched from camp toward the bridges below Deep Creek, head of column reaching the river 7.30 a.m., and waited in a sheltered position till bridges completed at 4 p.m. Opened artillery fire on houses on the plateau near the crossing, until masked by our skirmishers advancing. The troops were being rapidly thrown across when *an order came to retire*, owing to the difficulty of deploying and taking up defensive position at so late an hour. One brigade left to hold the bridge heads. December 12— 1st division crossed and relieved the outpost brigade; another division crossed and formed in line of battle on left of 1st division; 3rd division crossed and formed columns as reserve. The corps now advanced: 1st division to hold the Richmond road and Deep Creek, with one line in front of the Creek; 2nd division occupied the crest of a hill over which ran the Richmond road, their right at a sharp turn of Deep Creek. These movements were all concealed by a fog from the enemy who held the hills in front of us. "The troops were as well concealed as the topography would allow, and there was nothing to be done but maintain our skirmish line, which was engaged nearly all the time, and submit quietly to the feeble and spasmodic artillery fire of the enemy, which both encircled and commanded us."

Reynolds (1st) Corps.—December 11 at 5 a.m., the corps took up its line of march to the place of crossing. One brigade and two batteries had been posted at 2 a.m. to cover the working party on the bridges. The two bridges were completed at 1 p.m., the bridge heads secured for the night, and the corps waited orders to cross. December 12—crossed under cover of the fog, following 6th corps; enemy's skirmishers driven from ravines and houses in the vicinity of "Smithfield." All dispositions completed and pickets thrown out before 5 p.m., and troops bivouacked in the following positions: Gibbon's division formed on left of 6th corps, in two lines of brigades deployed; Meade's division in two lines of brigades deployed, his left resting on the river about "Smithfield," his right joining nearly at right angles with the left of Gibbon; Doubleday's division formed the reserve in column on the bank of the river, in rear of Meade's left; Meade's and Gibbon's artillery were placed to command the Bowling Green road. "The river bottom, on which we had debouched, was inclosed by a series of heights running from the rear of Fredericksburg on the right to the valley of the Massaponax Creek on the left, at which point the nearest crest approached the Rappahannock to within probably less than a mile. The ranges of heights formed an arc, of which the railroad from Fredericksburg to Richmond may be said to form the chord, the road to Bowling Green running nearly parallel to it for this distance, but some 500 yards nearer the river. On the left of this bottom the ground ascended gradually from the river bank to a point about half way between the two roads, when it fell off more suddenly to the line of the railroad, just beyond which the rise to the heights began. These were wooded from the rear to the crests in places, and in others the wood extended into the plain beyond the line of the railroad. All that could be seen of the enemy's position was that he occupied the crests of these heights with his artillery and infantry; also the edge of the wood and the cuts of the railroad with a line of skirmishers thrown out in front, and extending from the heights to a ravine and some houses on the river bank, opposite the extreme crest of hills on the left. This bottom was cultivated ground, and intersected by hedges and ditches running along the roads, but affording slight shelter of any description for our troops, while all our movements and dispositions were plainly visible to the enemy from the heights he occupied."

General Franklin thus describes his movements:—

" On December 11, at 4 p.m., I was instructed to cross my whole command, which order was shortly afterward modified, so that my orders were to cross about a brigade to insure the safety of the bridges. Devens' brigade

(Newton's division, Smith's Corps) crossed with great enthusiasm, and took position on the south bank about dark. Some of the troops of Brooks' division also crossed, but returned, in obedience to the orders as modified. Devens' brigade drove away the enemy's pickets from the houses near the crossing, threw out a line of pickets to the left and front, and held the position during the night. At daylight on the morning of December 12 Smith's Corps began to cross, and at 9.15 a.m. two divisions and three batteries were across the river. It was followed by Bayard's brigade of cavalry, which immediately proceeded to the front to make a reconnaissance. Reynolds' Corps followed Bayard, and by 1 p.m. the whole of the Grand Division was on the south bank of the river. The crossing was made in excellent order, without the slightest confusion or stoppage. Smith's Corps had been previously ordered, in compliance with the directions of the Commanding General, to form parallel to the old Richmond road, with two divisions in front and one in reserve. Reynolds' Corps was to form at nearly right angles to Smith's, his right resting on Smith's and his left on the river. Two divisions were to be in line of battle and one in reserve. The artillery was to be posted and used according to the discretion of the corps commanders, as the nature of the ground and position of the enemy might determine. The dispositions indicated were made in the face of some slight opposition by the enemy's skirmishers, and a spiteful, though nearly harmless, fire from his artillery, and by four o'clock the troops were in the positions assigned to them. The ground upon which the troops were disposed is, in general, a plain. It is cultivated and much cut up by hedges and ditches. The old Richmond road traverses the plain from right to left, about one mile from the river and nearly parallel to it. This road is bordered on both sides by an earthen parapet and ditch, and is an exceedingly strong feature in the defence of the ground, had *the enemy* chosen to hold it. On the right of my position is Deep Run, and on the left, about one mile in front of Reynolds, is Massaponax Creek. Both streams are tributaries of the Rappahannock. The plain is bordered by a range of high hills in front, which stretches from Fredericksburg to the Massaponax, nearly parallel to the river. In front of and nearly parallel to the old Richmond road, and about 500 or 600 yards from it, at the foot of the range of hills, is the railroad. The ravine, through which Deep Creek runs, passes through the hills near the centre of my front. Two brigades of Brooks' division (Smith's corps) were in front of Deep Creek, forming the extreme right. The remainder of Smith's troops was in rear and to the left of Deep Creek, Reynolds' Corps being about one mile from the Massaponax. The enemy had artillery on the hills and in the valley of Deep Creek, in the wood near Reynolds' right, and on the Massaponax, so that the whole field was surrounded by it, except the right flank. His infantry appeared in all directions around the position. In front of Reynolds' right the forest extends to the old Richmond road, coming nearer the river there than at any other point in the vicinity of my position. The railroad traverses the forest."

About this time " positive information " reached Burnside that the Confederates had improved their lateral communications by making a new road in rear of the ridge or crest from Hamilton's to the Telegraph road, and the Federal general thereupon decided to seize a point on this road. The particular object he had in view in ordering this point to be seized is somewhat enigmatically stated in the Report which he wrote three years after the battle : " I decided to seize, if possible, a point on this road near Hamilton's which would not divide the enemy's forces by breaking their line, but would place our forces in position to enable us to move in rear of the crest, and either force its evacuation or the capitulation of the forces occupying it. It was my intention, in case this point had been gained, to push Generals Summer and Hooker against the *left* of the crest, and prevent at least the removal of the artillery of the enemy, in case they attempted a retreat " Burnside further declares that his written orders of December 13 " were prepared in accordance with these views." Following are the orders in question :—

December 13, 5.55 a.m.

MAJOR-GENERAL FRANKLIN,—

General Hardie will carry this dispatch to you, and remain with you during the day. The general commanding directs that you keep your whole command in position for a rapid movement down the old Richmond road, and you will send out at once a division at least to pass below Smithfield, to seize, if possible, *the height near Captain Hamilton's,* on this side of the Massaponax, taking care to *keep it well supported and its line of retreat open.* He has ordered another column of a division or more to be moved from General Summer's command up the Plank road to its intersection with the Telegraph road, where they will divide, with a view to seizing the heights on both of these roads. Holding these two heights, with the heights near Captain Hamilton's, will, he hopes, compel the enemy to evacuate the whole ridge between these points. He makes these moves by columns distant from each other, with a view of avoiding the possibility of a collision of our own forces, which might occur in a general movement during a fog. Two of General Hooker's divisions are in your rear, at the bridges, and will remain *there as supports.* Copies of instructions given to Generals Sumner and Hooker will be forwarded to you by an orderly very soon. You will keep your whole command in readiness to move at once, as soon as the fog lifts. The watchword, which, if possible, should be given to every company, will be " Scott."

December 13, 6 a.m.

MAJ.-GEN. E. V. SUMNER,—

The general commanding directs that you extend the left of your command to Deep Run, connecting with General Franklin, extending your right as far as your judgment may dictate. He also directs that you push a column of a division or more along the Plank and Telegraph roads, with a view to seizing the heights in the rear of the town. The latter movement should be well *covered by skirmishers, and supported so as to keep its line of retreat open.* Copy of instructions given to General Franklin will be sent to you very soon. You will please await them at your present headquarters, where he (the general commanding) will meet you. Great care should be taken to prevent a collision of our own forces during the fog. The watchword for the day will be "Scott." The column for a movement up the Telegraph and Plank roads will be got in readiness to move, but *will not move* till the general commanding communicates with you.

December 13, 7 a.m.

MAJ.-GEN. JOSEPH HOOKER,—

The general commanding directs that you place General Butterfield's corps and Whipple's division in position to cross, at a moment's notice, at the three upper bridges, in support of the other troops over the river, and the two remaining divisions of General Stoneman's corps in readiness to cross at the lower ford, *in support* of General Franklin. The general commanding will meet you at headquarters (Philips House) very soon. Copies of instructions to General Sumner and General Franklin will be sent to you.

The interpretation of the above-quoted Orders has given rise to much controversy among students of the Fredericksburg campaign. The meaning they bore to the officers to whom they were dispatched on the morning of December 13 will be perceived when our narrative of the battle is reached; but in the meantime, we may attempt to discover in what respects these Orders harmonize with and illustrate Burnside's plan of attack, so far as that plan has been revealed to us in his official Report (page 130) written after the war and published by the U.S. Government.

We shall clear the ground somewhat by stating, on the authority of the Federal commander, that Franklin was ordered to seize immediately with a division the height near Hamilton's, "in order to enable the remainder of his forces to move down the Old Richmond Road with a view of getting in rear of the enemy's line on the crest." We may further state that Sumner was instructed not to permit any offensive movement until Burnside himself gave directions, because " I did not intend to move General Sumner until I learned that Franklin was about to gain the heights near Hamilton's."

Evidently Burnside's plan depended entirely upon Franklin's success in a preliminary operation with a comparatively small force directed against a point in the enemy's defences which might, or might not, be vulnerable to attack, an operation which Burnside expressly states he did not expect to result in dividing the enemy's forces by breaking their line (page 130), and which we may therefore assume was intended to cover the movement to a flank of a larger force. In fact, the remainder of Franklin's command, to which was attached two divisions from Hooker's Grand Division, was directed in certain circumstances to move southwards down the Old Richmond Road, and finally " to move in rear of the crest and either force its evacuation or the capitulation of the forces occupying it."

So far, at least, Burnside's plan is perfectly clear, and refreshingly simple on the supposition that Lee's right flank would be found *en l'air* and Jackson's men susceptible to such treatment as would enable the Federals to execute a military promenade in rear of the Confederate defences. Our real exegetical difficulties begin, however, as soon as we attempt to discover the parts to be played by Sumner, whose Grand Division was at Fredericksburg, and Hooker, whose mutilated command still remained on the left bank of the river.

The Federal leader appears to dispose of the matter in his Report by saying, "It was my intention in case this point [the height near Hamilton's] had been gained to push Generals Sumner and Hooker against *the left of the crest*." But a question of topography here arises. Surely the " left " of the crest was the assigned objective of the Left Grand Division ? And if we assume a *lapsus calami*—a dangerous practice in military matters —and read " right " for " left," we are still confronted with a few minor difficulties; for Burnside informs Franklin (page 131) that Sumner is to seize *two heights on the Telegraph and Plank roads* near the point at which those roads intersect, but in his Order to Sumner he indicates "the heights in the rear of the town " as the objective of a small force (held in readiness to move along the Plank and Telegraph roads), while the remainder of the Right Grand Division was to be extended southward, so that its left should connect with Franklin's command in the vicinity of the Massaponax. And out of such material in the shape of Operation Orders Burnside's subordinates were expected to evolve a Federal victory.

CHAPTER IX

THE MORNING OF DECEMBER 13—FINAL DISPOSITIONS FOR BATTLE—TACTICAL POINTS—FRANKLIN'S INTERPRETATION OF "ORDERS"—COST OF AN "ARMED OBSERVATION."

CHAPTER IX

THE morning of December 13 found the two armies—nearly 190,000 men—busy preparing for battle.

A plan of the battlefield would embrace an area of twenty square miles, in shape a right angled triangle, of which the long side traversed a ridge or range of low hills running due north and south, the base being a continuation of the same ridge running east and west, the hypothenuse representing the river about Fredericksburg, where the Rappahannock bends and takes a southeasterly course to the sea.

The general direction of Lee's front was north-east; but his entrenchments were made to follow the sinuosities of the ground, nearly touching the river on his left flank at Taylor's hill above Falmouth, and gradually receding until four miles lower down the river a clear space of nearly three miles of comparatively open ground, semicircular in shape between ridge and river, invited an enemy to deploy a large force for attack. Further south at Hamilton's Crossing the Confederate earthworks again approached the river, and if we may trust the large scale map which was prepared by the United States Government five years after the battle, at this point the ridge terminated in a neck of flat country a mile wide, sloping eastward to the Rappahannock, and southward to the Massaponax Creek. On this open space or neck Lee rested his right flank, posting there his cavalry and horse artillery. His defensive line was intersected by Hazel Run and Deep Run, tributaries of the Rappahannock, which caused the Confederate defences to group themselves naturally into " sections."

Along the front of the left or northern section for two and a half miles ran the town canal ; along the front of the centre and right sections for about four miles ran the Richmond railroad.

Between the railroad and the river, and parallel with them, the Richmond Stage road (often referred to as the River road or Bowling Green road) formed a covered way for troops, owing to a peculiarity in its construction, described on page 129. The entire extent of Lee's front as the crow flies, from the cavalry on the right to the artillery on the left flank of the defences, may be taken as seven or eight miles. His position in its general features is reproduced for us on the southern bank of the Thames, between Richmond Hill and Battersea ; and we may picture the Confederate forces occupying the high ground which runs eastward for seven miles from the Thames, through Richmond Park across Putney Heath and Wimbledon Common, through Wandsworth to Clapham Common (as it was before the advent of suburban builders), intersected at intervals by the river Wandle, by Beverly Brook and other water courses. To man his defences Lee had at his disposal a force of 68,000 men.

His infantry was organized in thirty-nine brigades or nine divisions : twenty brigades (five divisions) formed the 1st Corps under Longstreet, to whom was allotted the left and centre sections of defence : nineteen brigades, (four divisions) formed the 2nd Corps under Jackson, to whom the defence of the right section was entrusted. Each division had its proportion of artillery—a small division like that of Ransom, two batteries, a large division like that of A. P. Hill, seven batteries ; but these batteries (thirty-nine in all) appear to have been requisitioned very freely by the Chiefs of Artillery to support the Reserve Artillery (heavy guns) in selected positions, which (page 79) General Pendleton had been preparing ever since his arrival at Fredericksburg.

In the left section, Walton's heavy guns were in redoubts or pits (the terms are used indiscriminately in the official reports) on the eminence west of the town, now famous as Marye's hill, extending from the Telegraph road to the Plank road, otherwise known as the Orange Court House turnpike. Alexander's heavy batteries were posted, some on a hill south of the Plank road overlooking the country as far as the opposite bank of the river one and a half miles distant ; some (including howitzers) were near Stansbury's House, commanding the flats beyond the canal north of the town, and even the streets leading to the pontoon bridges. Many batteries were held in reserve, ready to be moved into prepared positions, or to relieve other batteries running short of ammunition—a frequent occurrence since the "train" or ammunition column was, in one case at least, several miles distant. Alexander's batteries expended over 1,000 rounds during the three days engagement, and one of Walton's batteries (nine guns) at the end of four and a half hours had "exhausted all the canister shell and case shot, and nearly every round of solid shot in the chests." Other batteries, however, were able to remain in action till the on-coming darkness compelled them to aim at the flashes of the enemy's muskets. Marye's hill—the point finally selected by the Federal general for his right attack—was defended by Ross's battery (brought back from its position three or four miles down the river), which posted its four long-range guns on the right of McLaws' division. Marye's hill was commanded by another hill near the Telegraph road, and this hill was occupied by a battery, whose mission it was to sweep the enemy off Marye's hill in the event of his seizing it. A similar duty was assigned to Rhett's battery of heavy guns, posted on another hill in rear of Marye's Hill, and near the Plank road. On the left of the line was Lane's battery of heavy guns, including the Whitworth and other large rifled ordnance; on Marye's hill was the Louisiana "Washington" artillery, with Alexander's, Maurin's and other batteries on its left. Many guns were in reserve, under cover of the hills. The centre section of defence was covered by a battery posted in front of Hood's division. One of the large Parrott guns enfiladed an unfinished cutting prepared for a projected railroad from Fredericksburg to Gordonsville. In the right section, Brown's heavy artillery did not take post until 12 noon, and then a battery of eight guns was emplaced on the right of the railroad near Hamilton's Crossing. At 2 p.m. a section (two guns) was posted on "the hill to the extreme right of our infantry line," and was reinforced later in the day by two howitzers. The eight-gun battery was also reinforced by a section, and we are told that "the ammunition of most of these pieces was exhausted before dark." The guns known as Parrott rifles were unfortunate ; few of the shells exploded, owing to imperfect fuzes ; both of the " large " Parrott guns burst after forty or fifty rounds had been fired. Where the right section joined the centre section of defence thirty-three guns were posted. These batteries were commanded by Captains Brockenbrough and Davidson. Emplacements had been prepared on both sides the railroad in the vicinity of Bernard's Cabins. In the centre of the right section about 1,000 yards of frontage was undefended by direct artillery fire, and only partly by the oblique fire of Brock's guns. This was " a point of woods runing out into the field," a sailent which occurred where the ground in rear was unfavourable, " being intersected by a deep ravine, and the undergrowth so thick as to require more time to clear it away than we had before the action began." No name had been given to this locality, and we shall refer to it therefore as " Woodpoint," since the Chief of Artillery had noticed that it would afford the enemy " early and good shelter," and so prove a probable objective. Brockenbrough and Davidson were instructed to reserve their fire for the enemy's infantry at close range, and not to engage his batteries, unless he advanced them to the support of his infantry, and then the Confederate guns were to concentrate their fire on the advancing battery, and not to retire so long as their own infantry supported them. The Whitworth gun mentioned on page 109 was put in position " beyond the Massaponax," probably in the neighbourhood of Jackson's headquarters, which were at Yerby's, half a mile south of the Massaponax, according to a map prepared by the topographical engineers of the 2nd Corps. Upon the same authority we may state that the headquarters of Longstreet were on the Telegraph road, half a mile north of Deep Run, and those of General Lee on the Mine road, between Deep Run and the Massaponax river.

Longstreet moved the 1st Corps into position as follows: one division (five brigades) at Taylor's Hill; two divisions (six brigades) at Marye's Hill; two divisions (nine brigades) between Hazel Run and Deep Run. The divisional commanders were: Anderson, McLaws, Ransom, Pickett and Hood, and their commands garrisoned the left and centre sections of defence. Anderson was on the left flank. McLaws supported by Ransom held Marye's hill. Pickett and Hood occupied the centre section, the former covering Longstreet's right flank, the latter Jackson's left flank.

Jackson distributed the 2nd Corps as follows to garrison the right section of defence: one division (six brigades) occupied the whole of the front between Deep Run and a road east of Hamilton's Crossing; two divisions (eight brigades) were placed in support; one division (five brigades) were placed in reserve. The principle, that each unit should form its own support and reserve, was evidently abandoned on this occasion by Jackson; but it must be remembered in extenuation that two of the four divisions had arrived late upon the field, after a long night's march, and were presumably in need of rest for some hours, which they obtained by being detailed to form the second and third lines. To this violation of a sound principle, however, we may fairly attribute the heavy losses that occurred in the 2nd Corps.

The divisional commanders were : A. P. Hill (first line), Early and Tailaferro (second line), and D. H. Hill (third line).

Certain writers with a penchant for statistics have endeavoured to prove that Lee's dispositions at the battle of Fredericksburg gave him six men per yard of frontage ; but the author of *Troops to the Yard* wisely points out that such statements serve only to raise another question, viz : What is the " active " as distinguished from the " demonstrative " front of an army in position for battle ? Evidently the inclusion of what we now call a false flank, as part of the frontage theoretically occupied, would materially affect any estimate of the number of rifles per yard of front. Assuming Lee's front to have covered 13,000 yards, and the force distributed thereon to have numbered 68,000 men, we may say that he defended the position with an average of five men to the yard ; but if we take into consideration the fact that his centre section, two and a half miles in extent, was garrisoned by only two divisions (nine brigades), or 14,850 men, we find that his left and right sections where the fighting took place—the active front—had nearly seven men to the yard including the reserves. Moreover, part of the force allotted to the " centre " section did in fact co-operate actively with the troops of the " right " section and therefore a brigade at least ought to be added to Jackson's Corps, and deducted from the force distributed along the " demonstrative " front, if the number of troops to the yard is to be ascertained for any practical purpose. The truth is, it is impossible for the military historian to push his enquiries far enough to make deductions of this kind of great value. The evidence available exists in the form of narratives by eye-witnesses, and the majority of such accounts are highly coloured by prepossessions on the part of the narrators. The faculty of accurate observation under fire is possessed by few, and the gift to record such observations with exactitude is still rarer; even in official reports we find that a position or a body of troops will be described as on the "right" or "left" of the observer, though the observer's point of view is itself not indicated; distances, too, are frequently misjudged. A dozen maps of the same battlefield will all differ in such important particulars as the names of places and the positions of troops. The important element, Time, is almost invariably ignored. Better training for a modern staff-officer could hardly be imagined than to require him to depict a given battlefield from contemporary records; for the task of reconciling the conflicting statements of a hundred eye-witnesses would never be forgotten, a valuable lesson would have been learnt, and whenever the occasion arose for him to prepare an official report of operations in the field, he would be careful to avoid such sources of error as he had discovered in studying for historical purposes the reports and sketches of others.

The Battle of Fredericksburg has been officially described by no fewer than 336 commanders of units, small and great, and yet there remain many questions of fact unanswered, and with regard to these the historian, writing forty years after the event, can only speak in general terms, if he would avoid perpetuating the obvious mistakes of his predecessors. There is, however, nothing more remarkable about Lee's preparations for defence, both as regards the construction of works and distribution of his troops, than the manner in which he anticipated the enemy's movements. By some mental process akin to divination he fathomed Burnside's intentions, as we may observe by comparing the official reports of subordinate commanders on both sides. It invariably appears that the reasons given by the Confederates for the construction of certain works or the disposal of troops in a particular locality correspond exactly with the Federal orders and instructions for attack. We know, for example, from Burnside's last order to Franklin, dated 7 a.m. December 13, what importance he attached to the seizure of the height near Hamilton's, and we may read in the report of Jackson's Chief of Artillery as follows : " The heights on the right of our lines were held by fourteen guns . . . the position was a commanding one . . . but what was more important, so controlled the ground in front as to force the enemy to open a heavy cannonade upon it, in hopes of silencing these batteries, before they could move their infantry down the plain to turn our right. . . . Other batteries were held ready to move out and take position in the fields to our right, so as to cross their fire with Walker's batteries."

We have seen (page 129) the importance to Burnside of his discovery of a new road constructed by the Confederates, and called by them " the military road." We shall find that this lateral communication was occupied by the supports to Jackson's firing line.

Opposite the Confederate entrenchments General Burnside had on the morning of December 13 concentrated the bulk of the Army of the Potomac. Sumner's Right Grand Division occupied the town east of Marye's

L

Hill and north of Hazel Run. Franklin's Left Grand Division lay along the river bank south of Deep Run, screened to some extent by the earthen parapets that fenced the Richmond Stage road. He protected his pontoons, the line of retreat, the line of supply, by means of a *tête de pont* in the shape of an earthwork for thirty-six guns. Hooker's Centre Grand Division had not yet crossed the river, but was disposed so as to afford support to either or both of the flanks, by crossing either the pontoon bridges opposite the town, or those which spanned the river a few miles lower down. Burnside's heavy batteries, as we have seen, fringed the Stafford Heights, from Falmouth to Pollock's Mill opposite the mouth of the Massaponax. The cavalry brigades attached to the commands of Sumner and Hooker were massed on the left bank of the river: Franklin's cavalry crossed with the infantry (see page 115). It would be interesting to know how this latter force was disposed, but the sketch in which Franklin elaborately depicted the positions of his infantry has no further reference to the cavalry than a note to the effect that its commander, General Bayard, was at "Mansfield"—Franklin's headquarters—along with General Smith and General Reynolds the corps commanders.

Sumner's two corps were distributed as follows: 2nd Corps (three divisions, nine brigades) occupied the centre and right of the town; 9th Corps (three divisions, seven brigades) prolonged to the left and connected with the right of Franklin's Grand Division.

Franklin's two corps were distributed as follows: 6th Corps (three divisions, nine brigades) was formed with its right on Deep Run, parallel to the Richmond

Stage road, two divisions in front, and one in reserve at the *tête de pont* : it was surrounded by a semi-circle of skirmishers and piquets reaching westward to the railway and south to the Massaponax, and a portion of the corps was over Deep Run to connect with Sumner's Right Grand Division. 1st Corps (three divisions, ten brigades) was stationed between " Smithfield " and " Mansfield," its right resting on the 6th Corps, its left upon the river, two divisions in front, and one in reserve, the whole fronting south, that is, towards the Massaponax Creek.

It will be observed that the Federal dispositions had placed them on interior lines with regard to the enemy, that all attempts at surprise by a wide turning movement had been frankly abandoned, and since Burnside's army had crossed the Rappahannock only to find itself enclosed within an angle formed by the river, and as the Confederate dispositions precluded tactical envelopment, it is clear that the Federals stood committed to a frontal attack upon an entrenched position, held by an enemy ably commanded, in excellent fighting condition, and even, for the defensive rôle Lee had assumed, comparatively superior in numbers. Burnside's three Grand Divisions represented 119,000, Lee's two Corps 68,000 men. The former was about to assume the tactical offensive with a proportion of less than two to one; but if the concentration of Sigel's (11th) and Slocum's (12th) Corps had been ordered a week earlier, Burnside would have added 30,000 men to his fighting strength.

When finessing has failed, when a general has been out-marched and out-manœuvred, salvation is often found, we are told, in a determination to come to grips with the antagonist. For such an enterprise, however, two things are deemed essential—Numbers and Resolution; and if one or the other must needs be lacking, numbers may be more easily dispensed with than resolution: for when a Frederick is opposed to a Soubise and strong pressure relentlessly brought to bear upon a weak spot in the defences of a slow-witted, immobile enemy, the result generally goes to prove what Von der Goltz asserts, namely, that the tactical frontal attack must not, even from a purely theoretical standpoint, be rejected as something in itself wrong: there are times when it is necessary to carry it out, and to perform this task with success is to accomplish a far more difficult feat than to make a successful enveloping attack. The author of *The Conduct of War* says: " One circumstance naturally favours the assailant in such a case. From having to face a difficult task, even a man of moderate attainments will often gain moral strength, and accomplish things of which we had not thought him capable. Qualities then appear which required a very strong stimulus to awaken them from their slumber. Exactly the same thing happens with the soldiery. The consciousness of having to carry out something difficult inspires the leaders in the first place with an enthusiasm which shows itself in an energetic manifestation of all their abilities, and this process is communicated to the men from their leaders." The Confederates were neither slow-witted nor immobile—were indeed remarkably alert in mind as in body, from Commander-in-Chief to the men in the ranks: and yet many latter-day tacticians, wise after the event, would ask no better gift at the hands of Fortune than to be placed in command of a large force of American volunteers such as the Army of the Potomac, in the situation which General Burnside had created on the morning of December 13.

Even at the eleventh hour many suppose the Federals might have emulated the Prussians at Torgau who won their battle after Frederick had ridden off the field ; and certainly few would envy Lee his position if General Burnside had been able to throw into the fight on that memorable Saturday the two corps which were slowly approaching Falmouth, and had been reported already at Dumfries and Fairfax Station.

General Burnside's course of action must now be attentively considered : he states, " By the night of the 12th the troops were all in position, and I visited the different commands with a view to determining as to future movements. The delay in laying the bridges had rendered some change in the plan of attack necessary, and the orders already issued were to be superseded by new ones. It was after midnight when I returned from visiting the different commands, and before daylight of the 13th I prepared the following orders." These orders have been already quoted on page 130, and military students may at this stage pause to examine them, and consider their purport and what action they demanded from the Grand Division commanders to whom they were addressed on a foggy morning in December, 1862. Since any movement on the right by Sumner was to be entirely dependent (see Burnside's statement, page 133) on the course of events on the left, where Franklin commanded, and where Burnside's representative, General Hardie, was stationed to watch and report progress, we will proceed to " Mansfield " and see what interpretation was put upon Burnside's orders by Franklin, without protest, or remark even, on the part of the Headquarters staff-officer then and there present. Three distinct commands are conveyed by the dispatch brought by General Hardie to Franklin at 7.30 a.m.

(1) To keep the whole of the Left Grand Division in position for a rapid movement down the old Richmond road " as soon as the fog lifts."
(2) To send out at once a force—a division at least—to seize, " if possible," the height near Hamilton's on the north side of the Massaponax.
(3) To keep the force mentioned in (2) well supported, and its line of retreat open.

Franklin was also informed that two of Hooker's divisions were in his rear at the bridges, and would remain there as supports. An hour and a half had elapsed between the time of writing the dispatch and the time of its delivery to Franklin; and another hour and a half was to elapse before Hardie could report at 9 a.m., " General Meade just moved out. Doubleday supports him." We must assume that General Burnside had anticipated this necessary delay. According to Frankline's sketch map, four out of his six divisions were on receipt of his " orders " already in position for movement down the old Richmond road. Howe's division was actually lining the road, and the divisions of Meade, Gibbon and Doubleday were only half a mile distant, and an oblique march forward would put them also on the road; it only remained, then, for Franklin to advance Newton's division a mile, and recall Brooks' division (which had crossed Deep Run) and face it in the contrary direction, in order to comply with the letter of his orders, in addition to putting the batteries (thirty-six guns) which now formed the bridge-head, in column of route upon the road in readiness to march. So far, then, no difficulty arose in carrying out the somewhat precise orders of the Commander-in-Chief. But the special injunction with reference to the force to be immediately advanced in spite of the fog namely, to " keep it well supported and its line of retreat open," certainly introduced complications. Is not the object of supporting a force to keep that force at fighting strength and preclude the idea of retreat ? To cover a retirement, as in the case of skirmishers at that period, another force would be employed; but would it not be called a relieving body ? The necessity of raising such questions as these, in attempting to judge the action of commanders in the field, points to the wisdom of exercising extreme care in the wording of Operation Orders. Franklin's dispatch of a division to the front in the direction of Hamilton's, followed by another division in support, would, however, seem a satisfactory compliance with the first part of his orders ; but the commander of the Left Grand Division might now be expected to seek further instructions from his somewhat pedantic Chief, who had not apparently taken his principal generals into his confidence, in spite of the numerous interviews, orders and messages we have recorded. Burnside was, perhaps, unaware that " the consciousness of having to carry out something difficult inspires the leaders in the first place with an enthusiasm which shows itself in an energetic manifestation of all their abilities, and this process is communicated to the men from their leaders." It does not appear, however, that Franklin made any effort to obtain further orders or explanations from General Burnside, though hour after hour passed by, and General Hardie was meanwhile reporting progress to Headquarters at 11 a.m., 12 noon, 12.5 p.m., 1 p.m., 1.15 p.m., 1.25 p.m., 1.40 p.m., and at 2.15 p.m. There was a field telegraph in operation between Army Headquarters and the Headquarters of the Left Grand Division, and yet no message was sent by General Burnside to Franklin until 2.25 p.m.

In five hours and a half much may occur on a battle-field, and we must now see what happened during the period which General Burnside apparently devoted to quite other matters than the offensive operations on his left, which he had started at 9 o'clock. And at this point it is material to note that the terms of Burnside's dispatch would justify three distinctly different lines of action on the part of Franklin

(1) A reconnaissance in force by a division. Against this theory is the absence of staff-officers to make observations, the existence of an order to seize Hamilton's Height, "if possible," and the order to "support" the force engaged.

(2) A decisive attack on that part of the enemy's position which faced north by two army corps as soon as the fog lifted, meanwhile attacking the locality called Hamilton's Height with a division. Against this interpretation is the absence of any clear statement as to the ultimate intentions of General Burnside, and his expression—"if possible"— is not

the language of one who has determined upon a vigorous offensive.

(3) Concentration of the whole command (less one or two divisions) for a march on an unknown object down the old Richmond road (occupying the enemy, meanwhile, by a Flank Guard action) under the personal direction of the Commander-in-Chief. Against this theory is the fact that, if General Burnside intended to lead the Left Grand Division in person, he need not have sent a dispatch which begins by saying that " General Hardie will remain with you during the day."

Unfortunately General Franklin did not adopt any one of these alternatives, nor follow out any plan consistently and to its logical conclusion ; nor did he apply for explanation of what was unintelligible. He states that he was guided by the following opinions : " General Burnside ought to have known, and doubtless did know, that to make his main attack, and thereby bring on a general engagement, on my front under an order of this description, sent after daylight in the morning, was to send his troops to a useless and unavailable (*sic*) slaughter, and therefore he could not have intended it." What, then, in Franklin's opinion, did General Burnside intend the Left Grand Division to do after so much preparation, and after reinforcing it by two divisions of Hooker's command ? Franklin, on his defence, says in answer to this question, " General Burnside's order, though incongruous and contradictory on its face, admitted of but one interpretation, viz. : that he intended to make an armed observation from the left to ascertain the strength of the enemy—an interpretation also given to it by both of my corps commanders."

General Franklin, in the light of subsequent events, must have often regretted that, instead of conferring with his subordinates as to the meaning of his superior's dispatch, he did not at once ask a question or two point blank of the sender by means of the telegraph, which had doubtless for some such purpose been established within half a mile of "Mansfield." For the operation he engaged in on December 13, calling it an "armed observation," cost the Left Grand Division over 3,000 casualties ; and a soldier stands self-convicted of want of judgment who pays such a price for mere "observation." Moreover, it is to be remembered that Franklin in the same letter (undated, but written in reply to the Report of the Committee of Congress on the Conduct of the War on April 6, 1863), after asserting his belief that Burnside intended an "armed observation," says that "General Burnside knew the strength in numbers and position, as well as the desperate determination of the rebel army." Why, then, should Franklin assume that an armed observation or reconnaissance in force was required ? And why, acting on that assumption, did not Franklin, after drawing the enemy's fire, retire and report the result of his observations ? Finally, why did Franklin make no allusion to the "armed observation" in his official report dated 2nd January, 1863, but, on the contrary, in that report continually refer to "the attack ? "

Clearly Franklin stands convicted of at least great folly in misinterpreting orders while a telegraph was available for the purpose of clearing up misunderstandings, doubts and difficulties, and the only palliation of his fault is that Burnside's own representative was present, and made no effort to obtain a decision from Army Headquarters on any point in dispute. This officer in turn may plead that his repeated reports to Army Headquarters evoked no response, no word of approval, blame, or even enquiry. It is indeed hard to find a parallel to a case, in which the commander-in-chief, his staff-officer, and the immediate commander of the troops engaged, cannot determine whether the operation they have started with a force of upwards of 47,000 men is an " armed observation " or a " vigorous attack." Modern students of war would for excellent reasons hesitate to describe the Battle of Fredericksburg by either of these terms.

The actual conflict between the divisions, brigades and batteries of Jackson and Franklin is an affair of minor tactics, that can be followed up in minutest detail or reduced to mere tables of losses, for the material afforded by the reports of the commanders of eighty-eight units, more or less concerned, is overwhelmingly voluminous. But in this small volume it is impossible to do more than indicate the general character of the battle by following the movements of those brigades which, judging by their casualty lists, were the principal instruments of American generalship on December 13. Broadly speaking, Franklin was opposed by Jackson, and Sumner by Longstreet, Hooker's Grand Division assisting Franklin and Sumner in turn. The average strength of brigades was (Confederate) 1,650 (Federal) 2,200 of all ranks. Down by the Massaponax two Federal divisions (seven brigades) struggled with six Confederate brigades drawn from the divisions of A.P. Hill, Ewell and Hood. Up at Fredericksburg, west of the town, Couch's 2nd Corps of three divisions, assisted by three brigades from Wilcox's 9th Corps, were easily held up by four brigades of Confederates from the divisions of Ransom and McLaws, and even in the last determined assault by Butterfield's four brigades (5th Corps) the Federals met with the same degree of resistance, and suffered corresponding losses.

CHAPTER X

THE AMERICAN SOLDIER; HIS SOCIAL STATUS AND PROFESSIONAL ABILITY—A VOICE FROM THE RANKS.

CHAPTER X

IT is at this stage of our narrative that we feel the need of some such human document as the diary of a private soldier, as an antidote to official despatches and reports, to remind us that behind the plan of campaign, the strategical dispositions and the " Orders " of generals—which constitute for so many of us the whole history of war—there remains the army, the organized and disciplined multitude, and the individual combatant, who counts for something after all. In vain a Napoleon contrives a Marengo, ordering his marches hither and thither, if he lack the means of winning the inevitable battle. As a strategical operation, Novara is often compared with Salamanca, but how different the result, since the tactical decision depended, in the one case upon Sardinian, in the other upon British troops. Do we not read far too much about generals and far too little about the armies that served them ? We hear of Waterloo and of Sedan, as the achievements of a Wellington and a Moltke; maybe it were wiser to study Saratoga and Valmy, where newly raised levies and extemporized generals humbled the proud leaders of " regular " forces. In regard to the campaign of Fredericksburg it is indispensable that we should become acquainted with the characteristics of the men who did the fighting, since on one side at least the generals were of little account, and serve only to show how far human fatuity may go before the mistake is perceived of sending forth an army equipped with everything but what has been called its "brain," and how largely the blundering experiments in war of inefficient leaders are redeemed by the resolute and intelligent fighting of tactical units.

As to the condition and morale of the Confederate forces we have the independent testimony of Lord Wolseley, who was then holding a staff appointment in Canada and spent his "leave" in visiting Lee's headquarters soon after the battle of Sharpsburg. "I have seen," he writes, "many armies file past in all the pomp of bright clothing and well-polished accoutrements; but I never saw one composed of finer men or that looked more like *work* than that portion of General Lee's army which I was fortunate enough to see inspected." The Confederates were however, according to one who had had the custody of some 12,000 rebel prisoners, exceedingly ignorant. "Many of them could not read or write. I often admired the military skill displayed by the Confederate officers in forging these ignorant men into the almost perfect soldiers they were. The discipline in the Confederate armies must have been exceedingly severe, to have enabled these officers to control these reckless, savage-tempered men. The prisoners at Elmira were exclusively Americans."

Lord Wolseley remarked that however slovenly the dress of any particular company might be (officers and men alike wore the hair long, passing the locks behind their ears as women do), their rifles were "invariably in good serviceable order." They marched, he says, with an elastic tread, the pace being somewhat slower than that of British troops of the period, and each man bore an " unmistakable look of conscious strength and manly self-reliance." Unfortunately so many of the chroniclers of events in 1862 have considered it necessary in giving praise to one side to belittle their antagonists. Lord Wolseley even could not suppress a sneer at " Mr. Lincoln's mercenaries," and in his zeal for the Confederates forty years ago indignantly exclaimed : " Will any one, who understands what it is that makes and unmakes armies, for a moment believe that such men are to be beaten by mobs of Irish and German mercenaries, hired at fifteen dollars a month to fight in a cause they know little and care less about ? " Surely Lord Wolseley forgot that this description hardly applied to the bulk of the Northern army in 1862. The author of *New England in War Time* says that the fitness of the New Englander, whether bred in town or country, for the duties of a soldier was abundantly demonstrated. " The man of the fields no doubt had a better physique to begin with ; but the more varied conditions of urban life, and perhaps a better knowledge of hygienic laws, gave the town-enlisted soldier an advantage in the malarial and fever-stricken districts of the South. The countryman often fared hardly, and in many places it was no mere figure to say that the climate slew more than the enemy. Living all his life in a climate of noted healthfulness, if of severe extremes, it is not surprising that the rural New Englander often found the conditions of less tonic latitudes more deadly than the enemy's bullets. One indispensable requisite for soldiering he possessed in common with most Americans; he had the hereditary instinct of marksmanship, the latent, if not always developed, capacity for shooting straight. The blood of the early Indian fighters still ran in his veins, though he was rarely cognisant of their exploits; and he had enjoyed a fair amount of practice upon the game of his native woods and fields; but I doubt if, in the country districts, one man in fifty had ever used a rifle or a musket in his life. If 'Zekiel, however, could not have given Huldah an exhibition of his prowess with the longer-ranged arm, as his countrymen of the West and South might still have done—whose shooting must at least have equalled Robin Hood's, for they used to drive nails into trees, and hit squirrels and rabbits in the eye to save the skins at incredibly long distances with their pea-rifles—the root of the matter was undoubtedly in him." With respect to military drill and discipline, a tradition of training and training-days lingered at that time in the country, and in the larger centres there were regular volunteer organizations of a good degree of efficiency.

It is not a little surprising that an ingenious people like the Americans, to whom so many inventions and improvements in machinery are due, should have been so ill-provided with weapons of precision at the battle of Fredericksburg, which was fought only four years before the Prussians at Sadowa startled the world with a firearm that Nicolas Dreyse had brought to perfection by experiments extending over thirty years. The Federals at any rate might have quickly re-armed their infantry with the needle gun, or with one of the breech-loaders invented by Sharp or Wilkinson their countrymen; but we find that in 1862 the American armies were employing muskets, Belgian, Springfield or flint-lock, and others which they designated "altered" and "improved" muskets. They had, it is true, a quantity of rifles (Springfield, Austrian, Belgian, Mississippi and Enfield), calibre ·54, ·57, ·58, and ·69) the best of which in the hands of skilled marksmen were dangerous at 600 yards. But the general impression evidently was that fire effect was to be produced by deliberate aiming at short ranges, not by rapid firing at a distant "beaten zone." Even this slow "aimed" fire apparently caused difficulties in regard to ammunition supply; we shall see that many units were put temporarily out of action for want of cartridges. Every infantry soldier was equipped with 40 rounds carried in a very thin and nearly square cartridge box. The box was so contrived that after expending 20 rounds it was necessary to withdraw the interior tin case and turn it upside down in order to get at the remainder—a difficult thing to do when the leather of the outer leather had shrunk from exposure to rain. Perhaps for this reason cartridge boxes were frequently left behind, and a deficiency of ammunition was so caused. Hundreds of these boxes might have been picked up on the battlefield of Fredericksburg.

Reverting to the subject of the social status of the Federal armies we read that, " Coming like Cincinnatus from the plough, or from the factory, the warehouse and the office, even from schools and colleges, these excellent citizen-soldiers were first hived in camps for instruction in the rudiments of war. Literally they were of all sorts and conditions. It is said that no other modern army ever had in its ranks so much talent and even genius as this first American volunteer force."

General Lee even took a juster view than Lord Wolseley of his opponents in December 1862, and though he mentions to President Davis that the Army of Northern Virginia was " never in better health or in better condition for battle than now," he has no illusions as to the military situation. " I would wish it to be double its present strength for the work before it." And he scouted the idea that he could spare a single battalion for coast or other local defences, stating plainly that " the people must turn out to defend their homes or they will be taken from them." It was said in after years, " given Grant in command of the Federal army in 1862 and the rebellion would have been crushed that year." If asked how McClellan would have done with the army of 1864 under his command, old soldiers shrugged their shoulders and replied, " Well, he would have ended the war in the Wilderness—by establishing the Confederacy."

An analysis of the American armies of 1862, and classification according to social status of the men who composed them, would solve a problem that has beset many writers on the Civil War. Attempts have been made to dispose of the subject by roundly asserting that the Northern armies consisted exclusively of townsmen and the Southern armies were composed wholly of men who lived the open-air life ; that the Confederates were born horsemen and the Federals skilled mechanics ; that Lee's men were all patriots, and Burnside's men all mercenaries ; that the rebels were the better shots, and the Yankees the better marchers ; and so on. Such generalizations are worthless as applied to the forces operating on the Rappahannock at the period of which we write. Save a nucleus of regulars (thirty regiments) with the Northern army, the whole of the combatants were volunteers ; and alike in point of discipline, zeal and intelligence, may be fitly compared with the French Revolutionary armies of 1792. Like Napoleon's first armies, too, the soldiers elected their own officers, though not to the same extent nor with the same results. There did not arise from the ranks of the American volunteers a Junot, a Lannes, a Massena, an Augereau, nor even a Serrurier, a circumstance which is possibly due to the administrative error of coupling the system of election for first appointments with the system of promotion by seniority. The French volunteers of 1792 elected their officers up to the rank of colonel, and in the course of twenty years threw up the generals who won Napoleon his empire—Lannes for example was the survivor of 300 combats, including fifty-four pitched battles.

On the American continent events went to prove that if, on the one hand, not every West Point graduate was a heaven-born soldier, on the other hand the peculiar qualifications for leadership of a modern army are not acquired in the backwoods nor the counting-house. Lee, Johnston, Jackson and Stuart on the one side, and Grant, Sheridan, Sherman and McClellan on the other, point the moral that military success, in wars that last only for a few years—often only a few months—depends almost entirely upon preparation by study undergone in time of peace ; and the fact of the Army of Northern Virginia possessing in 1862 at least three first-class leaders, while the Army of the Potomac had then discovered not a single one, probably accounts for the difference in fighting value of the two armies during the Fredericksburg campaign. Later on, no doubt, other factors in the problem would appear. Before finding its Grant, the Army of the Potomac had lost the best of its volunteers, of whom some 50,000 had perished, their places being taken by a type of soldier whom a Northern writer, having fought and marched with them, thus describes: "They are not Americans, they are not volunteers: they are the offscouring of Europe. They disgrace our uniform." Again writing in 1864 he says: "Take the volunteers away from the Army of the Potomac, and Lee could drown the rest of this army in the James River without firing a shot." By the term "volunteer," of course, was understood the voluntarily enlisted soldier as distinguished from the "bounty jumper;" the soldier of the field army as distinguished from the 100-day men who furnished local garrisons; the veterans of a dozen hard-fought battles as distinguished from that undrilled, undisciplined mob of conscripts and substitutes which, panic-stricken at the prospect of fighting, had to be prodded with bayonets to make them follow the column. The American volunteer who had survived such battles as Bull Run, Shiloh, Antietam, and the seven days' fighting round Richmond, was probably such a soldier as the world had never seen before. He needed no instruction as to his duty in the field, and in fact often exercised the functions of instructor both to officers and men less experienced than himself. To the novice he would say in action, "Don't fire so fast. This fight will last all day. Don't hurry. Cover your man before you pull your trigger. Take it easy, my boy, take it easy, and your cartridges will last the longer." Clever infantry fighters on both sides managed their battles in some such fashion as a Federal soldier describes in the following words:

"The infantry were almost constantly engaged in feeling of the Confederate lines to find a weak place, and finding all points staunchly defended. The artillery was pleasantly employed in burying good iron in Confederate earthworks. The list of our killed and wounded and missing grew steadily and rapidly, longer and longer, as their cartridge-boxes grew lighter and lighter. One day a brisk fight was going on in front of us: we—the light artillery—were ordered to the top of a hill, and told to fire over our infantry into the edge of the woods where the Confederates lay. The battery swung into action. Below us in the open was a pasture field: in it were two batteries and a line of infantry: the former were noisily engaged; the latter were not doing much of anything. The Confederates were behind an earthwork that stood, shadowed by trees, in the edge of the forest, and it was evident that they meant to stay there. Our infantry charged, and at some points they entered the edge of the woods, out of which they speedily came, followed by a disorderly and heavy line of Confederate skirmishers. The batteries in the open were skilfully handled and admirably served, but it was a matter of a very short time for them. As soon as our infantry got out of range in a ravine, the Confederate skirmishers dropped prone on the ground, disappeared behind trees, sank into holes, squatted behind bushes, and turned their attention to the Union batteries which were within rifle range, and the guns were almost instantly driven from the field, leaving many horses and men clad in blue lying on the ground. Then the Confederate skirmishers ran back to their earthworks and clambered over. The battery I served with was firing three-inch percussion bolts at the Confederate line and doing no harm." The Americans revolutionized infantry fighting in 1862, just as twenty-five years later they revolutionized prize-fighting, by methods which substituted for conventional attitudes swift movements, for hoary maxims subtle inventions, for stolid endurance fertility of resource.

The gunner whose battery had been parked, the battle having opened in dense timber where artillery could not be used, would satisfy his desire for fighting his thirst for experience by picking up a dead man's cartridge belt and rifle and spending the day in the firing line with the infantry, doing as he saw them do, changing front under fire to meet a flanking movement, and afterwards sizing up the situation as well as if he had studied infantry tactics all his life. "The Confederate charge against the portion of the 5th Corps, where I was fighting, was not delivered with *vim*. It impressed me as a sham. Their line, as I said, was thin, and it lacked *momentum*. I spoke to my fellows about it, and they all agreed that it was not earnest fighting, but a sham to cover the real attack on our left." The gunner thus enjoyed himself and served the Union cause, but for such works of supererogation the Federal army provided no Victoria Cross nor Distinguished Conduct Medal. On the contrary, for so participating in the battle of the Wilderness—absence without leave it was called—the gunner was punished by having to pack a stick of cordwood on his shoulder for many hours in front of a guard, who skilfully touched him up with the point of a sabre when he lagged.

The experience of a lifetime gets crowded into a few days such as were lived through by the American volunteers in the early " sixties ". Apter pupils no general ever had, nor more trenchant critics. When Grant was appointed Commander-in-Chief the enlisted men thoroughly discussed their new general's military capacity. Periodical literature which contained accounts of his past achievements was procured and attentively read. " I have seen an artillery private quickly sketch the water-courses of the West in the sand with a pointed stick, and ridge up the earth with his hands to represent mountain chains, and then seize successive handfuls of earth and drop them in little piles to represent Forts Henry and Donelson, and Pittsburg Landing, Vicksburg, and Chattanooga." And then the soldiers would gather round the model and take sides for and against Grant, as the story of the battle was read aloud." The men had their own Intelligence Department, too, and knew of defeats and victories long before the news was published ; in fact these volunteers never accepted as accurate the reports of battles appearing in General Orders unless confirmed by the " Camp walkers," who would trudge miles after dark to verify a rumour that affected the safety of the troops. " Seeing our fire with men around it, they would issue forth from the woods and join us. They would sit down, fill their pipes, light them with glowing coals, and then with their rifles lying across their knees ask for the 2nd Corps news, inquire as to our losses, and whether we had gained or lost ground, and what Confederate command was opposed to us. They would listen attentively to what we said—it was a point of honour not to give false information—and then they would briefly tell the 5th, 6th or 9th Corps news, and rapidly disappear in the darkness." Out of such material were fashioned the scouts and couriers who often for days and weeks lived within the enemy's lines, journeying from place to place (sometimes as prisoners of war), and return eventually to head-quarters with an elaborate report, which would guide the commanding generals in making their future dispositions.

There were strategists, too, in the ranks, as appears from the following :—

"It was a weary march, but a march during which there was no straggling. We could look back from hill-tops and see the long, steel-tipped column stretching for miles behind us. There was some anxiety among the men, but not much, as we were confident that we would not be called upon to fight more than half of Lee's army, if we had to fight at all, and we believed that the 2nd Corps, which we judged to number 30,000 men, could whip an equal number of Confederates in the open. At least we could try it, and a fight of that character would have been an agreeable change from assaulting earthworks. At noon we halted for dinner. . . . again we marched. By the middle of the afternoon one of my comrades called my attention to a dust column, which rose away off to our right behind the crest of a ridge, and which moved parallel with us. The news spread up and down the column that we had been out-marched, and that wherever we stopped there we would find Longstreet's Corps. How did we know that Longstreet's soldiers were to oppose us? I cannot tell. But I record the fact that we did know it, as an instance of the accuracy of the information the enlisted men of the Army of the Potomac possessed. That afternoon I dropped behind the battery to talk to some country boys who were serving in an infantry regiment—boys who were raised in Columbia County, New York, and who lived on farms that surrounded my family's homestead. To them I expressed my anxiety at being so far in advance of the main army. I was promptly reassured by a young line sergeant, who said:

"That dust you see over yonder is kicked up by Longstreet's men. They were on the Confederate right at Spottsylvania. As soon as the Confederates missed the 2nd Corps from the battle-line, they knew that we had been despatched on a flanking movement, and Lee started Longstreet towards Richmond to intercept us. Now we have been fighting Longstreet's Corps for two weeks and better, and we all know that he has not more than 15,000 men. The Confederates are not sufficiently numerous to fight us in the open: Longstreet will not attack the 2nd Corps unless he is heavily reinforced: there lies our only danger. Lee knows that the 2nd Corps has been detached from our main army. He knows that Grant has not more than 65,000 men remaining with him. Now, if Lee has a sufficient number of men in his entire army to enable him to whip Grant's 65,000, he would have jumped on him savagely the very instant he discovered that the 2nd Corps had been detached. The fact that he has not sufficient men to whip 65,000 Union soldiers is plainly indicated by that dust column. If Lee had even 50,000 men he would probably risk a battle with Grant's weakened army. *He has not got them.* The only danger we are in is that Lee may be marching with his entire army to jump on the 2nd Corps. If that is his plan—and I think it is not—he had better put it into execution speedily, because in less than an hour after we halt this evening we will be intrenched : and once behind earthworks the 2nd Corps can whip the entire Confederate army."

How did the rank and file acquire their information? From prisoners whom they captured, from comrades in the cavalry, from negroes, and above all from the "news-gatherers," the soldiers who walked the battle-lines at night. But such information is of little account if its possessor lack the faculty of deducing the military situation, and in this art the American volunteers excelled : nor did abstract reasoning prove detrimental to them as practical soldiers.

"Towards evening I saw troops defiling to the left of the road ahead of us, and as soon as they halted, dirt began to fly and intrenchments to rise out of the ground. Our line of defence was quickly chosen, and at once the men began to fortify it. Here they pushed the line out, there they drew it back, taking advantage of the ground and fortifying it, as their experience had taught them was best. In an hour a line of earthworks was thrown up which the 2nd Corps could have held for days against all the Confederates whom Lee could have massed to the assault."

After the battle of the Wilderness, where Grant was computed to have lost the fifth part of his army, the question of the general's next move excited keen controversy. " Grant's military standing with the enlisted men this day hung on the direction we turned at the Chancellorsville House. If to the left, he was to be rated with Meade and Hooker, and Burnside and Pope, the Generals who preceded him. At the Chancellorsville House we turned to the right. Instantly all heaved a sigh of relief : our spirits rose : we marched free. The men began to sing : they understood the flanking movement : that night we were happy."

These fine critics, however, did not approve Grant's subsequent dispositions. His doctrine of " attrition " pressed heavily on the American volunteer, who was flung day after day at the Confederate earthworks. The men in the ranks endured it for long ; they gave their fighting general every chance to prove at their expense the soundness of his theories. The ten days at Spottsylvania reduced their numbers by 12,000, on the North Anna they left 2,000, at Cold Harbour they assaulted the Confederate works for a period of twelve days at a cost of 15,000 ; and then the 'Thinking Bayonet' dropped an unmistakable hint to General Grant that his methods were wrong. Brigades had been reduced to 500 muskets, regiments to 100 bayonets, and two Delaware regiments could only muster 60 files between them. It became necessary to draw the general's serious attention to the matter, and this is how it was done :—" About 4 o'clock in the afternoon I heard the charging commands given. With an oath at the military stupidity which would again send good troops to useless slaughter, I sprang to my feet and watched the doomed infantry. Men whom I knew well stood rifle in hand not more than ten yards from me, and they continued so to stand. Not a man stirred from his place. The army to a man refused to obey the order, presumably from General Grant, to renew the assault. I heard the order given, and I saw it disobeyed. Many of the enlisted men had been up to, and over, the Confederate works, had seen their strength, and knew that those works could not be taken by direct assault. They refused to make a second attempt. That night we began to intrench."

It must be admitted that the Union troops had much to complain of. There is another picture worth studying, of soldiers who had grasped the strategical situation, who knew exactly what ought to be done, who were madly impatient to do it, and who, when baulked of their desire by their own generals, grew furious. Those who would know of war, says the author of *The Yellow War*, should learn of it from the standpoint of the humblest atom that goes to furnish the whole, and the following record is therefore of value to the student of the American Civil War:—

"We were off for Petersburg. We crossed on the pontoon bridge, which had a peculiar earth-quaky motion, and entered the village of tents. Thousands of boxes of hard bread and barrels of pork and coffee were there, but instead of being open, lining the road, and we helping ourselves as we marched, the troops were halted and jammed, and irritated by having to stand around with open haversacks while a few commissary employees slowly dealt out the provisions to us. Hours were worth millions of dollars each on this flank movement, and we dawdled away three of them in getting a little food into our haversacks. Then we marched. We were in high spirits, for every enlisted man in the 2nd Corps knew that we had outmarched the Confederates. We were tired, hungry, worn with six weeks of continuous and bloody fighting and severe marching; but now that we knew that at last a flank movement had been successful, we wanted to push on and get into the fight and capture Petersburg. We knew that we had outmarched Lee's veterans, and that our reward was at hand. On all sides I heard men assert that Petersburg and Richmond were ours, and that the war would virtually be ended in less than twenty-four hours. Night came. The almost full moon arose above the woods, and gold-flecked the dust column which rose above us. We had heard heavy firing about sun-down, and judged that we should be drawing near the battle-line. We entered a pine wood, and there we met a mob of black troops who were hauling some brass guns. The eager infantrymen asked: "Where did you get those guns?" They replied: "We 'uns captured them from the rebels to-day." "Bah!" exclaimed an infantry sergeant who was marching by my side, "you negroes captured nothing from Lee's men. The city is ours. There is not a brigade of the Army of Northern Virginia ahead of us." And we all exclaimed: "The city is ours! We have outmarched them!" And we strode on through the dense dust clouds, with parched throats, footsore and weary. Not a grumble did I hear. But with set jaws we toiled on, intent on capturing Petersburg before the Army of Northern Virginia got behind the works. It was "March, march, march! No straggling now. It is far better to march to-night than to assault earthworks defended by Lee's men tomorrow. Hurry along! hurry, hurry, hurry!" And the Northern army marched its best.

The soldiers examined their rifles, and shifted their cartridge-boxes to a position where they could get at them easily, and they drank deeply from their canteens. Then belts were tightened, blanket rolls shifted, the last bits of hard tack were swallowed, and mouths again filled with water and rinsed out. Then throughout the ranks arose murmurs: "Now for it." "Put us into it, Hancock, my boy." "We will end this d——d rebellion to-night!" Soon we heard commands given to the infantry. My battery moved forward, twisted obliquely in and out among the stumps, and then the guns swung into battery on a cleared space. "And then—and then—we went to cooking! That night was made to fight on. A bright and almost full moon shone above us. The Confederate earthworks were in plain view before us, earthworks which we knew were bare of soldiers. There was a noisy fire from the Confederate pickets in front of us. So unnerved and frightened were they [local militia?] that their bullets sang high above us. We cooked and ate, and fooled the time away, while every man knew that not many miles away the army of Northern Virginia was marching furiously to save Petersburg and Richmond and the Confederacy. We could in fancy see those veteran troops, lean, squalid, hungry and battle-torn, with anxious-looking eyes, striding rapidly through the dust, pouring over bridges, crowding through the streets of villages, and ever hurrying on to face us. And we knew that once they got behind the earthworks in our front we could not drive them out. Still we cooked and ate, and sat idly looking into one another's eyes, questioningly at first, then impatiently, and then angrily. Gradually the fact that we were not to fight that night impressed itself on us. I walked over to the limber of my gun, opened my knapsack, and took out a campaign map and a pair of compasses. Returning to the fire, the map was spread on the ground. As I measured the distances a group of excited soldiers gathered around and watched the work. We had the less distance to march, about nine hours the start, and allowing for the time lost at the crossing of the James River, we were at 11 p.m. four or five hours ahead of Lee's army. " Will they be in the works by morning, men ? " I asked ; and all answered, " By God, they will ! " The rage of the enlisted men was devilish. The most blood-curdling blasphemy I ever listened to I heard that night, uttered by the men who knew that they were to be sacrificed on the morrow. Seated on the ground I rested my back against one of the ponderous wheels of my gun, and slept. At early dawn I was awake and tried to examine the Confederate line. I noticed that the noisy, wasteful picket-firing of the night before had ceased ; that the main line of earthworks, indistinctly seen in the grey light, was silent. It grew lighter and lighter, and there before us, fully revealed, was a long, high line of intrenchments, with heavy redoubts where cannon were massed at the angles, silent, grim. No wasteful fire came forth from that line. Now and then a man rose up out of a Confederate rifle-pit, and a ball flew close above us, no longer singing high in the air. Sadly we looked at one another. We knew that the men who had fought us in the Wilderness, at Spottsylvania, North Anna, and Cold Harbour were in the works sleeping, gaining strength to repulse our assault, while their pickets watched for them."

Even divisional generals and brigadiers were not exempt from the volunteers' criticism. " We knew the fighting generals and we respected them ; and we knew the cowards and despised them," said a Union soldier. He had prepared statistics to show that only one general had been killed to 44,000 enlisted men, whereas there should have been—he averred—at least 20 killed and 80 wounded " if they had done their duty as recklessly as the Confederate generals did theirs." No doubt local and political influences were often at work to place in positions for which they were unfitted a class of officers whom the men derided as " shoulder-strapped office-holders." On the other hand, especially on the Confederate side, the volunteers were often the social superiors of their regimental commanders. General Jackson showed no surprise when invited by his orderly one day to take up his quarters in a roomy mansion hard by, the owner of which he discovered to be the soldier who was at that moment holding his horse. Wealthy Southern planters in the ranks often went shoeless for weeks at a time. On another occasion General Lee was accosted after a fight by a powder-blackened artillery man, who on closer inspection turned out to be his own son, then serving as a " No. 1 " in a light battery.

Of course the Confederate army possessed an enormous moral force in the personality of its leaders.

" The feeling of the soldiers for General Lee," says Lord Wolseley, " resembles that which Wellington's troops entertained for him, namely, a fixed and unshakable faith in all he did, and a calm confidence of victory when serving under him. But Jackson, like Napoleon, is idolized with that intense fervour which, consisting of mingled personal attachment and devoted loyalty, causes them to meet death for his sake, and bless him when dying." All the more honour to the volunteers who fought on the opposite side, who espoused the cause of the Union without any other stimulant than loyalty to their own Government and pride of race, who had taken heavy punishment so gamely time after time, and who now in December 1862 were ready again to face the enemy, to assault intrenchments, and unless stricken down in the advance, to close with the fierce Confederates and settle matters at the point of the bayonet.

The fight done, the wounded and prisoners fraternized. Americans all, volunteers most of them, they would be seen exchanging food for tobacco, and indulging in badinage such as " Say, sonny, did you clover-leaf chaps get a belly full ? " as though a hotly contested football match had just concluded. But it was different when the negro was in question. The negro was a servant, not an equal in the South, and when coloured troops faced the Confederates there was no quarter given. A Northern negro sergeant and a Confederate line sergeant were discovered dead together, having fought a duel with bayonets in the midst of the battle and literally stabbed each other to death. The employment by President Lincoln of about 120 regiments of coloured troops as combatants was hotly resented by the Southerners, who used negroes only for fatigue purposes and as working parties, impressing them as hewers of wood and drawers of water. And in this aspect of the slave question there was doubtless more fellow-feeling between, say, Jackson's men and Hancock's men, than between Hancock's men and the Federal Government. From the politician's point of view the Confederates were rebels, but the Union volunteer who came to grips with them respected and admired these men of his own race and class, and the Northern fighter who penned the following account of the battle in the Wilderness had evidently more sympathy with Longstreet's men than with the "foreign-born" soldiers of the type described on page 166, who for valuable consideration helped to save the Union.

"About five o'clock we (2nd Corps) were ordered to advance, and pushed ahead fighting as we went and forced Hill's men back, killing many, wounding more, and taking scores of prisoners. We crossed a road which a wounded Confederate told me was the Brock road. I saw many dead Confederates during this advance. They were poorly clad. Their blankets were in rolls, hanging diagonally from the left shoulder to the right side where the ends were tied with a string or a strap. Their canvas haversacks contained plenty of cornmeal and some bacon. I saw no coffee, no sugar, no hard bread in any of the Confederate haversacks I looked into. But there was tobacco in plugs on almost all the dead Confederates. Their arms were not as good as ours. They were poorly shod. The direful poverty of the Confederacy was plainly indicated by its dead soldiers. But they fought! Yes, like men of purely American blood. We had charged and charged again, and had gone wild with battle fever. We had gained about two miles of ground. The Confederates seemed to be fighting more stubbornly, fighting as though their battle-line was being fed with more troops. They hung on to the ground they occupied, and resolutely refused to fall back further. Then came a swish of bullets and a fierce exultant yell, as of thousands of infuriated tigers. Our men fell by scores. Great gaps were struck in our lines. There was a lull for an instant and then Longstreet's men sprang to the charge. It was swiftly and bravely made, and was within an ace of being successful. There was great confusion in our line. The men fired wildly. I feared the line would break; feared that we were whipped. The line was fed with troops from the reserve. The regimental officers held their men as well as they could. We could hear them close behind us, or in line with us, saying : " Steady, men, steady ! " as one speaks to frightened and excited horses. The Confederate fire resembled the fury of hell in intensity, and was deadly accurate. Their bullets swished by in swarms. Again our line became wavy and badly confused, and it was rapidly being shot into skirmishing formation. Speedily a portion of the 9th Corps came to our assistance—and they came none too soon. They steadied the line and we regained heart. The Confederates then got a couple of batteries into action, and they added to the deafening din. The shot and shell from these guns cut great limbs off the trees, and several men were knocked down by them. Our line strengthened, we in our turn pushed ahead, and Longstreet's men gave ground slowly before us, fighting savagely for every foot. The wounded lay together. I saw in the heat of this fight wounded men of the opposing forces aiding each other to reach the protective shelter of trees and logs, and as we advanced I saw a Confederate and a Union soldier drinking in turn out of a Union canteen, as they lay behind a tree. There was another lull, and then the charging line of grey again rushed to the assault with inconceivable fury. We fired and fired, and fell back fighting stubbornly. We tore cartridges until our teeth ached. But we could not check the Confederate advance, and they forced us back and back, until we were behind the slight intrenchments along the Brock road. A better charge or a more determined one I never saw. We fought savagely at the earthworks. At some points the timber used in the earthworks was fired, and our men had to stand back out of the line of flame and shoot through it at the Confederates, who were fighting in front of the works. And the woods through which we had fallen back were set on fire, and many wounded soldiers were burned to death. We beat off the Confederates and they, with the exception of the picket line, disappeared. Our line was straightened, reserves were brought up, and some of the battle-torn troops were relieved. We had half an hour's rest, during which time many of us ate and smoked, and drank out of our canteens; and we talked, though not so hopefully as in the early morning.

"Firing had almost ceased. It was as the cessation of the wind before a cyclone. A tempest of fire and yells broke out on the right. We were now out of it. The real battle raged furiously in the woods to the right, while a heavy line of Confederate skirmishers, who lurked skilfully behind trees and fired briskly and accurately, made things decidedly unpleasant for us, and effectually prevented any men being drawn from our portion of the line to strengthen the right. How we fretted while this unseen combat raged! We judged that our men were being worsted, as the battle-sounds passed steadily to our rear. Then the fugitives, the men quick to take alarm and speedy of foot when faced to the rear, began to pass diagonally through the woods behind us. While we stood quivering with nervous excitement, and gazing anxiously into each other's eyes, we heard a solid roll of musketry as though a division had fired together, cheers followed, and then the battle-sound rapidly advanced towards the Confederate line. Then all was quiet. The day's offensive fighting on the part of the Confederates as we, the enlisted men, summed it up, had consisted of two general assaults delivered all along our line, as though to feel of us and discover where we were the weakest ; and to promptly take advantage of the knowledge gained, to attack in force, and with surprising *vim* and staunchness, first one flank and then the other. Both of the assaults were dangerously near being successful. " The sun sank, and the gloom among the trees thickened and thickened, until darkness reigned in the forest where thousands of dead and wounded men lay. The air still smelled of powder-smoke. Many soldiers cleaned out their rifles. We ate, and then large details helped to carry their wounded comrades to the road, where we loaded them into ambulances and wagons."

For these vigorous sketches of the American soldier

in battle we are chiefly indebted to a Northern gunner, who afterwards became Lieutenant Frank Wilkeson of the United States army ; and although his personal experiences are restricted to Grant's last campaign, all students of the Civil war must recognize the essential truth of his pen-pictures. With the artist's instinct he has undoubtedly seized upon the salient characteristics of his countrymen, and his narrative vividly depicts the method of fighting on both sides. It is however generally conceded that the armies put in the field in the spring of 1864 were inferior in *morale* to those engaged in the autumn of 1862, and whose achievements at the battle of Fredericksburg space does not allow us to describe in greater detail than the reports of brigadiers and divisional commanders exhibit.

CHAPTER XI

The Battle of December 13—The Left Attack by Franklin—Jackson's Defence of the Confederate Right Section—The Right Attack by Sumner—Longstreet's Defence of the Confederate Left Section—General Burnside's Failure—General Lee's Decision.

CHAPTER XI

THE broad facts in connection with the fiasco known as the Left Attack appear to be these : Franklin, in compliance with Burnside's instructions to seize " at once " Hamilton's Height—the enemy's strongest point in the Right Section of defence—and to do so with a comparatively small force, deputed the task to a corps commander (General Reynolds), who in turn selected Meade's (3rd) Division to attack the hill, promising that it should be supported by the 1st and 2nd Divisions. Neither of these units, however, appear to have been warned for the occasion, and in the result Doubleday stood fast on the left, while Gibbon became involved in some independent enterprise upon the right, and himself demanded " support " instead of rendering help to Meade.

Meade himself allowed his supporting brigade to incline outwards, so that it was not in position to reinforce the leading brigade at the moment when, having strayed somewhat from the objective (Hamilton's Height) Meade had by some lucky chance struck the weakest spot in the whole of the enemy's position and caused a temporary panic in the Confederate ranks.

Birney's Division, of Hooker's command, which had crossed the river and joined Franklin at noon was instructed to support Meade, but soon afterwards was ordered to retire to a road for shelter (retirement is hardly commendable as a preparatory movement to support a force already engaged with the enemy), and ultimately the burden of sustaining a severe local counter attack fell upon this auxiliary unit.

We will now follow the movements of each of these commands in turn. Reynolds ordered Meade to form for attack, and told him he would be supported on his right by Gibbon and on his left by Doubleday. Meade had three brigades (fourteen regiments) and four batteries, but his fighting strength was hardly 4,500 men. Meade says the " point " to attack was indicated as " near the left of the ridge where it terminated in the Massaponax Valley." Between the place of assembly and the ridge the railroad ran through a hollow. About 9.30 a.m. the column of attack was formed as follows : 1st Brigade in line of battle on the crest of the hollow and facing the railroad with one regiment deployed as skirmishers. 2nd Brigade took post 300 paces in rear of 1st Brigade. 3rd Brigade formed by the flank [column of fours], its right flank [head of column] being a few rods to the rear of the 1st Brigade, with one regiment deployed on its left as flankers. The artillery (sixteen guns) was placed between the 1st and 2nd Brigades.

When the Confederate guns opened fire on the left and rear of Meade's Division the 3rd Brigade was faced to the left, thus forming with the 1st Brigade two sides of a square. Three batteries moved out to return the enemy's fire, and assisted by Doubleday's guns they silenced the Confederate battery in twenty minutes. Meade's batteries then shelled the position, to prepare the infantry advance, and the 3rd Brigade changed front and formed in line of battle on the left of the 1st Brigade. The left of Meade's line thus prolonged extended very nearly opposite the end of the ridge to be attacked.

The Confederate guns again opened fire on the left, and Meade's guns replied, silencing the enemy's battery in thirty minutes. The infantry advance was now commenced.

The 1st Brigade or right of the line advanced a few hundred yards over cleared ground, driving the enemy's skirmishers back to a wood in front of the railroad; then through the wood as far as the railroad, "where they were found posted in ditches and behind temporary defences." The 1st Brigade drove the enemy out of these intrenchments and up the heights in their front and, though suffering from enfilade fire on their right, forced the Confederates over the crest of the hill and, still advancing, crossed a main road which runs along the crest and finally reached open ground on the other side. According to the brigadier, the 1st Brigade had captured " a large number " of Confederates before they could remove their guns [muskets] from the order in which they had been stacked, but on the other hand the five regiments of the brigade had become " greatly confused." At this stage, no doubt, the brigadier looked round for his supports, and sought in particular the 2nd Brigade.

The 2nd Brigade had followed the 1st Brigade at a distance of 300 yards as far as the railroad. There two regiments were induced by the enemy to form to a flank and fight independently. The other three regiments continued to follow the 1st Brigade for some distance, and then, instead of filling up the gaps on the 1st Brigade, these regiments inclined to the left and prolonged Meade's line in that direction, perhaps in consequence of an accident that befell the 3rd Brigade.

The 3rd Brigade (five regiments), as we have seen, had formed on the left of the 1st Brigade, and so advanced as far as the railroad; but here it was checked, and by halting uncovered the left flank of the 1st Brigade. The commander of the 3rd Brigade says that he " gained the railroad and penetrated into their camps, holding the position for over an hour, when, the last round of ammunition being exhausted and no support coming up, the brigade was forced to fall back, leaving the brigadier dead upon the field."

Meade had, nevertheless, pushed on with the 1st and part of the 2nd Brigade and, as we shall see, was almost justified in his belief that " the attack was for a time perfectly successful." And yet the story of Meade's Division ends lamentably enough :

" With one brigade commander killed, another wounded, nearly half their number *hors de combat* ; with regiments separated from brigades, and companies from regiments, and all the confusion and disorder incidental to the advance of an extended line through wood and other obstructions ; assailed by a heavy fire, not only of infantry but of artillery, not only in front but on both flanks—the best troops would be justified in withdrawing without loss of honour."

But where were the supports which General Reynolds ad promised ? Meade had sent to Gibbon and sent to Doubleday for assistance. What had happened to Gibbon's (2nd) Division ?

The 2nd Division appears to have fought its own way

to the front without any special orders and with no particular object, and Gibbon afterwards said: "I had exhausted my last man in capturing the position. Meade's men were retiring on the left, and without the speedy arrival of reinforcements the position would have to be abandoned." Gibbon himself was wounded at 2.30 p.m., and his successor in the command reported—"No reinforcements coming to my support, and amid a universal cry of a want of ammunition I deemed the position no longer tenable." The notion, that the mission of the 2nd Division was to afford support to the 3rd Division in the attempt to seize Hamilton's Height, does not seem to have entered the mind of either Gibbon or his successor. Perhaps no such instructions had ever reached them. Indeed, Hardie had reported to Burnside at 1.25 p.m.—"Reynolds will push Gibbon in, if necessary," as though the 2nd Division were, even then, awaiting orders. Meade had also been promised the support on his left of the 1st Division under Doubleday; but this general states that—"Between the Bowling Green Road and the river there is a wide open plain, and upon this plain most of the operations of my division took place." He was apparently never within a mile of Meade. It remains to be seen how General Birney played his part. Birney says that he reported to Reynolds about 11.30 a.m. and was ordered to deploy " in the field in rear of Meade's division, as a support to the intended attack by that division." Hardie notes at 12 noon—"Birney's division is now getting into position. That done, Reynolds will order Meade to advance."

Birney deployed two brigades in two lines and held one in reserve; but being under artillery fire in the open and losing heavily, he was ordered by Reynolds to retire and take shelter behind the " high embankments with ditches next to road some six feet deep." And through these embankments were two narrow wagon-ways, making it possible to retire from the field only by the flank of a regiment [*i.e.* in column of fours], which perhaps accounts for Meade's statement that "a brigade of Birney's advanced to our relief just as my men were withdrawn from the wood." Birney's own account is that while retiring as ordered to find shelter, Meade sent to him for assistance; that he at once relieved Meade's batteries (out of ammunition) with his own, and reversed the movement of his infantry so as to send them forward " to the support of the troops in front," but he found " Meade's and Gibbon's divisions were in full retreat . . . the retreating troops passed through my ranks, and at General Meade's request I ordered the 99th to try and stop his troops. It was useless, as they sullenly and resolutely marched to the rear." Birney then had to sustain a counter attack, and states that a brigade deployed in line and one " doubled on the centre " on each flank charged upon his four batteries.

According to Burnside's Staff-officer, General Hardie, who as a non-combatant on December 13 is perhaps for some purposes its most trustworthy historian, Meade moved out at 9 a.m., his advance was checked at 9.40 a.m.; he again advanced half a mile at 11 a.m., and at 12.5 p.m. " is advancing in the direction you [Burnside] prescribed this morning ". At 1.15 p.m. Meade is assaulting the hill; at 1.25 p.m. his division is in the wood and " seems able to hold on "; but " Reynolds will push Gibbon in if necessary." At 1.40 p.m. Meade has carried a portion of the enemy's position in the wood and Gibbon has advanced to Meade's right. At 2.15 p.m. Gibbon and Meade are driven back from the wood.

It was about this time—before 2.30 o'clock—that Franklin received an order through Burnside's aide-de-camp to " make a vigorous attack with his whole force." Nothing, however, was done. Franklin and his advisers were no doubt well aware that the golden opportunity had been lost, and that the Confederates' appetite for fighting had been merely whetted by four hours of intermittent assault.

The Left Attack or " armed observation " expired of inanition at 5 p.m., when General Reynolds ordered Birney to take command of his front, where for three nights his division remained on the field without blankets and under the fire of sharpshooters until " an informal arrangement " was made between him and the Confederate general opposite [Ewell] to stop the picket firing. The outposts on both sides then rested peaceably within a hundred yards of each other.

Meade's opponent was General A. P. Hill, who, as we have seen (page 108), had occupied the 1st line in the right section of the Confederate defences with his six brigades; but the brunt of the fighting fell upon the two centre brigades, whose commanders have described the combat from the defenders' point of view.

Archer's report may be summarized as follows: " My brigade was posted in the edge of a wood before Bernard's House, overlooking the plain through which the railroad and Bowling Green turnpike pass (the former about 250 yards, the latter about 1,350 yards from my front), my left resting where the wood extends forward

O

to a point beyond the railroad. Lane's Brigade was on my left, with an interval of about 600 yards between us, while," as I was informed," Gregg's Brigade was immediately behind the interval, close enough to prevent my being flanked. On my right I found fifteen light guns supported by Field's Brigade. As the fog cleared away, the enemy was seen advancing from the Bowling Green Road, and about 8 a.m. some of his batteries, posted about 1,000 yards from us, were fired on by our batteries, far off to the right. They carried on a brisk exchange of shots for about an hour, occasionally throwing shell into the wood where I was posted. About 10.30 a.m. the enemy turned all his guns on our position for about thirty minutes, and then lines of infantry formed and advanced. I perceived them massing in front of, and entering, the point of wood projecting on my left beyond the railroad. I sent to warn General Gregg to move forward into the interval to prevent my being flanked, and shortly after, fearing that Gregg might be too late, I drew out my right battalion (5th Alabama) and moved it to the left. When the enemy got near the railroad my brigade opened fire, which forced them to take shelter in the railroad, from which they kept up a desultory fire. In the meantime the columns which had entered the point of wood on my left succeeded in passing round my flank, and attacked the 19th Georgia and 14th Tennessee in rear and flank. These regiments left about 160 prisoners in the enemy's hands; and part of the 7th Tennessee also, seeing the regiments on their left give way, and hearing the cry that the enemy was in their rear, quitted the trenches in disorder. The 1st Tennessee and part of the 7th held its ground, and after its ammunition was exhausted charged across the railroad with Hoke's [Trimble's] Brigade of Early's Division, afterwards returning to its original position. The 5th Alabama, which I had sent from the right to aid in opposing the enemy on the left, discharged their duty faithfully. I now sent my aide-de-camp to bring up another brigade in support of my line, which had nearly exhausted its ammunition. Gregg's and Lawton's Brigades and the 5th Alabama drove back the enemy, who had passed my flank, and part of Hoke's Brigade returned to the edge of the wood (my original position), which I still maintained with the right of my brigade, but with empty rifles and cartridge-boxes. Finally I drew back my troops about thirty yards, reformed my brigade, and remained in support of Hoke's Brigade, which had relieved me in the trenches. No enemy ever got within fifty yards of my front; and even after my left was broken by the attack in rear and flank, the enemy in front did not venture to come again.

Lane reported to the following effect: " On December 12, at 6.30 a.m., we left our bivouac and took the position assigned us on the railroad, my right being about 250 yards to the left of the small piece of woods beyond the track, and my left resting on a dirt road which crosses the railroad near the bend. Several batteries were to my left and rear, and Pender's Brigade was some distance farther back, my left nearly covering his right. Archer's Brigade was posted in the woods some 400 yards from the railroad: there was an open space between us of about 600 yards: Gregg's command (my support) was on the military road opposite this opening, and some 500 or 600 yards from the railroad.

On December 13 the 7th and 18th Regiments were moved beyond the railroad, to support three batteries on a hill in their front. As soon as the fog lifted, heavy skirmishing commenced along my whole line, and the enemy were seen advancing. Our skirmishers fell back except Turner's company on the left. The batteries just alluded to opened fire and checked the enemy's advance, while Turner withdrew his company as his men were suffering. Several guns, after firing a few rounds, hurried from the field, saying they were choked. The 7th Regiment then moved to the crest of the hill in front of the guns and fired a volley at the enemy's sharpshooters, the artillery all limbering up and driving to the rear. About two hours later the enemy advanced in strong force across the open field to the right of my front. Colonel Barbour (37th Regiment) being on the right informed me of the advance, and on being ordered to hold his position should he be flanked, he deflected his three right companies and formed them to the rear, at right angles to the track. I sent my courier to inform General A. P. Hill that the enemy were advancing in force upon the opening. Eight regiments were seen to pass to my right, and another 'by the right flank by file left' moved between the small body of woods and the fence beyond the track, and then 'faced by the rear rank' and opened fire upon my right. The three right companies of Barbour's 37th became hotly engaged. Although my right was turned by such a large force, our position was deemed too important to be given up, and the brigade awaited the approach of another force along our entire front. As this force was concealed from the 33rd, 18th, and 7th Regiments by the hill about 40 yards beyond the track, they were cautioned to reserve their fire, but the 28th and 37th had open, level ground in their front; and when the enemy had gotten within 150 yards of our line these two regiments opened fire, repulsing the enemy's first and second lines and checking the third. These two regiments were however subjected not only to a frontal, but to right and left oblique fires, and as the right of my command had become engaged with an overwhelming force, I had dispatched an officer to General Gregg for re-enforcements. My command held their ground until the 28th and 37th had fired away the whole of their own ammunition, and that of the killed and wounded. Then the enemy 'in column doubled on the centre' bore down in mass from behind the hill upon the left of the 28th and right of the 33rd and forced them across the railroad. The 28th and 37th being flanked right and left fell back, and were re-supplied with ammunition. A volley from the 33rd checked the enemy for a time, and their commander ordered a charge, but being unsupported on his right, he countermanded the order and withdrew his regiment into the woods, about 75 yards from the railroad. The 18th Regiment then fell back about 100 yards, the right companies firing into the foe until he reached the woods. The 7th being on the left fell back about 50 yards. General Thomas came to my assistance, but too late to save my line. His brigade met the enemy in the edge of the woods and, with the 18th and 7th Regiments of my brigade on his left, chased them to their first position. The 33rd held the position in the woods to which it had fallen back until I could move up the 28th and 37th, when all again resumed their positions on the railroad. That night the whole brigade was aligned on the track and skirmishers thrown forward, preparatory to a general advance. After this order was countermanded my brigade rested on their arms until morning, having been on duty forty-eight hours. On December 14 there was heavy skirmishing along my whole front, a number of men being killed and wounded. On Monday, December 15, we formed a portion of the second line and, as we occupied an exposed position, the men soon constructed a very good temporary breastwork of logs, bush and dirt, behind which they rested until Tuesday morning, when it was ascertained that the enemy had all recrossed the Rappahannock."

Field's Brigade formed the right brigade in the first line and was not itself attacked, but its commander observed the Federals penetrating the centre of the line, and at once quitted his portion to act as support to the brigades of Archer and Lane. He says: "We moved up by the left flank [in column of fours to the left]; and so urgent and repeated were the calls for reinforcements that my two leading regiments—the only regiments actively engaged—advanced in a run, separated themselves from the brigade, passed well to the left, and encountered the enemy in rear of our front lines about midway between Archer and Lane. Firing one volley into the enemy's left flank and charging them with a yell, they drove the enemy to the shelter of the railroad cut. Here a Georgia brigade co-operated in a second charge, which drove the Federals from the railroad. Pursuing the enemy, they came under a fire of grape, canister and minie balls." The men were all

Virginians, and many were fighting within sight of their homes; their loss was only ten killed and sixty wounded.

Pender's Brigade was posted on the extreme left of the Right Section in first line "in the skirt of wood where we had no protection from the enemy's artillery." Davidsons and Latimers' batteries in front drew a severe artillery fire when the Federals advanced in the afternoon, and Pender's men suffered from this bombardment. One regiment was detailed as escort to the guns and held the enemy's sharpshooters in check on the south side of Deep Run; but the Federals, working up this wooded ravine, captured a flanking party of sixteen and brought enfilade fire to bear upon the main body. Supports arrived and charged the Federals, driving them back upon their batteries. Many men were without cartridge-boxes and got out of ammunition. The brigade lost 169, of whom sixteen were killed. Pender was supported on his right by Thomas' Brigade, which took post on the Military Road, and on his left by Laws' Brigade of Hood's Division, which had been attached to General Hill's command. Thomas, as we have seen, moved to his right in order to support Lane, and it was Law who came to the assistance of Pender. Law states—"At 3 p.m. a force of the enemy defiled from the wood on Deep Run, and forming into line of battle advanced upon Latimer's battery. I then moved my brigade forward to the edge of the timber in rear of the battery, and advanced two regiments to attack the Federals, who had gained the line of railroad about 200 yards in front of the battery. The 57th drove the enemy back to within 300 yards of the Bowling Green Road, but was enfiladed from the wood bordering Deep Run, until the 54th changed front to the left in order to face the wood. The 57th lost thirty-two killed and 192 wounded; the 54th lost six killed and forty wounded. Law's Brigade successfully held the railroad until the close of the day.

Such was the Confederate account of the Federal attack on the left. Lane and Archer between them lost 604 men and their supports, the brigades of Gregg and Thomas 664 men. On Lane's left was Pender's Brigade supported by Law's Brigade. Pender lost 169, and Law 315, before the enemy was routed. There was undoubtedly some blundering in General A. P. Hill's Division in regard to the positions taken up by the supports. An imaginative writer has suggested that Jackson left a gap in his line of defence as a trap for the Federals, but Jackson himself disposes of that theory in saying—" before General A. P. Hill closed the interval which he had left between Archer and Lane it was penetrated, and the enemy pressing forward through that interval turned Lane's right and Archer's left." As often happens in military history, the chief witness is absent. General Gregg was killed, and his successor in command throws no light on the circumstances in which his brigade, on which Lane and Archer depended for immediate support, was itself surprised. Even the reports of the regimental commanders have unaccountably disappeared. But Jackson states that " the enemy penetrated the wood in rear of the position occupied by the brigades of Lane and Archer, and came in contact with Gregg's Brigade. Taken by surprise, Orr's Rifles were thrown into confusion."

An independent counter attack by a part of the 2nd

line cost Lawton's (Atkinson's) Brigade a loss of 424 men, including the brigadier who was taken prisoner; and the best brigades in Jackson's 1st and 2nd Lines were apparently so far used up in the effort to expel Franklin's attacking force that we are able to see how small a margin often lies between defeat and victory. General Lee had lost 3,000 men by the passive defence of a comparatively small frontage attacked by a force which General Burnside somewhat bitterly described as one of the smallest divisions in Franklin's command; and yet the Fog of War caused the Confederate general to believe that he had gained an easy victory, while the Federal commander could not persuade his dispirited troops to renew the attack. Comparing the losses (killed and wounded) in Jackson's command with those in Franklin's command, there is only a balance of 1,000 in favour of the defenders.

Burnside's written " Orders " to Franklin had however been strictly carried out, and since Hamilton's Height was still in the hands of the enemy, the Battle of Fredericksburg might here have ended, in accordance with Burnside's own determination expressed twelve hours previously (5 a.m.) to make Sumner's movement dependent on Franklin's success. Unfortunately, General Burnside's unstable mind had caused him six hours later, for the first time since his arrival at Fredericksburg, to " feel the importance of haste," and acting under this impulse, he had at 11 a.m. directed General Sumner " to commence his attack."

Sumner had been waiting for permission to advance, in accordance with his orders. He had selected French's Division to prepare the attack, and Hancock's Division to support French. Each division comprised three brigades and two batteries. French says—" the divisions were ordered to attack in column by brigades, covered by a strong line of skirmishers."

At 12 noon French moved from the town of Fredericksburg to carry Marye's Height, about 1,400 yards distant. His skirmishers debouched from the streets, deploying right and left as soon as they crossed the bridges of the canal at the railroad depot and beyond Hanover Street. They immediately came under heavy fire from Confederate guns and infantry. The 1st Brigade followed, marching directly towards the centre of the Confederate line. The 3rd Brigade followed, and the 2nd Brigade brought up the rear. This was the column of attack, the head of which had not ceased steadily to advance until the 1st Brigade arrived in front of the enemy's rifle-pits, at short musket range. The Federal skirmishers having driven the enemy to cover were now scourged with rifle fire on the front and flanks, and compelled to lie down, slightly protected by the undulations of the plain. The 2nd and 3rd Brigades, shattered by the Confederate fire, "filled up the serried lines of the 1st Brigade" and "poured their fire into every part where the enemy appeared"; but the length of time required to cross the bridges and the extent of the plain to be crossed "under the fixed batteries and covered ways of the enemy" caused the column of attack to become so reduced that "it could make no serious impression upon the works to be carried." Still the head of the column pushed on, though melting away before the Confederate fire. "My troops," continues French, "now covered themselves to the right and left of the front of attack, opening a cross fire upon it."

Hancock's Division followed in support, and reinforced the line of skirmishers; and a section of rifled guns co-operated from a commanding position at the head of Prince George Street. Nevertheless, after being four hours in this useless position, the two divisions were "relieved by fresh troops," after losing over 3,000 men. The table of casualties accounts for them as follows:—

French's Division: 1st Brigade, 520; 2nd Brigade, 291; 3rd Brigade, 342; and seven Artillerymen. Hancock's Division: 1st Brigade, 952; 2nd Brigade, 545; 3rd Brigade, 527; and five Artillerymen.

General Hancock gives a more detailed account of the operation which General Burnside hoped would—coupled with Franklin's anticipated success—cause the Confederates to evacuate the whole ridge. "My division followed that of General French without intervals, so long as we moved by the flank (in fours), through the streets of the town, under a heavy fire. Owing to obstacles, among them a mill race, it was impossible to deploy, except by marching the whole length of each brigade by the flank [in fours] in a line parallel to the enemy's works, after we had crossed the mill race by the bridge. The troops then advanced, each brigade in succession, under fire of artillery and musketry, the artillery fire even reaching the troops in the town. The distance was probably 1,700 yards. The planking of one of the bridges was found to be partly taken up, requiring the men to cross on the stringers. Zook's Brigade formed line and advanced to the attack, being joined, as it passed them, by other regiments of French's Division; it failed however to take the stone wall, although our dead were left within twenty-five paces of it. The Irish Brigade next advanced to the assault, the same gallantry was displayed, but with the same results. Caldwell's Brigade was next ordered into action and failed to carry the enemy's position. All the troops then formed one line of battle, extending from a point to the right of Hanover Street to the left of the culvert. This line was held for some hours after the troops had exhausted their ammunition, and that of the killed and wounded within reach, and some of the regiments did not quit the field until 10 a.m. the following morning."

The Confederate general, McLaws, who repulsed the attack with two brigades of his division, gave the following account of the fighting behind the stone wall at the foot of Marye's Hill, where part of Cobb's Brigade was posted. "On the 13th skirmishing commenced at early dawn, the enemy shelling in that direction until about 11 o'clock, when the advance of the enemy drove in our pickets, and his column approached our left by the Telegraph Road and deployed to our right, planting stands of colours along our front. Before their deployment was completed our fire had so thinned their ranks that the survivors retreated, leaving their colours. Soon another column, heavier than the first, advanced to the colours, but were driven back. They were met on retiring by re-enforcements and advanced again, but were again repulsed. About 1 p.m., Kershaw was directed to send two regiments from his brigade to the support of Cobb, who was getting short of ammunition.

The 16th Georgia of Cobb's Brigade was sent forward at the same time. Not long after this, Kershaw was directed to take his whole brigade and assume command of the position under Marye's Hill, as General Cobb had been disabled." Cobb's untimely death doubtless deprived us of an interesting account of the first fight at the stone wall; even the reports of his regimental commanders are missing, and the report of the officer who temporarily succeeded to the command of the brigade is obviously inadequate.

A fuller account is given by General Kershaw, whose five South Carolina regiments reinforced Cobb early in the afternoon. Kershaw writes:

"On the morning of December 11 the brigade was formed in line of battle in the position assigned me, the right resting at the left of Howison's Hill and the left near Howison's Mill, on Hazel Run. One regiment (15th) went on picket at Deep Run until withdrawn on Friday morning, after a night of such intense cold as to cause the death of one man and disable others. With this exception the brigade was kept in position, strengthening our defences nightly, until Saturday, December 13, when about 1 o'clock I was directed to send two regiments to the support of General Cobb, then engaged with part of his brigade at the foot of Marye's Hill. Within a few minutes I was directed to take my entire command to the same point, and assume command there. Leaving my staff to conduct the brigade I proceeded to the scene of action, reaching the position at Stevens' House at the moment the 2nd and 8th Regiments arrived, and just in time to meet a fresh assault on the left.

"The position was excellent. Marye's Hill, covered

with our batteries—the Washington Artillery—falls off abruptly toward Fredericksburg to a stone wall. The Telegraph Road winds along the foot of the hill: the road is about 25 feet wide, and is faced by a stone wall about 4 feet high on the city side: the road having been cut out of the side of the hill, in many places this last wall is not visible above the surface of the ground. The ground falls off rapidly to almost a level surface, which extends about 150 yards; then with another abrupt fall of a few feet to another plain which extends some 200 yards, and then falls off abruptly into a wide ravine, which extends along the whole front of the city and discharges into Hazel Run. I found on my arrival that Cobb's Brigade occupied our entire front, and my troops (2nd and 8th) could only get into position by doubling on them. This was accordingly done, and the formation along most of the line during the engagement was consequently four deep. As an evidence of the coolness of the troops, I may mention here that though their fire was the most rapid and continuous I have ever witnessed, not a man was injured by the fire of his comrades. The first attack being repelled at 2.45 p.m., the 3rd and 7th Regiments were moved into position on the hill to the left of Marye's House, with 15th in reserve and under cover of the cemetery at Willis' Hill. (One battalion I had left in position at Howison's Hill, to protect our right from any advance of the enemy up Hazel Run). While the 3rd and 7th Regiments were getting into position another fierce attack was sustained, and these regiments suffered severely: six officers in succession fell at once on assuming the command of the 3rd Regiment. In the meantime, line after line of the enemy deployed in the ravine about 400 yards from the stone wall, and advanced to the attack at intervals of fifteen minutes until 4.30 p.m., when there was a lull of half an hour, during which a mass of artillery was placed in position west of the town and opened fire upon our position. At this time I brought up my reserve—the 15th Regiment. Our batteries on the hill were silent, having exhausted their ammunition, and the Washington Artillery was relieved by a part of Alexander's Artillery. Under cover of the enemy's artillery fire the most formidable column of attack was formed, which about 5 o'clock emerged from the ravine, and no longer impeded by our artillery impetuously assailed our whole front until after 6 o'clock. Some few, chiefly officers, got within 30 yards of our lines, but in every instance the columns were shattered by the time they got within 100 paces. Then the firing gradually subsided, and by 7 o'clock our pickets were established within 30 yards of those of the enemy. Our chief loss after getting into position in the Telegraph Road was from the fire of sharpshooters, who occupied some buildings on my left flank and were only silenced by directing a continuous fire of one company upon the buildings. The regiments on the hill suffered most, as they were less perfectly covered. Cobb's Brigade during the engagement was re-enforced by the 16th Georgia, and Ransom's Division was in position in rear of Marye's House. That night we materially strengthened the position, and I more perfectly organized and arranged my command, fully expecting the attack to be renewed next day. I placed the 3rd Regiment in reserve, in consideration of their heavy loss. My command fired about 55 rounds a man.

At daylight in the morning the enemy was in position, lying behind the first declivity in front, but the operations on both sides were confined to skirmishing. Monday morning discovered the pickets of the enemy behind rifle-pits, constructed during the night along the edge of the ravine. From this position they were nearly all driven by our batteries. General Semmes relieved Cobb's Brigade Monday night. As soon as the haze lifted on Tuesday morning, the enemy's pickets being no longer visible, I sent out scouts from my own brigade to the left and from General Semmes' to the right. The former soon returned, reporting the evacuation of the town, which the latter soon confirmed, with the additional information that the bridges had been removed. I sent forward two companies, one from each brigade, and afterward two regiments to occupy the town, as ordered."

The topography of this part of the battlefield, as viewed from the Confederate lines, is ably described by the Chief of Artillery (McLaw's Division). " In front of my position the low grounds extended in an apparent plain from the base of the hill to the river bank. Through these low grounds the Richmond Railroad and the old Stage Road pass. Though apparently a plain, there are many inequalities of the ground which, with these roads, enabled the enemy to mask his approach. All but five of our batteries were so placed as to command not only the approach of the enemy on our right, but also the Telegraph Road and the abandoned railroad to Gordonsville. The guns back of Howison's House commanded the left of the Telegraph Road, and enabled us to give an oblique fire upon the enemy advancing from the various streets in Fredericksburg, and who were drawn up under the protection of the inequalities of the ground in front of Marye's Hill. The main battle on our left was fought to obtain this hill. Between this hill and the town, it is said, the Rappahannock formerly flowed. The conformation of the ground, therefore, enabled the enemy to mass their troops out of view of our infantry in position at the foot of Marye's Hill, and even screened them from our artillery on the hill itself. My position enabled me to observe the enemy's left flank, upon which our guns opened a most destructive fire: it was easy to perceive, from previous knowledge of the ground and the location of their left flank, where their troops were massed. Through the valley in front of Marye's Hill a sluice for the waste water of the canal passes. There is no passage for the enemy's troops between the road in front of Marye's House and the road leading from the Telegraph Road to the railroad depot. The approach by this latter road was completely commanded by our guns. Once a whole brigade was dispersed in confusion to the rear. Once they made for the railroad cut, attempting to cross by running down one side and up the other, and to escape in the same manner; but several shells from our batteries exploded among them before they could escape from it. I am confident that not only upon the approach and the successive repulses of the enemy was the fire of our batteries most efficacious, but that also it did great execution upon the masses of the enemy in front of Marye's Hill. The right of Marye's Hill terminates almost precipitously. The Telegraph Road passes on the right of the hill, and then turns almost directly at right angles at the foot and in front of the hill. The railroad cut and embankment would have enabled the enemy to come in almost perfect security within a short distance of the right flank of our troops drawn up behind the stone wall on the Telegraph Road. Their advance could not have been effectively checked by the artillery on Marye's Hill, owing to the conformation of the ground. It is due to the divisional artillery to say that their fire not only aided materially in repulsing the direct attack on Marye's Hill, but in preventing the right flank of this position being turned by the enemy. Forty-eight guns were placed under my charge. Read's Battery (three guns) occupied the position immediately to the right of the Telegraph Road. Next to this battery one of the 30-pounder Parrott guns (Richmond manufactory) was placed, and was replaced by a Whitworth gun, of Lane's Battery. Next on the right and on the hill back of Howison's House were placed two 6-pounder smooth bore guns and two 10-pounder Parrotts: the smooth bore guns fired only round shot. Next, a battery of three pieces (Parrotts), which was withdrawn to another position and replaced by one Parrott and two 3-inch rifles. Next, two Parrotts and one 30-pounder Parrott (Richmond manufactory). Next, one 3-inch rifle. Next, one 10-pounder Parrott. Next, a battery of five pieces consisting of two 10-pounder Parrotts (1st Company Richmond Howitzers) and three rifled guns. Manly's Battery of six pieces had been placed west of Marye's Hill, with a view to fire upon the enemy in case they succeed in taking that position. There was also twelve short-range pieces, two pieces of McCarthy's Battery, and three pieces of Carlton's Battery. These guns did not fire during the engagement. Both of the Richmond Parrotts did good service until they exploded."

We have seen that General Burnside's first experiment in frontal attacks—without personal reconnaissance, without artillery preparation, and without adequate supports—had cost the Federals over 5,000 men, and if the Union general had been content with experience so dearly purchased, he would have withdrawn his troops at the earliest possible moment and framed fresh plans for the future. Far from this, however, Burnside, having stultified himself by causing Sumner to attack, without fulfilling the conditions laid down in his own orders, had abandoned every tactical principle and all ordinary precautions, and by means of staff-officers and the field telegraph had ordered a series of similar attacks, as though bent upon the destruction of the Federal army. His commands were, however, obeyed so reluctantly, that in the result half the army was kept intact, and so preserved, by Franklin Sumner and Hooker; but the remaining nine divisions shared between them a total loss by 6 p.m. of near 13,000 men. The stone wall position at the foot of Marye's Height had been assailed in turn by the divisions of Hancock (loss 2,032), French (loss 1,160), Howard (loss 914), Griffin (loss 926), Sturgis (loss 1,007); and a last attempt was made at dusk by General Humphreys with the Pennsylvania Division which had crossed the river at 2.30 p.m. Now, Humphreys had not as yet seen any part of the ground, but an officer of Hancock's staff accompanied him, " first to a ravine crossing the Telegraph Road, where the troops could form under partial cover; then to the high ground above on which, some 200 yards in advance, were the troops I was to support, slightly sheltered by a small rise in the ground. In front of them was a heavy stone wall, 150 yards distant, a mile in length, strengthened by a trench and lined with infantry; this stone wall was at the foot of the heights, the crest of which, 400 yards back from the wall, was crowned with batteries." Humphreys led his 2nd Brigade forward, but found that they merely joined the troops already lying down under cover in their front and opened fire. "I was satisfied that our fire could have but little effect upon the enemy, and that the only mode of attacking him successfully was with the bayonet." Accordingly Humphreys called on his 1st Brigade to charge, but "the deadly fire of musketry and artillery broke it after an advance of fifty yards." General Humphreys now rode towards the 1st Brigade to conduct it forward, and while doing so "received three successive orders to charge the enemy's line, the last order being accompanied by the message that both General Burnside and General Hooker demanded that the crest should be taken before night. It was already growing dusky. The 1st Brigade was not yet entirely formed, and was impeded in doing so by a battery whose limbers occupied a part of its ground. With great difficulty I caused this battery to cease firing. Then riding along the two lines I directed the men not to fire, telling them it was useless and that the bayonet alone was the weapon to fight with here. Anticipating, too, the serious obstacle they would meet with in the masses of men lying under shelter, who could not be got out of the way, I directed the brigade to disregard these men entirely, and to pass over them. I ordered the officers to the front and, with a hurrah, the 1st

Brigade led by the brigadier and myself advanced gallantly over the ground under fire, which poured upon it from the moment it rose from the ravine where it had fromed for attack. As the brigade reached the masses of men referred to, every effort was made by the latter to prevent our advance. They called to our men not to go forward, and even attempted to prevent their doing so. The effect upon my command was that the line got somewhat disordered and in part forced to form into a column, but still it advanced rapidly. The fire of the enemy's musketry and artillery now became still hotter. The stone wall was a sheet of flame that enveloped the head and flanks of the column. Officers and men were falling rapidly, and the head of the column was at length brought to a stand. Up to this time not a shot had been fired by the column, but now some firing began. It lasted but a minute when, in spite of all our efforts, the column turned and began to retire slowly. I attempted to rally the brigade behind the natural embankment so often mentioned, but could not arrest the retiring mass. I was again dismounted, my second horse having been killed under me, and my force being too small to try another charge, I communicated the result of the contest to the Corps commander, and received orders to bring back my troops to the ravine. The greater part of the loss (nearly 900 killed and wounded) occurred during the brief time they were charging and retiring, which scarcely occupied more than ten or fifteen minutes for each brigade.

General Lee, writing a few months later his official report on the operations, says: "The attack on December 13 had been so easily repulsed, and by so small a part of our army, that it was not supposed the enemy would limit his efforts to an attempt which, in view of the magnitude of his preparations and the extent of his force, seemed to be comparatively insignificant. Believing therefore that he would attack us, it was not deemed expedient to lose the advantages of our position, and expose the troops to the fire of his inaccessible batteries beyond the river, by advancing against him; but we were necessarily ignorant of the extent to which he had suffered." It is allowable, however, to remark that General Lee overlooked another most important circumstance which certainly should have influenced his decision. He had sustained a very heavy loss. The Confederates, occupying a carefully chosen and perfectly prepared position, might have been expected to repel an attack which Lee considered " comparatively insignificant " without having to report a loss of 7.5 per cent. of his entire force—the Federals attacking only lost 10.5 per cent. of their strength —but the fact is that the Right Section of defence suffered almost as severely as Franklin's attacking force. Jackson lost in killed and wounded 2,997, Franklin only 4,028; the numbers reported " missing " are respectively, Confederates 538, Federals 809, but these figures are not so reliable as those furnished by the Medical Directors, which include the attached divisions of Hood, Birney and Sickles. The Left Section of defence, however, repelled Sumner's attack with small loss comparatively. The proportion is 1 to 6. Longstreet, moreover, only reported 115 men missing, including 110 taken prisoners on December 11; but the Federals opposed to him reported 960 officers and enlisted men "captured or missing" on December 13.

Advocates of the "decisive" counter attack—an operation rarely attempted, and still more rarely successful in war—condemn the Confederate leader for permitting the escape of Burnside's army. But it must be remembered that in 1862 it was not customary to retain a General Reserve for such a purpose, after taking up a position for defence. And on the present occasion it is evident that against the four divisions of Pickett, Anderson, D. H. Hill, and Taliaferro (say twenty-four brigades or 40,000 men), whose morale had been slightly affected by losses, the Federals could have massed eight divisions in a similar condition of efficiency (Burns, Getty, Whipple, Sykes, Doubleday, Brooks, Newton, and Sickles), say twenty-three brigades or 51,000 men—to say nothing of the reserve corps of Sigel and Slocum fast approaching the battlefield.

That counter attack on December 13 was indeed difficult we have the opinion of General Jackson, who after sustaining Franklin's assault all day desired to retaliate. He says: "The artillery of the enemy was so judiciously posted as to make an advance of our troops across the plain very hazardous; yet it was so promising of good results, if successfully executed, as to induce me to make preparations for the attempt. In order to guard against disaster, the infantry was to be preceded by artillery, and the movement postponed until late in the evening, so that if compelled to retire it would be under the cover of night. Owing to unexpected delays, the movement could not be gotten ready until late in the evening. The first gun had hardly moved forward from the wood 100 yards, when the enemy's artillery re-opened and so completely swept our front as to satisfy me that the proposed movement should be abandoned."

With the decision of General Lee to remain on the passive defensive the last hope of General Burnside to emerge with credit from the battle of Fredericksburg disappeared. The Federals lay under the shelter of their heavy batteries inviting attack for two days, but beyond a scourging fire of skirmishers, and an occasional salute from a Confederate battery which had discovered a new target to vex with enfilade fire, the Army of the Potomac was let severely alone, although permitted to see the Confederates digging fresh rifle trenches and gun pits, and to hear them chopping logs for parapets and abatis: for even on the night of the battle Ransom borrowed tools from McLaws and connected the redoubts in his front with rifle trenches, beginning to work with full fatigue parties at moonrise, after Lee had announced his decision not to attempt a counter attack on the morrow.

It is an interesting illustration of the Fog of War that Burnside, ignorant of the severe blow which his Left Grand Division, in spite of all the disabilities Franklin laboured under, had delivered on the Confederate right, determined at a Conference held in the evening to renew the attack on Lee's left. He subsequently was induced to alter his decision, but then he abandoned the fight altogether. General Franklin states: " On the night following I was with General Burnside at his headquarters, when he informed me that he intended to renew the attack from the right and to lead the 9th Corps [his old command] in person. At two interviews during that night . . . I urged upon him that if the attack was to be renewed, to renew it from the left, but with such force and preparations as would command success. An order, however, for an attack from the right was given by him. Next day I had another interview with General Burnside, when he informed me that strong protests were made against a renewal of the attack by Generals Sumner and Hooker, and he abandoned the plan of another attack with expressions of the greatest reluctance. I had another interview with him, in which, so far from expressing any dissatisfaction with me, he stated very distinctly that I alone of his generals had " held up his hands " (as he expressed it): that he had fully determined to resign his command, and to recommend me as his successor."

At a later date, however, finding out how near success the left attack had been (Jackson's casualties were 3,523, Franklin's 4,653), Burnside turned upon his subordinate Franklin and laid upon him the blame of failure for not making greater efforts on December 13. Looking back upon events it is easy to see that Franklin had, even at the end of the day, at least 35,000 effectives, and the presumption that he might have renewed his attacks is by no means unreasonable; but the impression at the time undoubtedly was that " another advance on the enemy on our left cannot be made this afternoon ": and this is the message which Burnside's staff officer, General Hardie, sent him at 3.40 p.m. Of course, it is at such junctures that the personal intervention of the Commander-in-Chief is needed, to infuse fresh energy into the operations, if he has determined to end them successfully: it is at such a time that officers who have been in contact with the enemy for many hours begin to feel the strain of responsibility, and the pessimistic view which is likely to prevail throughout an attacking force brought to a standstill needs combatting with all the commander's will-power.

The labour of years would hardly prove sufficient to reconstruct the battle of Fredericksburg in all its details, if even the *terrain* were specially surveyed for the purpose; and in the absence of a perfect knowledge of the whole of the circumstances of the moment, it is rash to do more than speculate upon the possibilities of the situation, upon what might have been achieved by one side or the other. It is always easier to criticize than to explain a great battle. But something has perhaps been attempted to indicate approximately the character of the fighting and the methods of commanders at this period of the history of tactics, when the resourcefulness of the backwoodsman was grafted on the European system of drill. Assuming that the official reports of the brigadiers and divisional generals are reasonably accurate, our extracts from them suffice to show how the strain of battle was borne at two points, six miles distant from one another on the field; where the defenders on the right and the attackers on the left were in the sorest straights; where the heavy bullet of the old muzzle-loading rifle, fired at short ranges, did its greatest execution in the hands of stout infantry, fighting in much the same fashion as fifty years back Wellington's men had fought in Spain; and where shot and shell ploughed their way through battalions massed for shock action.

Despite Lee's assertion that the Federal attack was

easily repulsed, the facts remain that on his right the first line of defence was actually broken through, and on his left the attackers effected a lodgment in dangerous proximity to the stone wall and other defences in which he had reposed so much confidence; and an examination of the casualty returns will show that the defenders in the first line at both points were severely handled by the Federal firing line and its immediate supports. Erratic as Burnside's methods were, he might easily have blundered into a great success, if he had only possessed the saving grace of knowing how to use his reserves; and in this respect he erred not more than did Ney at Waterloo or Bazaine at Gravelotte. That the battle of Fredericksburg ought to have resulted in a decisive victory for the Federals there is no reason to doubt. Every condition of success was present save one—a first class general who brooked no interference. A Grant would have won by massing his forces and driving home the frontal attack bludgeon-wise regardless of cost: a Lee-Jackson combination would have deftly enveloped the enemy's right flank, the flank that was weakest both strategically and tactically: a Kuroki and, let us hope, the student of *Combined Training* would have adopted the less heroic measure of fortifying the localities which the Federals had already seized on the southern bank of the river, and prolonging a defensive line across the Massaponax until Lee's army was invested from the south and the east, while an impassable river cut off retreat northwards: the two corps of Sigel and Slocum would have crossed the Upper Rappahannock and the Rapidan and moved on Gordonsville, where much of Lee's baggage had been sent, the cavalry protecting the outer flank against Jones' small force in the Valley : the Washington and other forces north of the Potomac would have moved south to furnish a General Reserve for the march on Richmond : the decisive attack would perhaps have been postponed for a week; but the result could hardly have failed to give satisfaction to the Federal government.

CHAPTER XII

After The Battle—the Departments of an Army—The Federals on the Defensive—Burnside's Retreat—Cavalry Reconnaissance—Burnside's Last Effort—The "Mud" March—End of Campaign.

CHAPTER XII

IT is in the nature of things that a narrative such as this should be lifeless. To gain the breadth of view necessary to discern the lessons of a campaign, much interesting detail must be sacrificed; the picturesque can have no place in a strategical and tactical study, and the moving accidents that go to make up "regimental" records must be ruthlessly excluded from these pages. The "march" orders, the plan of attack, the official report of duty performed, and the compilation of a casualty list must sum up a thousand combats which Homer might have sung. But in pursuance of our scheme of exhibiting every important feature of the Fredericksburg Campaign, some space must nevertheless be afforded for a glimpse behind the scenes of a great battle, where the non-combatants labour in the hospitals, in the field forges, in the headquarter offices, in the supply depots, and even in the camp of discipline. On the battlefield perhaps more than elsewhere Milton's immortal line must be remembered—

"He also serves who only stands and waits."

The "departments" of an army have increased in importance as the art of war has developed, and even in 1862 the American armies appear to have profited by the object-lesson furnished by the Old Country a decade previously in the Crimea, where a fine army had been decimated by Want in every form and shape.

At the battle of Fredericksburg the Confederate wounded were collected in ambulance wagons and taken to field infirmaries for the primary operations; and thence moved to the railroad depot for transfer to General Hospital. Some citizens had formed themselves into an Ambulance Committee for the occasion, who administered as an experimental diet to the wounded "portable soup meat," and superintended their removal by rail—the railroad was not under the control of the military authorities—to the base at Richmond. Tents were few and the farmhouses already filled with refugees from the bombarded town, so that immediate evacuation of the field infirmaries was necessary, especially in the vicinity of Jackson's Corps, which contributed nearly the whole of the casualties reported on December 13. Railroad communication, with the base only 60 miles distant, however, prevented at Fredericksburg a repetition of such scenes as were described after Sharpsburg, when in the town of Warrenton every house was filled with wounded and sick, lying on the floor "wrapped in a poor blanket with seldom a straw pillow under their heads." A Federal officer declared that when he passed through Warrenton, ten days after the battle, in some houses " the sick and wounded were literally decaying in their own filth"—a strange story, if true, since he admits that about forty Confederate surgeons were in charge, and that the number of patients did not exceed 1,300, whom, of course, he proceeded to "parole," giving them documents to exempt them from further service against the Federals, unless regularly exchanged as prisoners of war. The Federal wounded at Fredericksburg were less fortunately situated than the southerners, having to endure a long journey by road to Acquia Creek, there to embark for the Base Hospital at Alexandria. Boats for 3,500 casualties were requisitioned on December 14, but only two of the transports had been fitted up for the purpose. In every Federal division a certain number of combatants were detailed for ambulance duty and organized into a "corps" for each brigade. Stretcher-bearers were formed into regimental "squads." A divisional (field) hospital was established near the scene of action and two-horse ambulances removed the wounded to General Hospital. The chief of the 1st Division Ambulance Corps reported subsequently that "the working of the ambulance corps during the recent engagement has demonstrated the usefulness and efficiency of the organization"—from which we may infer that it had been recently established. The hospital arrangements were, however, deplorably deficient, according to the Report of the Medical Inspector-General.

"After the battle of Fredericksburg for three or four days some of the general depots for wounded men were without food except hard bread and such aid as private individuals brought to them, and on Monday night many wounded men lay upon the ground without shelter over them during the heavy rain. There were no stoves in any of the hospitals until a week after the battle, although the weather was very cold."

The Federals had organized a Signal Corps, and a G.O., dated March 1862, had granted special inducements to signallers to become proficient, rewarding every officer " who shall skilfully and bravely carry in action and use his signal flag " by a decoration called a battle-flag, which became his own property. At Fredericksburg parties of signallers crossed the river with the advanced guards of the Grand Divisions, but the fog and smoke interfered greatly with flag signalling during the battle, and moreover it was found that flags drew the enemy's fire, so that when signal-stations were in close proximity to the field hospitals the wounded were exposed to such danger that surgeons implored the signallers to desist from their labours. On December 5 a party of signallers had been sent on board the gunboats then lying off Port Conway, to enable them to communicate with the land forces in the combined operations then contemplated.

The Confederates also possessed a Signal Corps, and though no evidence of its use on December 13 is available, we know that while McLaws' pickets held the town they kept up communication with divisional headquarters by this means. On December 13, however, in striking contrast to the continuous employment of signallers by the Federal commander, General Lee was found penning his brief message to Jackson in regard to ammunition, just as Wellington had penned his field orders at Waterloo. The special interest of the Federal signal corps to us is the fact that the new " magnetic " telegraph was in December 1862 for the first time used in the field: and the northerners appear to deserve all the credit for the innovation. A wire was laid from Phillips' House along the pontoon bridge, thus connecting Franklin with Army Headquarters, and this wire conveyed the messages as to the progress of the fight to which reference has been made on page 152. It was found however necessary to guard the wire by means of a cavalry patrol, since teamsters and soldiers, " in order to satisfy an idle curiosity " as to the wonders of electricity, attempted to cut and carry off the wire. In the Appendix we give what is probably the first official report ever made upon the working of the electric telegraph on the battlefield. A balloon too had been sent to Falmouth and was used by the Federals for purposes of reconnaissance when weather permitted.

The functions of the Confederate provost guard during an engagement have been already indicated on page 110. The Federals possessed a similar organization a thousand strong, distributed among the corps and divisions of the army, and a circular issued by the Provost-Marshal-General thus defined its duties : On the march, provost-marshals will follow up and flank with cavalry the columns to which they respectively belong, driving up every loiterer, straggler and skulker to his company, or placing him under guard. During action, provost-marshals will station themselves in rear of their respective corps and divisions, out of range but within sight of the field, in order that stragglers and skulkers may be gathered and forced to return to their regiments, permitting none but the driver, with two privates of the ambulance corps, to accompany each ambulance ; they will select positions for the reception of prisoners captured by the division, and establish guards suitable for their safe custody, with orders to the officers to require the prisoners to account for their arms, etc., as they are brought in; they will assist the quartermaster in keeping open the Line of Communication; they will ascertain the position of division hospitals and ambulance parks, and of ammunition, quartermaster and subsistence trains, and will place guides at prominent points to direct persons to them. They will charge trusty non-commissioned officers with keeping themselves acquainted with the whereabouts of generals of brigades and divisions, in order that they may furnish the necessary information to staff-officers.

In the Confederate army, among the duties of Ordnance Officers was that of accounting for captures of personnel and material of war. McLaw's division, according to the report of its ordnance officer, captured 1,500 small arms, 200,000 rounds of S.A.A., 400 sets of accoutrements, 300 knapsacks, 145 cartridge-boxes, 695 rounds of 12 pr. shell and spherical case, 120 shot (12 pr), 240 rounds of Parrott shell (various calibres), and 200 three-inch shell of various kinds. The shells had been collected in the streets and houses of the town. Jackson's Corps captured 4,446 small arms and 521 prisoners, including 11 officers; and as 18 officers and 508 men were missing from the 2nd Corps, the exchange of prisoners which took place after the battle enabled Hill's division to recover part of its terrible loss, though 1,609 killed and wounded would still be absent from its ranks. We have no means of knowing whether Lee recovered 1,100 men in exchange for the prisoners taken by Longstreet at Fredericksburg; but if the reports were accurate, the balance in favour of the Confederates under the head of " Missing " was 1,114 (see Comparative Tables of Losses), and this number of " rebels " may have been restored to the southern army.

The fighting on December 13 was hardly over when General Lee, anticipating a renewal of the attack the next morning, directed Jackson to empty his ammunition wagons, by distributing their contents among the battalions and batteries, and then to send the wagons immediately to be refilled at Guiney's Station, where " all the ammunition prepared in Richmond " was about to be delivered. Lee then wrote to the War Office requesting that nobody be sent to the army at Fredericksburg except on duty— " all others are hindrances "—and pointing out that he could spare no troops for local defence. " The people must turn out to defend their homes or they will be taken from them," was his reply to a demand from Wilmington for military protection. The infantry divisions were at once set to work to dig. Ransom connected the redoubts in his front with rifle trenches, beginning to work with full fatigue parties at moonrise, and calling on McLaws for intrenching tools.

Pendleton, the Chief of Artillery, now redistributed his batteries, calling up Milledge's Battery of light rifles from the river below to strengthen Pelham's command on the extreme right. He caused incendiary shells to be made at the ordnance workshop, to be used if necessary by the batteries on Maryes Height in firing certain buildings on the outskirts of the town to expose the enemy's working parties, if he ventured during the night to construct works near the

Confederate lines. On Sunday morning, December 14, a dense fog again prevailed, and fearing a surprise attack upon the centre and right, especially upon the heights where the Whitworth and the large Parrott were emplaced, Pendleton posted Nelson's short-range guns to command all the approaches. Lane's guns (except the Whitworth) were to be moved from the extreme left to the extreme right of the defences, and this battery accordingly marched on Sunday night. On Monday morning Pendleton and Stuart carefully emplaced Lane's guns, and made all preparations for the decisive battle now expected. The Confederate plan, according to Longstreet's letter to Hood, was "to sustain the enemy's attacks and repel them, until they become exhausted and demoralized; when this takes place, General Jackson from the right will bear down on them, and if possible force them back, when the opportunity for the advance of our front will present itself."

At last all the batteries of the general reserve, as well as those of the two Confederate army corps, had been posted on the lines, except the other large Parrott which had burst after its fifty-fourth discharge; the cavalry was maintaining its position, two brigades being massed along the left bank of the Massaponax, guarding Jackson's right flank, while Hampton's brigade was still on Longstreet's left flank, having returned to the Upper Rappahannock after the raid on Dumfries (page 113). Jackson had redistributed his command immediately after the battle, placing the divisions of Early and Taliaferro in the 1st line, D. H. Hill's division in 2nd line, and sending A. P. Hill's division in reserve on the Old Mine Road; but on Sunday night, Early and Taliaferro were moved back to form the reserve, the other two divisions forming the 1st and 2nd lines respectively.

All these preparations, however, proved to be works of supererogation, for General Burnside, to the amazement and disgust of the Washington authorities—who had just telegraphed " we have every confidence in your judgment and ultimate success," and recommended him to " make some use of the spade "—recrossed the river on the night of December 15, and so rendered abortive the gunboat commander's plan to assist the Federal land forces by a feint attack on Port Royal. Burnside had on Sunday telegraphed to the President, " I have just returned from the field. We hold the front ridge outside the town and three miles below. We hope to carry the crest to-day. Our loss is heavy—say 5,000 " (a report which must be described as grossly misleading in the circumstances), and three days later Burnside, in reply to Lincoln's demand for his reasons for recrossing the Rappahannock, stated that " the army was withdrawn to this side of the river because I felt the positions in front could not be carried, and it was a military necessity either to attack or retire. A repulse would have been disastrous to us." The Federal general " hoped this explanation would be satisfactory " to the President! Burnside further took credit for having " remained in order of battle two days, long enough to decide that the enemy would not come out of his strongholds and fight us with his infantry " and at the same time he amended his casualty list, now reporting 1,152 killed, 9,000 wounded, and 700 missing; but omitting, even so, a further loss of 1,800 men.

The course of events on December 15 was thus described by the Federal officer, who was charged with the defence of the town against a counter attack. General Butterfield writes:

"At noon on the 15th, that portion of Fredericksburg bounded by Hanover Street on the left, and the Rappahannock River on the right, was assigned to me, to be put in a state of defence and held. The different portions of the line of defence were apportioned according to the strength of the various divisions: General Whipple on the right, from the river to the junction of the canal and Fall Hill Road; General Griffin on his left, to Fauquier Street; General Humphreys on Griffin's left, to Amelia Street; and General Sykes on Humphrey's left, to Hanover Street, his left connecting with the command of General Couch (who had been intrusted with the remaining portions of the defences of the town); General Warren was charged with the construction of the barricades and earthworks; Captain Weed, Chief of Artillery of the Corps, was charged with the distribution and disposition of the artillery. As soon as darkness permitted, the work was carried on as rapidly as the limited number of implements, at hand and to be obtained, would allow. No work could be done before dark. At about 10 o'clock at night the main body, assigned to the portion of the town on the left of Hanover Street, was withdrawn, and the defence of the entire town was assigned to me. I was directed to relieve the pickets on the left of Hanover Street. The darkness, and the wearied condition of both officers and men of the command, incident to exposure and the duties performed since breaking camp, made this a severe task upon them. Generals Griffin and Humphreys were withdrawn from the right and assigned to the line from Hanover Street to the left. General Sykes and General Whipple covered the line from which the other two divisions were withdrawn. At 3.30 a.m. orders came to withdraw the command from Fredericksburg and recross the river, covering the withdrawal of the bridges. Captain Weed was directed to move all the artillery immediately; the provost-guard ordered to patrol the town, wake up all stragglers, search all alley ways and byways, and make every possible exertion to get all absentees to their commands. Precise and detailed orders in writing were given for the withdrawal of the forces. Under direction of General Sykes, one of his brigades covered the whole. The order was carried out in the most admirable manner. No confusion occurred, no haste or disorder. Contrary to my understanding, and without notice, the engineers in charge took up two of the pontoon bridges before all the troops directed to cross them had done so. This action necessitated a change in the order of withdrawal. It was a most fortunate circumstance that this unwarrantable blunder caused no confusion. The bridges were immediately ordered to be relaid, and the crossing continued successfully. Buchanan's brigade, of Sykes' division, crossed last, at about 8 a.m., in most excellent order. Several boatloads of stragglers were brought over after the taking up of the bridges, which was completed at 9 a.m." Apparently one company was left unrelieved on picket, but a volunteer swam across the river and fetched a boat in which the greater part of the command ultimately crossed, after evading attempts to capture them.

General Warren thus describes his intrenchments:

"In obedience to the order assigning to me the duty of arranging a line of earthwork defences on the south side of the city on the night of December 15, battery epaulements and rifle-pits connecting with brick houses and walls intended to be loop-holed and barricading all the streets were built, extending from the plateau to the right of the Gordon House to the street on the left (east) of Hanover Street. Those to the right of Amelia Street were built by Humphrey's division and the batteries assigned to that portion. Those extending from Amelia Street to the Plank Road, the barricade for artillery across that road connecting with the graveyard wall, and the barricade on the left of the same wall across Commerce or William Street, were built by the details from the 2nd division. The barricades of Hanover Street and the rifle-pits to the left of it were built by a detail from the 146th New York Volunteers. The whole presented to the view of the enemy the next morning a complete line, and could have been connected and strengthened during the day without interference from him. I designed to assign this duty to the 140th New York Volunteers, and they were kept in reserve for this purpose during the night. I cannot omit to praise the energy exhibited by the working details, as shown by the work accomplished with a great deficiency of tools. The 5th New York Volunteers performed the guard duty in front of our lines during the whole night, and during the withdrawal at daylight disputed the advance of the enemy's pickets, so that no attempt was made to pursue us. It also constructed rifle-pits in advance of the main line."

The disappearance from his front of the Federal host on the morning of December 16, and in spite of a false alarm three days later, their continued silence caused General Lee some perplexity. Not for the first time, he attributed to Federal strategy what was apparently due to Burnside's bewilderment. However, Anderson's division and others were sent to their camps; McLaws occupied the town with a brigade, under orders to conceal his troops from the enemy and do nothing to draw artillery fire again upon the town; and Jackson's Corps and a brigade of cavalry was dispatched down the river to Port Royal, the point where Lee supposed the enemy would now attempt to cross. General Lee had heard from prisoners that two corps had reinforced Burnside on Sunday evening at Fredericksburg, and accordingly he wrote to Richmond, " Should the enemy cross at Port Royal in force before I can get this army in position to meet him, I think it more advantageous to retire to the Annas and give battle . . . my design was to have done so in the first instance, and my purpose was changed, not from any advantage in this position, but from an unwillingness to open more of our country to depredation, and also with a view of collecting such forage and provisions as could be obtained in the Rappahannock Valley . . . the crossing can be made at almost any point without molestation; it will therefore be more advantageous to us to draw him further away from his base of operations."

On December 18 Jackson camped in the woods near Moss Neck, about twelve miles south of Fredericksburg, but Federal scouts caused Burnside to believe that "Stonewall" was at this time moving on Brentsville north of the Rapidan, in support of a division which was covered by Hampton's Cavalry. In fact, Lee had sent another brigade of cavalry up the Rappahannock, and on December 17 Hampton repeated his exploit of the week before, crossing the river with 465 horsemen and proceeding to the Occoquan, surprising one after the other the Federal pickets between that place and Dumfries. He captured a train of wagons and brought them over the river, afterwards destroying the ferry boat, in the presence of a Federal brigade of cavalry which had been sent to the rescue of the convoy, finally recrossing the Upper Rappahannock with twenty wagons and 150 prisoners "without the loss of a man." The Federal cavalry in reporting their loss added "from the fact of its being cavalry of Hampton's Legion we infer there is a strong force back of it."

On December 20 postal communication with Richmond was resumed and drafts for the army came up, detraining at Guiney's Station for Jackson's Corps, or at the terminus (Hamilton's Crossing) for Longstreet's Corps. The artillery camps were now formed where forage was more plentiful than at Fredericksburg, Longstreet's spare batteries going to a point on the Telegraph Road about midway between the rivers Mattapony and North Anna, Jackson's surplus artillery going into bivouac within five miles of Bowling Green. The reserve artillery went into camp near the 1st Corps camp. Special directions were given as to the care of the horses, "to resuscitate and restore them to proper condition for the spring campaign."

On December 23 General Stuart received the following order from headquarters: "You are desired to proceed with a portion of the cavalry across the Rappahannock, penetrate the enemy's rear, ascertain if possible his position and movements, and inflict upon him such damage as circumstances will permit. I recommend that you cross the river as low down as you can without disclosing your purpose, leaving the upper fords for your return. At this inclement season I need not suggest to you the propriety of selecting such men and horses only as can undergo the expedition, and of taking every other precaution for their conduct and safety. I have directed 5,000 bushels of corn and 5,000 rations of hard bread to be placed at Culpeper Court-House to your order."

In compliance with these orders General Stuart, on December 25, with detachments of Hampton's, Fitz Lee's and William H. F. Lee's Brigades, made a forced reconnaissance in rear of the Federal lines, attacked the enemy at Dumfries, capturing both men and wagons. Then he advanced toward Alexandria, drove the Federal cavalry across the Occoquan, captured their camp, and burned the Accotink Bridge on the railroad. Afterwards, passing north of Fairfax Court-House, he returned to Culpeper with over 200 prisoners and twenty-five wagons. His total loss was one killed and six wounded.

Washington was duly notified of the occurrence as follows: "Stuart has, it seems, slipped through the Army of the Potomac, and was reported crossing the

Potomac to-day (December 30) at Harrison's Island. He had a telegraph operator with him on his raid, and took all messages from the wires."

On December 29 Ransom set a party to work at the trenches on Marye's Hill, in order to make them better and more comfortable (a battery of the divisional artillery was ordered to occupy the hill if the alarm signal was given), and then he shifted his camp a mile or two away. Anderson moved his strongest brigade with three days rations to the crossing of the Old Mine and Plank Roads, to communicate with the pickets at the United States Ford, and be ready to march either to that ford or westward to Culpeper. His movement was carefully concealed from the enemy's observation.

The Federals, hoping to emulate the activity of General Lee's cavalry, sent a scout up the Rappahannock to discover some spot which was fordable and unguarded, where a mounted force might cross and fall upon the Confederate picket, but the scout returned to Averell with the tidings that from the United States Ford to Kelly's Ford there was a complete line of Stuart's pickets, who sent patrols over the river every few hours to approach the Federal lines and take back information.

Down at Petersburg at this date a regiment of Confederate cavalry, 300 strong, was attempting to patrol a front of forty miles. This cavalry was of poor quality, " and when attacked are invariably worsted unless they have time to dismount and throw themselves in the thickets, where alone they can use their arms with effect." They complained of having no sabres or pistols, " only the old Harper's Ferry rifle, which is entirely unsuitable for mounted men," but a general remarked that " Cavalry cannot handle rifles, sabres and pistols at the same time : if some of the companies turn in their rifles and equipments, those companies might be armed with sabres and pistols alone. When armed with rifles they are for vedettes, and in a fight must dismount." We hear of a " battalion " of cavalry being dismounted " owing to their want of care for their horses." The facts are interesting as evidence of the influence upon the mounted arm of leaders like Stuart, Sherman and Sheridan. To invert a well-worn phrase, cavalry *fit non nascitur*.

The detailed reports of Stuart and those of his antagonist, Pleasonton, the Federal cavalry commander, furnish abundant evidence that American cavalry had in 1862 already adopted the method of fighting which Lord Roberts recently introduced into the British army ; that is to say, the men were prepared for either shock action or fire action, to charge in column of squadrons or dismount and use their carbines from behind cover. Sometimes a body of cavalry would employ both methods at the same time, one squadron opening fire as infantry while another squadron charged the enemy. Under Stuart the cavalry division with its horse artillery had become for all practical purposes a force of the three arms, at all times capable of attack or defence. He had little fear apparently that the true cavalry spirit would be extinguished because his men could shoot straight; though on occasion his cavalry might in defence form line of battle at the edge of a wood, or climb to the top of a haystack to deliver their fire. In his orders for the raid into Maryland is condensed the whole duty of cavalry, as distinguished from the work of the ancient dragoon of Cromwell's time, or the later theory that " without his horse the cavalry soldier as such becomes entirely useless." Stuart's creed was that " the attack when made must be vigorous and overwhelming, giving the enemy no time to collect, reconnoitre or consider anything except his best means of flight."

Some notion of the constantly recurring dissension among the Federal leaders may be gathered from a series of letters which bear date December 30, 1862. Halleck writes to Burnside, pointing out that, in order to assist operations elsewhere, he should " occupy and press the enemy, so as to prevent large detachments "; but at the same time Lincoln, the President, telegraphs " you must not make a general movement of the army without letting me know "; then Quartermaster-General Meigs (who had been Lee's subaltern in the engineers twenty years before, and surveyed the Mississippi with him) offers friendly advice to Burnside as follows : " It seems to me that the army should move bodily up the Rappahannock, cross the river, and aim for a point on the railroad between the rebels and Richmond ; " while a semi-private communication to Lincoln, signed by Generals Franklin and Smith, prophesies that " the plan of campaign already commenced will not be successful," and proposes a new campaign on the James river. In the result, Burnside countermanded orders he had already given to Averell's cavalry and Barnes' division of infantry, for an expedition into North Carolina, via the Rappahannock, Rapidan and James rivers, and himself proceeded to Washington, there to interview the President and "have it out" generally. But Abraham Lincoln was essentially a politician, and contrived to maintain the *status quo*, persuading Burnside to return to his duty at Falmouth, without, however, affording him any real support in his daily increasing difficulties as a commander.

On January 1 General Burnside committed to writing his view of the situation. "I have attempted," he says, "a movement upon the enemy in which I have been repulsed, and I am convinced, after mature deliberation, that the army ought to make another movement in the same direction, though not necessarily at the same points of the river; but I am not sustained in this by a single Grand Division commander." Burnside even suggested that he should resign the command and retire into private life. In this dilemma, Lincoln sought the aid, as mediator, of his general-in-chief at Washington, but Halleck bluntly declined to interfere, and likewise tendered his resignation. The strife at Washington was healed, the quarrel patched up, and Burnside returned to Falmouth, only, however, to revert to the subject a few days later, stating that he was not disposed to go into winter quarters, and had already given orders preparatory to moving the army across the river again, notwithstanding the opposition of his subordinates. Anticipating the President's disapproval of his plan, Burnside enclosed an application to resign his commission; but Halleck replied to this communication on January 7, endorsing Burnside's plan generally—"it will not do to keep your large army inactive"—and forwarding a note from Lincoln in these terms: "I deplore the want of concurrence with you in opinion by your general officers, but I do not see the remedy. Be cautious, and do not understand that the Government or country is driving you. I do not yet see how I could profit by changing the command of the Army of the Potomac; and if I did, I should not wish to do it by accepting the resignation of your commission." With such comfort as might be derived from this diplomatic note, in which the essence of Burnside's grievance is studiously ignored, the Federal commander addressed himself anew to his task—the defeat of Lee's army on the Rappahannock—and in a few weeks succeeded in rendering the disaster of December 13 dramatically complete, so terminating the Fredericksburg campaign.

Some encouragement in the meantime, no doubt, was derived from a widespread illusion in regard to the enemy. On January 6 " Foster is very certain that General Hill has been detached with 30,000 to North Carolina." A few days later " a portion, or all, of Longstreet's corps is ordered to Tennessee." On January 14 " Longstreet has been sent west," and on January 19 " Rosecrans announces arrival of Longstreet's forces." Longstreet, however, was still busy across the river, adding rifle-pit to rifle-pit, breastwork to breastwork, at every defensible point between Port Royal below, and the United States Ford above, the Federal army.

The three Grand Divisions were at this time encamped between Falmouth and White Oak church, which is some three miles east of Falmouth. Pleasonton's cavalry watched their left flank, with piquets at King George Court House, patrolling down to the river opposite Port Royal. On the right flank of the Federals a cavalry brigade under Averell circled about Warrenton, communicating with Headquarters through Catlett's Station and Hartwood. Sigell's 11th Corps was at Stafford Court House with Cesnola's cavalry brigade at Hartwood, patrolling between Richard's Ford on the Rappahannock and Dumfries on the Potomac. Slocum's 12th Corps had been stationed at Fairfax Court House, with similar protective duties to perform. The Maryland frontier and the Shenandoah valley was in charge of Schenek's 8th Corps (headquarters at Baltimore), under orders to cover the railroad from Baltimore to the Ohio river. This general had a cavalry detachment at Point of Rocks (between Berlin and Leesburg), a force under Kelly at Harper's Ferry, and another force under Cluseret holding Winchester. A new Federal command (4th corps) was at this time operating on the Peninsula from Yorktown, assisted by the Federal gunboats.

It would seem, then, that the Army of the Potomac, guarded at all points, might have recuperated at leisure while framing its plans for the future. But soon it had to reckon with the Confederate cavalry, which was now let loose upon it with such effect as to dismay the Washington authorities; and Halleck writes despairingly, "I am almost at a loss what to say or do." When reports had reached him on December 27, that the Confederates in the Valley were re-appearing in large force at Strasburg and at Front Royal, and it was pointed out that Lee would probably take advantage of Burnside's inactivity to make another raid on Harper's Ferry, Halleck replied, "this is certainly very disheartening; we have no forces here to send to Harper's Ferry without again stripping Washington";

and he remembered that Barnard, the chief engineer, then busy about the local defences of the capital, had threatened to give up his task if his working parties were again interfered with.

Down the Rappahannock at Leedstown the Confederates were found to be drawing supplies from territory on the northern bank within the Federal lines. Pleasonton's cavalry proved no match for the smugglers, who by means of concealed ferry-boats conveyed salt, blankets, shoes, sugar and other necessaries to the "rebel" camps. At the other extremity of the line the Confederate general, W. E. Jones, commanding the 4th cavalry brigade and holding the Valley district as Jackson's *locum tenens*, was incessantly engaged in attempts to drive Cluseret's force back over the Potomac. From a central position Stuart watched the upper fords of the Rappahannock, and by means of cavalry "expeditions" kept the right wing of the Federals in a continual state of anxiety. Their alarms grew more and more frequent, until Schenck was provoked to reply in terms more forcible than polite. His chief-of-staff wrote to the commandant at Harpers' Ferry as follows: "The general commanding wants you to say to General Milroy that he thinks his scouts must be fools, or else too nervous in their alarms to be reliable. They cry 'Wolf, Wolf' when there is no wolf, and by and by the wolf may come in fact, and we shall not believe them."

Halleck had been informed on December 23 that "the enemy has thrown a large force from Fredericksburg into North Carolina"; and he had then urged Burnside to "do something before these forces returned."

A week later Halleck wrote to Burnside again to say "it will be necessary that you occupy and press the enemy, so as to prevent large detachments, and so assist in the operations in North Carolina." General Lee, on the other hand, regarded the movements of the Federals in North Carolina as a feint to induce the Confederate government to withdraw troops from Fredericksburg, and so assist Burnside's next attempt to cross the Rappahannock, and though Lee had in fact detached two brigades from Longstreet and two from Jackson's corps, he had made good these losses, and declared "we shall be much stronger in position than we were before."

On January 19 Lee was collecting at Hanover Junction on the Virginia Central railway all the wheat in the country between the Rappahannock and the Pamunkey. The Richmond commissary department were advised to requisition all the wheat in Greene, Madison, and Culpeper counties, since "our necessities make it imperative that every exertion be made to supply the army with bread." Lee had to impress all the bacon in Culpeper, and obtain other necessary articles of food by bartering sugar, which then had a market value of five shillings a pound. The Confederate commander had in fact been corresponding with the Government since the beginning of the year about subsistence for his army, explaining why he could not live upon the country to the same extent as formerly, and why the resources at the base must now be drawn upon more freely. Salt meat was being issued in order to keep the beeves to fatten for the spring, and every flour mill in the vicinity of the troops was now in constant use, the farmers hauling their wheat to be ground covered by a force of cavalry—a novel form of convoy.

Lee's troops had meanwhile dug rifle-pits, and constructed breast works for their pickets, from the United States Ford down to King George county, and obtained information of the enemy from northern soldiers, who were freely deserting the Federal ranks at this period. On January 17 two brigades (those of Pender and Lane) were detached from A. P. Hill's division, proceeding by rail from Hanover Junction to reinforce the defences at Richmond. On January 20 Lee forwarded the following letter to Hampton, at the same time directing the two Lees to have their brigades ready to move at a moment's warning, and to suspend all furloughs to officers and men. Lee's orders ran as follows:

" From the reports of the scouts on both flanks of the enemy, he appears to be on the eve of making an advance. Sigel's corps, which is stationed at Stafford and Dumfries, I understand, has marching orders, and the impression among the men is that they will go in the direction of Warrenton. I think it probable that he will attempt to cross the Rappahannock at Kelly's Ford, or at Rappahannock Station. He will hardly go higher at this inclement season. Infantry is said to be collecting near Richmond Ford. The infantry pickets in front of Fredericksburg have been withdrawn this evening, and columns of infantry are reported to have been seen marching up the river. I think it probable that the enemy will cross the upper Rappahannock with a view to turn our left flank. Make such resistance as you can to retard or defeat him, and should he cross with a force too large for you to encounter, concentrate your troops, hang upon his flank and rear, cut up his communications, cause him embarrassment, and report all that you can discover of his movements and designs."

Longstreet, too, on January 21 instructed McLaws, Pickett and Hood to the following effect : " The enemy will soon make another effort to advance on this line. You must be prepared to prevent any landing by him in your front. This can be done by a small force well protected by rifle-pits. If your men are not comfortably fixed for a successful resistance, they must be made so at once. Our latest advices indicate that the crossing will be attempted at Falmouth and Port Royal, but we must be prepared at all other points as well as these. If the enemy should succeed in effecting a lodgment at any point in your front, I may wish to drive him into the river under cover of night. I desire, therefore, that you will make yourself familiar with the ground along the river bank, with that view. Give orders to your pickets, however, that they are to prevent any landing. This is confidently expected of them. It would be well to have pits made for single pieces of artillery, to cut the other end of the bridges wherever it is likely that they may be thrown across. Complete arrangements should also be made to prevent any landing by using boats."

On January 22 Lee wrote to the officer commanding at Staunton, to the President, to the chief of ordnance and the war secretary at Richmond, and to Colonel Imboden (commanding a corps of Partisan Rangers), upon the eternal question of supplies, upon the new guns (Whitworths and Napoleons) then being manufactured, and upon the subject of recruiting. He proposed in certain contingencies to unite the Valley force and the Staunton garrison with the Fredericksburg army, and the day following (January 23) Lee wrote again to the President as follows: "Appearances now indicate that the enemy intend to advance. They seem to be moving to the line of the Rappahannock. They have shown themselves opposite Port Royal. Our scouts also report the preparation of bridges on Seddon's farm, to which point they are conveying their pontoons and artillery. In addition to the force reported near the mouth of the Rapidan, a force of cavalry with 12 guns (reported as marching up the White Ridge road) may be intended to join hands with General Milroy in the Shenandoah Valley, who has abandoned Moorefield and the south branch of the Potomac, and has his advance at Front Royal. It is also reported that a force near Alexandria, presumed to be General Slocum's command, crossed the Wolf Run Shoals on the 19th, and resumed its march on the 20th in the direction of Dumfries or Fredericksburg, with a large train of wagons. It looks as if they intended to concentrate all their forces, and make a vigorous effort to drive us from our position. The storm of yesterday and the day before will prove unfavourable for their advance, as the roads have become heavy and the streams swollen. It will also operate unfavourably to our rapid concentration to oppose them at the point they may select. Direct all men and officers belonging to this army now in Richmond without authority to return to their posts. I have directed General U. S. Jones, should Milroy cross the Blue Ridge, to follow with his whole force and unite with General Hampton. If there are any available troops about Staunton or Richmond it will be well to advance them towards this line ".

General Lee was correctly informed as to the Federal intentions, for at last, after three weeks of complete inactivity, during which period the horses had consumed 6,000 tons of hay and 225,000 bushels of corn, the Army of the Potomac was again to be put in motion. A fresh scheme had been hurriedly concocted, some semblance of harmony at headquarters had been restored, and Burnside in a General Order announced to the army that they were " about to meet the enemy once more."

The immediate danger to the Confederates, however, was passing away even while Lee penned his letter. That powerful auxiliary, " general January " had come to the help of the defending army, as we shall see by following the course of events on the other side of the Rappahannock.

The delay in the Federal operations had been fatal in regard to Burnside's new plan, for the winter season was beginning to exert its full influence on the military situation in northern Virginia, and the elements quickly furnished an example of their power in the case of a portion of the 12th corps, (2 brigades and 2 batteries) then moving from Fairfax Station towards Falmouth. The itinerary for six days reads as follows :

Jan. 19. Broke camp and marched three miles.
Jan. 20. Marched to Dumfries, fifteen miles.
Jan. 21. Progress delayed by rise in Quantico Creek, caused by heavy rains ; marched between three and four miles.

Jan. 22. Returned to Quantico Creek and again marched forward to Chopawamsie Creek (four miles) the roads being almost impassable.

Jan. 23. Marched to Acquia Creek, four miles.

Jan. 24. Marched to Stafford Court House, four miles.

Nearly a week had been occupied by this small force in moving about thirty-five miles. Near Fredericksburg the engineers had begun in the second week of January to corduroy the road between the camps and Banks' Ford, and (the 11th Corps furnishing a whole brigade as a fatigue party) to make separate roads for artillery and infantry. The Grand Divisions of Hooker and Franklin had been ordered to concentrate near Banks' Ford, and moved accordingly about seven miles on January 20, but a storm rendered the bad roads worse, and the troops were halted to repair them while waiting for the pontoon train. The chief of artillery (Hunt), however, succeeded in some marvellous fashion in placing in position, along the northern bank of the river no fewer than 184 guns. Three batteries remained opposite the town; Hay's batteries extended from Falmouth to England's; Tompkins' batteries prolonged the line as far as Bank's [Randolph] House; and thence De Russy's batteries extended westward to Ballard's farm. The whole of the forty-one batteries were posted between midnight and 8 a.m. on January 21, and were intended to concentrate an overwhelming fire on each of the enemy's batteries as discovered.

Instructions were issued to the commanders of Grand Divisions, to be ready to move at an early hour on January 21. Two bridges were to be constructed a mile apart, one at a point just below Banks' Ford, where Franklin was to cross and seize the heights immediately above the crossing. Franklin was then to hold the Fall Hill Road which leads from Fredericksburg in front of Dr. Taylor's house to the Plank Road, and so establish communication with Hooker's command on his right; afterwards he was to throw his right flank forward to a point on the other side of the Plank Road, designated on the map as Guest's, an operation which Burnside supposed would cause "the heights in front of the town" to be evacuated by the enemy. Hooker was to cross by the other bridge, at a point above Banks' Ford, and support Franklin's right. Sumner was to follow in rear.

An hour before midnight on January 20 Burnside had penned a lengthy folio of bewildering instructions to Hooker as to his movements after crossing, "in addition to the orders already given you," and he promised Hooker to be "in frequent personal communication" with him during the operation. We should judge from this document that General Burnside had learnt nothing from the December disaster. A demonstration was also to be made below Fredericksburg, at two points 4 to 5 miles apart near the Massaponax; and in giving detailed instructions to the officer commanding —even prescribing the particular class of men to be left as camp-guards—Burnside concludes: "you will keep in constant communication with the commanders of your brigades during the day by orderlies." We can but wonder whether divisional commanders in the Federal army in 1862 really needed such elementary instruction. Unfortunately, General Burnside, in lecturing the combatant officers on the administration of their commands, had forgotten that it rested with himself to provide the means of crossing the river, and he was apparently astonished to find, on January 21, that the pontoon bridges were not yet commenced. The only explanation forthcoming was given by Woodbury, the engineer general. "Before the rain began," he said, "we had every prospect of being able to throw three bridges over at daylight. The rain has prevented surprise, and changed our condition entirely. It seems to me the part of prudence to abandon the present effort, not only because the enemy must be aware of our intention, but because the roads are everywhere impassable . . . all my men are tired out by their nightwork, and cannot give to the fatigue parties that energetic attention necessary to efficiency. We can, I have no doubt, be ready to build our bridges at daylight tomorrow morning; hardly before."

Thus Burnside learnt that in bridging operations though commanding generals may "propose," their engineer officers "dispose." His comment on Woodbury's communication is not recorded, but he wrote in reply, "it is not probable that we will attempt to cross tomorrow." In fact, on January 22 fresh orders were issued to the army, in consequence of which the troops marched back to their respective camping grounds between the river and the base at Acquia Creek. And so the Fredericksburg campaign ignominiously ended.

General Lee's original programme in regard to the Federals, namely, to "throw them into the winter," had been fulfilled to the letter, and Burnside's expiring effort is known to this day as The Mud March. The remarks of General Hooker upon the occasion may be easily imagined, since on the following day Burnside commenced an Army Order in the following terms :

"General Joseph Hooker, having been guilty of unjust and unnecessary criticisms of the actions of his superior officers . . . is hereby dismissed the service . . . this order is issued subject to the approval of the President of the United States." The "order" also dismissed from the service, or removed from duty from the Army of the Potomac, Franklin and seven other general officers.

Burnside's "order" was however not approved in all its details by President Lincoln, who accordingly amended it on January 25, and as subsequently published it relieved General Burnside of his command, appointing as his successor—General Joseph Hooker !

The Federal cavalry pickets watching the river below the Massaponax, reported from Seddon's farm on January 24 "a much larger force massed opposite here than ever before," while up at Fredericksburg, General Pickett had moved to a new position on the Plank Road near Salem church, about 6 miles west of the town, where an important line of defence had been laid out for him to work, after collecting all the available tools in his own and Hood's divisions ; for already it was whispered that the Federals would next attempt to cross above Banks' Ford, where Anderson's division was stationed ; and in fact this is what they attempted three months later. But General Lee on the defensive, within the angle formed by the Rappahannock near Fredericksburg, possessed all the advantages of interior lines, and the longer his army was permitted to stay there, the smaller grew the chance of driving it south

For more than two months already, the axe and the spade had been busy, earthworks and timber entrenchments had grown up, new communications had been opened; and with the Rappahannock's swollen stream between the two armies, the Confederate leader bid defiance to the invaders of the Old Dominion.

The Army of the Potomac now consisted of about 10,000 officers and 188,000 men "present for duty," including over 13,000 cavalry, 1,000 guns, 6,000 wagons and 1,400 ambulances. Of this host, 75,000 men and 638 guns were still retained for the defence of Washington and the protection of communications, so that the field army which Hooker was destined to lead against Lee in the spring may be estimated at 110,000 bayonets and 400 guns, with abundant transport. The use which General Hooker made of his opportunity is the story of the Chancellorville campaign, which we must reserve for a future volume in the Special Campaign Series.

* * * * *

There is, after all, a wide difference as Clausewitz observes, between the strategical conception of war and war in reality; and if it were not so, hostilities between states of very unequal strength would never take place. The total destruction of the enemy's forces is not always and necessarily a general's sole aim; for in practical politics there occur two considerations which often take the place of inability to continue the contest. The first is the improbability, the second is the cost, of ultimate and complete success; and in order to "raise the price of success" there is no more effective method than that of wearying out the enemy. This was the method adopted by Frederick in the Seven Years' War. Frederick was never strong enough to overthrow the Austrian monarchy, but by the skilful application of a system of husbanding his resources, he at length demonstrated to the Powers allied against him that the price of success, if success were ever attained, would be excessive ; and then they made peace. It was the method adopted by Wellington. During six years of persistent effort in Spain, he economized the lives and treasure of his countrymen, while the resources of the enemy wasted, and finally wrung from Napoleon the confession that "the Spanish ulcer" had destroyed him. General Lee's system of warfare in northern Virginia was modelled on that of Frederick and Wellington, and though the result was different—from causes which we cannot here discuss—the series of defensive compaigns of which "Fredericksburg" is an example will remain a pattern for future leaders of the oppressed ; and will serve as a warning to rulers and peoples whom military ambition or political greed might tempt into wars of aggression.

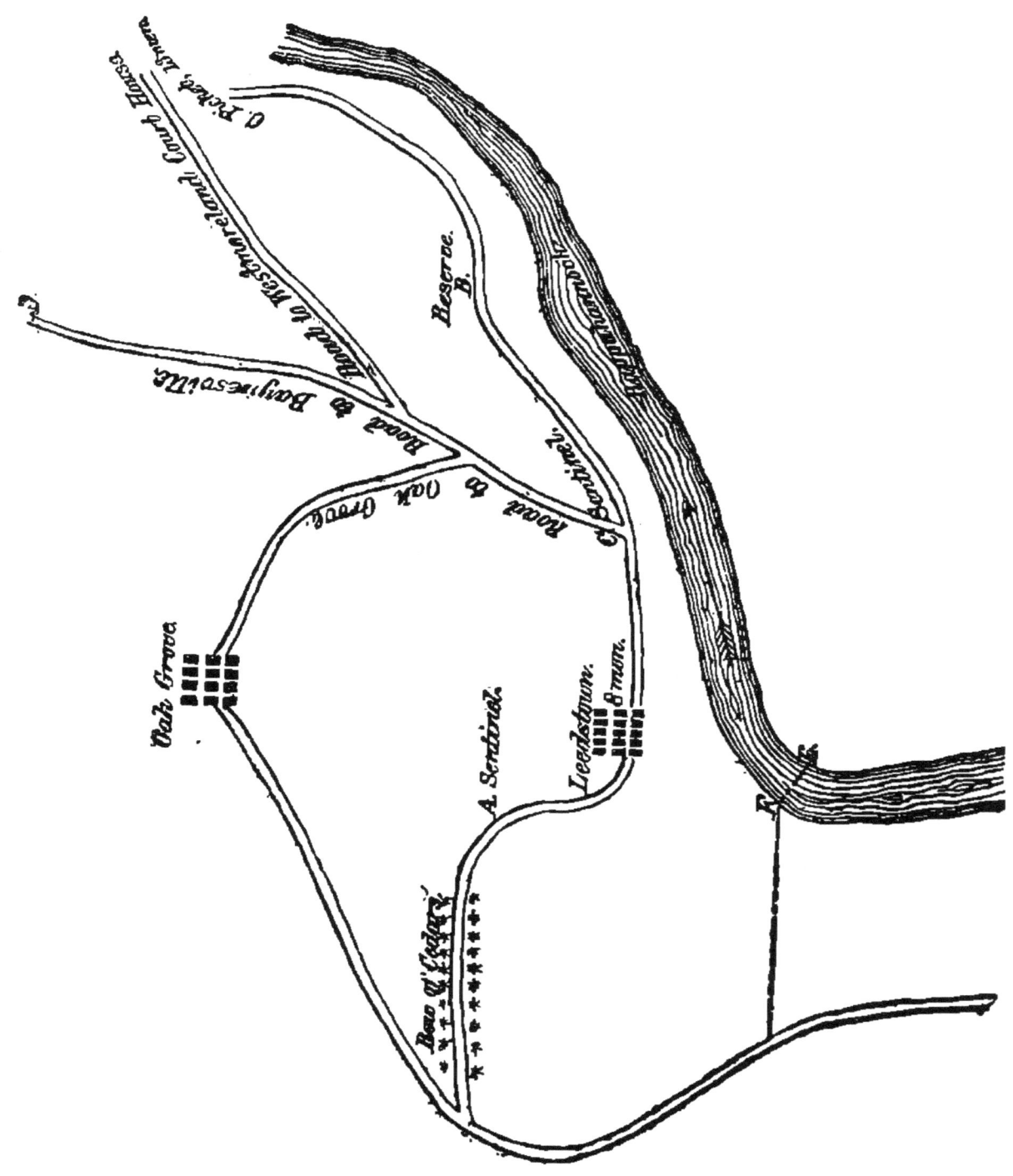

APPENDIX

A

RAILROAD COMMUNICATIONS.

[The following " Railway guide " is extracted from *Hunts' Gazetteer*, 1863.]

RICHMOND, FREDERICK AND POTOMAC RAILROAD.

Richmond (Burkesville 46 miles—Gordonsville 76 miles), the capital of Virginia, in Henrico County, on the left bank of James River, is the largest town in Virginia, and one of the handsomest in the United States. Richmond has about twenty-five churches, numerous benevolent institutions, governor's residence, court-house and jail, an armory, two market houses, a theatre, three banks, several insurance offices, and a large newspaper and periodical press. Of late years, and since the opening of canals and extension of railways, Richmond has greatly increased in wealth and population. The chief manufactures produced here are tobacco (the staple article), flour, cotton and woollen goods, paper, and iron ware. The city enjoys an abundance of water-power from the Falls in the vicinity, and is also supplied with water works. The population is 35,000. Richmond has a daily steamboat communication with Baltimore and Norfolk, and with Philadelphia and New York semi-weekly. The institutions of the city comprise the Virginia Historical and Philosophical Society; Richmond College, founded by the Baptists in 1832; St. Vincent's College, under Catholic direction; and the Medical Department of Hampden and Sydney College, established in 1838. A number of good hotels are also among the "institutions" worthy of note. In the matter of railroads, Richmond has long been recognized as important among southern centres. Its connections with the northern and southern cities upon the Atlantic coast have been sufficiently direct; but the great Southwest, which has been thus far only accessible by most circuitous routes, *now* invites " the head and front " of " the Mother of Presidents " to a cordial interchange of friendship and business. The Virginia Central Railroad, already completed 173 miles to Goshen, leads to a connection with the Ohi. James River, which affords constant navigation with Chesapeake Bay on the east, completes the communication toward all the compass-points. These facilities of business intercourse augur wealth and prosperity to Richmond. Richmond is now the seat of Government of the so-called Confederate States of America, 75 miles from Acquia Creek.

Hungary (Richmond 8 miles—Acquia Creek 67 miles) is a small post village on the R. F. & P. R. R.

Ashland is a flag station on the R. F. & P. R. R.

Taylorsville (Richmond 20 miles—Acquia Creek 55 miles), a post village in Hanover County, on the R. F. & P. R. R.

Junction (Richmond 23 miles—Acquia Creek 52 miles), a branch road runs from here to Gordonsville 49 miles west.

Chesterfield (Richmond 25 miles—Acquia Creek 50 miles), a post village on the R. F. & P. R. R.

Milford (Richmond 38 miles—Acquia Creek 37 miles). a post village of Caroline County, Va., on the R. F. & P. R. R.

Guineas (Richmond 48 miles—Acquia Creek 27 miles), a wood and water station on the R. F. & P. R. R.

Fredericksburg (Richmond 60 miles—Acquia Creek 15 miles), the chief town of Spottsylvania County, Va., on the right bank of the Rappahannock River, at the head of tide water.

Acquia Creek (75 miles from Richmond) is the terminus of the R. F. & P. R. R. on the Potomac River. During the fall and winter of 1862, this place was used as the base of supply for the federal army during their stay about Fredericksburg.

VIRGINIA CENTRAL RAILROAD.

Atley's (Richmond 9 miles—Gordonsville 67 miles).

Hanover Court-House (Richmond 18 miles—Gordonsville 58 miles) is the capital of Hanover County, Va., and situated about a mile from Pamunkey River.

Junction (Richmond 27 miles—Gordonsville 49 miles), in Hanover County, is the point where the Richmond, Fredericksburg and Potomac Railroad, leading northward, crosses the Virginia Central. The singular position of these two roads may be likened to an arc and its chord.

Beaver Dam (Richmond 40 miles—Gordonsville 36 miles) Depot is a post village of Hanover County—a hilly district, presenting much diversity of soil, and drained by streams which afford considerable water power. The dividing line between the primary and tertiary formations passes through Hanover County.

Frederick Hall (Richmond 50 miles—Gordonsville 26 miles) is situated in Louisa County, Va., formed in 1742. The adjacent country is hilly; the soil, originally fertile, has been partly exhausted. Gold mines have been worked in this county, but with little remuneration.

Tolersville (Richmond 56 miles—Gordonsville 20 miles), in Orange county.

Louisa Court-House (Richmond 62 miles—Gordonsville 14 miles) is the capital of Louisa County, and contains a population of about 550.

Trevilian's (Richmond 67 miles—Gordonsville 9 miles), Depot, in same county.

Gordonsville (Richmond 76 miles—Alexandria 88 miles) is the present southern terminus of the Orange and Alexandria Railroad, and intersecting point with the Virginia Central. It contains 700 inhabitants. Its railroad connections have given it considerable importance. When the proposed connection is made between Gordonsville and Lynchburg (by the Lynchburg and Charlottesville, and a short extension of the O. and A. Roads) the majority of northern travel which now goes via Burkesville or Petersburg, Richmond, and Fredericksburg, will undoubtedly seek this more direct and expeditious route. From Gordonsville, also, the Virginia Central continues, via Charlottesville and Staunton, through the spring, mountain and cave region, 97 miles to Goshen.

Virginia Central Railroad,

FROM CHARLOTTEVILLE TO JACKSON RIVER.

Charlotteville (described elsewhere), (Jackson River 94 miles).

Mechum's River (Charlotteville 7 miles—Jackson River 87 miles).

Greenwood (Charlotteville 15 miles—Jackson River 79 miles), a station at the base of the Blue Ridge Mountain.

Waynesboro' (Charlotteville 26 miles—Jackson River 68 miles), a post village of Augusta Co., Virginia, situated at the west base of the Blue Ridge, 108 miles WNW. from Richmond. The village contains 2 or 3 churches, and an academy. Population estimated at 800.

Fishersville (Charlotteville 31 miles—Jacksonville 63 miles), a post office of Augusta Co., Virginia.

Staunton (Charlotteville 38 miles—Jackson River 56 miles), a flourishing town, capital of Augusta Co., Virginia, is situated on a small branch of the Shenandoah River, near its source, and 120 miles WNW. from Richmond. Staunton is the seat of the Western Lunatic Asylum, and of the Virginia Institution for the Deaf and Dumb, and Blind. Staunton contains 4 or 5 churches, 2 academies, 2 female seminaries, and 2 banks. Three newspapers are published here. The surrounding country is highly productive, and beautifully diversified, forming part of the great valley of Virginia. In the limestone formation of this region extensive caverns occur, among which the most celebrated is Weyer's Cave, about 18 miles northeast from Staunton. Population about 3,500.

Orange and Alexandria R. R.

Madison (Gordonsville 4 miles—Alexandria 84 miles), situated in Orange Co., Va., which derives its name from the colour of the soil in the highlands, which were included in its original boundary. Population of the town, 500.

Orange Court-House (Gordonsville 9 miles—Alexandria 79 miles) is the capital of Orange Co., and at present contains 900 inhabitants. Orange Co. contains limestone, iron ore, and small quantities of gold. It has a hilly, fertile and well-watered soil, producing corn, wheat, oats, hay, and tobacco.

Rapidan (Gordonsville 14 miles—Alexandria 74 miles) derives its name from a river which divides Green and Orange Counties on the right, and Madison and Culpeper on the left, and empties into the Rappahannock near Fredericksburg.

Mitchell's (Gordonsville 19 miles—Alexandria 69 miles).

Culpeper Court-House (Gordonsville 26 miles—Alexandria 62 miles), the capital of the county, was originally called "Fairfax," after Lord Fairfax, well-known as a wealthy proprietor in the early days of the "Old Dominion." It was subsequently named after the county, which derives its title from Lord Culpeper, who was Governor of Virginia, in 1681. The town was founded in 1759, and contains about 1,200 inhabitants. The adjacent country is a finely diversified and productive region, boasting a high state of cultivation.

☞ Stages from this point to Luray and Newmarket.

Brandy (Gordonsville 32 miles—Alexandria 56 miles) Station is in same county.

Rappahannock (Gordonsville 37 miles—Alexandria 51 miles) is familiar as being the name of a county, and one of Virginia's noble rivers.

Bealeton (Gordonsville 41 miles—Alexandria 47 miles), a post village of Fauquier Co.—a district named in honour of Francis Fauquier, Governor of Virginia in 1759.

Warrenton Junction (Gordonsville 47 miles—Alexandria 41 miles), in same county.

☞ Change cars for Warrenton.

[Warrenton (on Branch Road—Junction 9 miles), the beautiful capital of Fauquier Co., boasts a delightful situation, in a picturesque and fertile region of country, and

APPENDIX

possesses an active trade. It contains a fine court house, churches, 2 academies, and newspaper offices. Population 1,800. Stages run from Warrenton to the " Fauquier White Sulphur Springs."]

Weaversville (Gordonsville 50 miles—Alexandria 38 miles), in same county, Fauquier, which region contains valuable beds of magnesia and soapstone.

Bristoe (Gordonsville 57 miles—Alexandria 31 miles).

Manassas (Gordonsville 61 miles—Alexandria 27 miles) is in Prince William Co. It is the Junction-point of the Manassas Gap Railroad, which now operates 88 miles to Strasburg, a town in Shenandoah Co. This route (as contemplated) runs in a north-westerly direction, through Manassas Gap, towards Winchester, and then deflecting southward, traverses one of the Alleghany Valleys—almost parallel with the Orange and Alexandria Road—until it connects with the Virginia Central at Staunton : the whole district being 162 miles.

Union Mills (Gordonsville 65 miles—Alexandria 23 miles), a post village of Fluvanna Co., and located on Rivanna River, which flows through the centre of the same. The river affords excellent water power facilities for manufacturing, which advantage is appreciated in the operating of a cotton factory and several other mills. Population 300.

Fairfax (Gordonsville 71 miles—Alexandria 17 miles) Court-House, a small town of 350 souls, is the capital of Fairfax Co. This district lies between the Potomac and Occoquan, and borders also on Maryland and the District of Columbia ; was established in 1742, and immortalizes the name of Lord Fairfax.

Burke's (Gordonsville 74 miles—Alexandria 14 miles), a post office in same county.

Springfield (Gordonsville 79 miles—Alexandria 9 miles).

Alexandria (Gordonsville 88 miles—Washington City, by steamboat, 8 miles), the northern terminus of the Orange and Alexandria Railroad, is the capital of Alexandria Co., Virginia. It is situated on the right bank of the Potomac River, which is here one mile wide, and being of sufficient depth for the largest ships, affords a commodious harbour. The city and county of Alexandria were once comprised within the boundary of the District of Columbia, forming part of the national and congressional territory, but were retroceded to Virginia by an act of Congress, in 1845-46.

The Potomac River (Alexandria to Washington, 8 miles), throughout its entire length, forms the State-line between Maryland and Virginia. Its general course is south-east; and along the entire distance of 350 miles, from its mountain source to Chesapeake Bay, the scenery is varied and celebrated for its magnificence. Its largest affluent is the Shenandoah, which, at the confluence-point, is as great a volume as the main stream. At this point is "Harper's Ferry," famous for its beautiful scenery. The bay-tide ascends 120 miles, to Georgetown, and affords ample depth for the largest class of vessels to visit Washington.

ALEXANDRIA, LOUDON, AND HAMPSHIRE RAILWAY.

Alexandria (Leesburg 38 miles), the capital of Alexandria Co., opposite Washington City. A canal extends from this city to Georgetown.

Arlington Mills (Alexandria 6 miles—Leesburg 32 miles), flag station.

Carlinville (Alexandria 7 miles—Leesburg 31 miles), flag station.

APPENDIX

Fall's Church (Alexandria 11 miles—Leesburg 27 miles), a post office, Fairfax Co.

Vienna (Alexandria 15 miles—Leesburg 23 miles), post village.

Hunter's Mill (Alexandria 18 miles—Leesburg 20 miles), post office.

Thornton (Alexandria 21 miles—Leesburg 17 miles), post village.

Herndon (Alexandria 23 miles—Leesburg 14 miles), post office.

Guilford (Alexandria 27 miles—Leesburg 11 miles), post office.

Farnwell (Alexandria 31 miles—Leesburg 7 miles), post office.

Leesburg (Alexandria 38 miles), a handsome post borough, capital of Loudon Co., is situated near the Kittoctan Mountain, 3 miles from the Potomac River, and 150 miles north of Richmond. The streets are well paved, and the town is built in a neat and substantial manner. It contains a court house, 3 churches, a bank, an academy, and a newspaper office. It is surrounded by a beautiful variety of landscapes. Population 2,500.

MANASSAS GAP RAILWAY.

Manassas Junction (Mount Jackson 85 miles). The two great battles of Bull Run were fought near this place, the former under Gen. McDowell, and the latter under Gen. Pope.

Gainesville (Manassas Junction 8 miles—Mount Jackson 77 miles), a small post village.

Thoroughfare (Manassas Junction 14 miles—Mount Jackson 71 miles), water station.

Salem (Manassas Junction 24 miles—Mount Jackson 61 miles), a post village of Fauquier County, Virginia, 52 miles from Alexandria, and 114 miles NNW. of Richmond. The situation is high and pleasant. The village contains 1 church, an academy, and several stores. The post office is Salem Fauquier.

Piedmont (Manassas Junction 34 miles—Mount Jackson 51 miles), a post village of Fauquier Co., Virginia.

Mackham (Manassas Junction 39 miles—Mount Jackson 46 miles), a post office of Fauquier Co., Virginia.

Front Royal (Manassas Junction 47 miles—Mount Jackson 38 miles), a flourishing post village.

Buckton (Manassas Junction 70 miles—Mount Jackson 29 miles), a wood and water station.

Woodstock (Manassas Junction 74 miles—Mount Jackson 11 miles), a beautiful post village of Shenandoah Co., Va., is situated on the Valley Turnpike, 1 mile from the north fork of the Shenandoah River, 160 miles northwest of Richmond.

Mount Jackson (Manassas Junction 85 miles), a post village of Shenandoah Co., Virginia, on the Valley Turnpike from Staunton to Winchester.

APPENDIX

B

INVASION OF VIRGINIA BY THE ARMY OF THE POTOMAC, SEPTEMBER 26–NOVEMBER 9.
MARCH TABLE.

9th Corps.—26th, Two divisions cross at Berlin and move on Lovettsville. 27th, Remainder cross at Berlin. 29th, Wheatland and Waterford. 2nd, Bloomfield Union and Philomont. 3rd, Upperville. 5th, Manassas Gap, Piedmont and Salem. 6th, Waterloo.

Pleasonton's Cavalry.—26th, Lovettsville. 27th, Purcellville. 1st, Philoment and Bloomfield. 2nd, Union. 3rd, Upperville. 4th, Piedmont. 5th, Barber's Cross Roads. 6th, Flint Hill. 7th, Towards Culpeper Court House *via* Little Washington and Sperryville. 9th, Amissville, Jefferson and Hazel Run.

1st Corps.—27th, Towards Berlin. 28th, At Berlin. 30th, Lovettville. 1st, Purcellville and Hamilton. 3rd, Philomont Union and Bloomfield. 5th, Rectortown and White Plains. 6th, Warrenton.

Reserve Artillery.—29th, Cross at Berlin and move on Lovettsville. 9th, At Warrenton.

Stoneman's Division.—29th, To Leesburg.

Averell's Cavalry.—29th, Towards Berlin. 2nd, Towards Union. 5th, Manassas Gap.

2nd Corps.—29th, Cross at Harper's Ferry and move into the valley, east of Loudon Heights. 31st, Hillsborough. 1st, Woodgrove. 2nd, Snicker's Gap. 3rd, Upperville. 4th, Ashby's Gap. 5th, Cross

Roads, Paris-Upperville. 6th, Rectortown. 8th Towards Warrenton. 9th, Warrenton.

5th Corps.—30th, Towards Harper's Ferry. 31st, Harper's Ferry. 1st, Hillsborough. 2nd, Snickersville. 3rd, Snicker's Gap. 6th, Towards White Plains. 8th, New Baltimore. 9th, Warrenton.

6th Corps.—31st, Boonsborough. 1st, Berlin. 2nd, Wheatlandland. 3rd, Purcellsville. 4th, Union. 5th, Aldie Pike, east of Upperville. 9th, New Baltimore.

Bayard's Cavalry.—5th, Salem. 6th, Rappahannock Station.

11th Corps.—6th, New Baltimore, Gainesville, Thoroughfare Gap, Hopewek Gap.

Sickles' Division.—6th, Orange and Alexandria railroad between Manassas Junction and Warrenton Junction.

C

ABSTRACT FROM FIELD RETURN OF THE DEPARTMENT OF NORTHERN VIRGINIA, COMMANDED BY GENERAL R. E. LEE, DECEMBER 10, 1862; HEADQUARTERS FREDERICKSBURG, VA.

Command.	Present for duty. Officers	Present for duty. Men.	Total present.
FIRST ARMY CORPS.			
Lieutenant-General LONGSTREET.			
General staff	13	—	—
Staff	15	—	—
Anderson's Division	556	7,083	8,745
Hood's Division	539	6,795	7,969
McLaws' Division	587	7,311	8,640
Pickett's Division	707	6,860	8,216
Ransom's Division	260	3,505	4,116
Alexander's and Walton's Battalion of Artillery	37	586	634
Total	2,714	32,230	38,320
SECOND ARMY CORPS.			
Lieutenant-General JACKSON.			
Staff	13	—	—
Ewell's Division	616	7,100	8,520
A. P. Hill's Division	811	10,743	12,091
D. H. Hill's Division	617	8,327	9,465
Jackson's Division	479	4,526	5,514
Brown's Battalion of Artillery	24	449	488
Total	2,560	31,145	36,087
Stuart's Cavalry Division	634	8,512	10,016
Pendleton's Reserve Artillery	41	677	752
Grand total	5,949	72,564	85,175

Note.—Lee, writing to Jackson on December 3, states: "I find that deducting the batteries in the General Reserve Artillery, composed of Colonel Cutts' and Major Nelson's battalions, and consisting of six companies which are for general service, there are 127 pieces of artillery in your corps and 117 pieces in Longstreet's; in your corps there are 52 rifles, 18 Napoleons, and 58 smoothbores; in Longstreet's 46 rifles, 13 Napoleons, and 58 smoothbores." This statement agrees with Pendleton's statement of November 1, to the effect that Longstreet had 24 batteries (108 guns), Jackson 25 batteries (112 guns), Stuart 3 batteries (16 guns), if we assume the Reserve Artillery to consist of 48 guns.

D

ABSTRACT FROM TRI-MONTHLY RETURN OF THE ARMY OF THE POTOMAC, MAJ.-GEN. AMBROSE E. BURNSIDE COMMANDING, FOR DECEMBER 10, 1862.

Command.	Present for duty.	
	Officers.	Men.
General Staff	67	1
Escort (McIntyre)	7	148
Provost Guard (Patrick)	56	1,040
Regular Engineer Battalion (Cross)	2	379
Volunteer Engineer Brigade (Woodbury)	34	914
Quartermaster's Guard (Ingalls)	26	233
Signal Corps (Cushing)	39	111
Right Grand Division (Sumner)	1,741	29,918
Centre Grand Division (Hooker)	2,132	38,264
Left Grand Division (Franklin)	2,388	44,509
Eleventh Corps (Sigel)	688	14,874
Twelfth Corps (Slocum)	614	11,548
Defences Upper Potomac (Horrell)	280	5,302
Defences of Washington (Heintzelman)	2,005	44,383
Total	10,079	191,624

Note.—The Right Grand Division (Second and Ninth Corps), the Centre Grand Division (Third and Fifth Corps), and the Left Grand Division (First and Sixth Corps), at Fredericksburg; the Eleventh Corps at Fairfax Court-House; and the Twelfth Corps at Harper's Ferry.

E

FEDERAL TRANSPORT, JANUARY 1, 1863.

	Number of men present for duty.	Means of transportation.				Horses.		Number of animals.
		Horses.	Mules.	Wagons.	Ambulances.	Cavalry.	Artillery.	
RIGHT GRAND DIVISION.								
Second Corps	19,742	1,425	2,725	649	185	112	915	—
Ninth Corps	17,566	1,086	2,112	514	123	141	934	13,730
Pleasonton's Cavalry	3,807	327	198	113	21	3,585	170	—
LEFT GRAND DIVISION.								
First Corps								
Sixth Corps	} 48,370	3,506	4,880	1,427	406	4,357	2,292	15,035
Gregg's Cavalry								
CENTRE GRAND DIVISION.								
Third Corps								
Fifth Corps	} 42,700	2,732	4,848	1,249	357	3,399	2,130	13,109
Averell's Cavalry								
Artillery Reserve	1,734	462	1,039	367	11	—	1,434	2,935
Army headquarters [1]	1,049	669	1,036	355	19	1,020	—	2,725
Engineer Brigade	1,976	1,146	284	113	8	—	—	1,430
Eleventh Corps, General Sigel	19,858	1,740	1,213	539	117	2,647	894	6,494
	[2] 156,802	13,093	18,335	5,326	1,247	15,261	8,769	55,458
Twelfth Corps [3]	23,000	1,030	1,199	447	110	82	747	3,058
General Kenly's Brigade	5,856	160	309	103	22	1,512	339	2,320
1st New York Cavalry	} 1,073	125	75	40	5	1,294	—	1,494
12th Pennsylvania Cavalry								
Total	186,731	14,408	19,918	5,916	1,384	18,149	9,855	62,330

[1] Includes transportation in charge of Captain Pierce.
[2] Number actually present with this army.
[3] Report of November 1, 1862.

F

COMPARATIVE TABLE OF LOSSES (*Dec.* 11–15).

Engineers	57
Artillery Reserve	8
Right Grand Division	4,804
Centre Grand Division	2,852
Left Grand Division	3162
(1,284 Killed ; 9,600 Wounded)	10,883
Add 1,767 missing	1,767
FEDERALS : Grand Total	12,650
1st Corps	1,519
2nd Corps	2,682
(458 Killed ; 3,743 Wounded)	4,201
Add 653 missing	653
CONFEDERATES : Grand Total	4,854

APPENDIX

SUMNER'S (RIGHT) GRAND DIVISION.

Divisions.	Brigades.	Killed and Wounded.	
Hancock	1. Caldwell	837	
	2. Meagher	471	
	3. Zook	487	
	Artillery, 1 battery (5); staff (3)	8	
			1,803
Howard	1. Sully	91	
	2. Owen	230	
	3. Hall	482	
	Artillery, 2 batteries (18); staff (1)	19	
			822
French	1. Kimball	456	
	2. Palmer	227	
	3. Andrews	303	
	Artillery, 2 batteries	7	
			993

The above formed Couch's (2nd) Army Corps.

Burns	1. Poe	13	
	2. Christ	7	
	3. Leasure	3	
	Artillery, 1 battery	2	
			25
Sturgis	1. Nagle	452	
	2. Ferrers	453	
	Artillery, 2 batteries (15); staff (1)	16	
			921

Divisions.	Brigades.	Killed and Wounded.
Getty	1. Hawkins	201
	2. Harland	31
		—— 232

The above formed Willcox's (9th) Army Corps.

	Reserve Artillery	7
		—— 7

Total, 2nd Army Corps (Couch): 412 killed, 3,214 wounded = 3,626; reported missing, 488.

Total, 9th Army Corps (Willcox): 111 killed, 1,067 wounded = 1,178; reported missing, 152.

Total, Right Grand Division: 523 killed, 4,281 wounded = 4,804; reported missing, 640.

HOOKER'S (CENTRE) GRAND DIVISION.

Divisions.	Brigades.	Killed and Wounded.	
Birney	1. Robinson	120	
	2. Ward	476	
	3. Berry	163	
	Artillery, 3 batteries	10	
			769
Sickles	1. Carr	79	
	2. Hall	16	
	3. Revere	2	
	Artillery, 1 battery	0	
			97
Whipple	1. Piatt	3	
	2. Carroll	107	
	Artillery, 1 battery	1	
			111

The above formed Stoneman's (3rd) Army Corps.

Griffin	1. Barnes	411	
	2. Sweitzer	216	
	3. Stockton	176	
	Artillery, 2 batteries	3	
			806
Sykes	1. Buchanan	47	
	2. Andrews	126	
	3. Warren	6	
	Artillery, 1 battery	1	
			180
Humphreys	1. Tyler	373	
	2. Allabach	511	
	Staff	5	
			889

The above formed Butterfield's (5th) Army Corps.

Total, 3rd Army Corps (Stoneman): 145 killed, 832 wounded = 977; reported missing, 202.

Total, 5th Army Corps (Butterfield): 206 killed, 1,669 wounded = 1,875; reported missing, 300.

Note.—The divisions of Birney and Sickles were attached to the Left Grand Division; the remainder of Hooker's command supported the Right Grand Division, on December 13.

APPENDIX

FRANKLIN'S (LEFT) GRAND DIVISION.

Divisions.	Brigades.	Killed and Wounded.	
Doubleday.	1. Phelps	27	
	2. Gavin	26	
	3. Rogers	64	
	4. Meredith	49	
	Artillery, 3 batteries	26	
			192
Gibbon	1. Root	421	
	2. Lyle	428	
	3. Taylor	299	
	Artillery, 2 batteries	17	
			1,165
Meade	1. Sinclair	433	
	2. Magilton	491	
	3. Jackson	466	
	Artillery, 4 batteries	26	
			1,416

The above formed Reynold's (1st) Army Corps.

Brooks	1. Torbert	112	
	2. Cake	17	
	3. Russell	10	
	Artillery, 3 batteries	8	
			147
Howe	1 Pratt	23	
	2. Whiting	142	
	3. Vinton	15	
	Artillery, 1 battery	1	
			181

Divisions.	Brigades.	Killed and Wounded.	
Newton	1. Cochrane	21	
	2. Devens	17	
	3. Rowley	6	
	Artillery, 1 battery	10	
			54

The above formed Smith's (6th) Army Corps.

Cavalry	Bayard	4	
			4

Total, 1st Army Corps (Reynolds): 347 killed, 2,429 wounded, including cavalry escort (3)=2,776; reported missing, 561.

Total, 6th Army Corps (Smith): 53 killed, 329 wounded = 382; reported missing, 64.

Total, Left Grand Division: 401 killed, 2,761 wounded = 3,162; reported missing, 625.

LONGSTREET'S (1st) ARMY CORPS.

Divisions.	Brigades.	Killed and Wounded.	
M. Laws	1. Cobb	167	
	2. Barksdale	65	
	3. Kershaw	249	
	Washington Artillery	25	
			506
Anderson	1. Perry, including artillery (6)	51	
	2. Featherston, including 3 batteries (6)	34	
	3. Wright	2	
	4. Wilcox	8	
	5. Mahone	8	
			103
Hood	1. Law [1]	315	
	2. Toombs	12	
	3. Robertson	6	
	4. Anderson	10	
			343
Ransom	1. Cooke	354	
	2. Ransom	154	
			508
Pickett	1. Kemper	38	
	2. Jenkins	8	
			46
Cavalry, W. H. F. Lee, including Henry's Artillery		13	
			13

Total: 130 killed, 1,389 wounded, (but the number of "slightly wounded" was unusually large) = 1,519, and 127 were reported "missing."

Longstreet's losses on December 11-12, included in above totals, were 40 killed, 209 wounded, and 110 missing. Net loss of 1st Corps on December 13 = 1,287.

[1] Attached to 2nd Army Corps on December 13.

JACKSON'S (2ND) ARMY CORPS.

Divisions.	Brigades.	Killed and Wounded.	
A. P. Hill	1. Field [Brockenbrough]	83	
	2. Gregg	334	
	3. Thomas	330	
	4. Lane	375	
	5. Archer	229	
	6. Pender	169	
	Artillery, 7 batteries	99	
			1619
Ewell	1. Hays, including artillery (3)	48	
	2. Trimble [Hoke]	106	
	3. Early	141	
	4. Lawton	424	
			719
Taliaferro	1. Paxton, including 1 battery (26)	70	
	2. Jones, including 2 batteries (4)	41	
	3. Warren, including 1 battery (13)	22	
	4. Starke, including 1 battery (7)	39	
			172
D. H. Hill	1. Rodes	16	
	2. Iverson	13	
	3. Ripley	27	
	4. Colquitt	15	
	5. Anderson	59	
	Artillery, 2 batteries and 2 regiments	42	
			172

Total: 328 killed, 2,354 wounded, (but the number of "slightly wounded" was unusually large) = 2,682, and 526 were reported "missing," of whom 406 were from A. P. Hill's division.

G

REPORT OF SIGNAL OFFICER.

BELLE PLAIN, *December* 18, 1862.

SIR: In accordance with your instructions, I inclose you a report of the work done by the United States army telegraph during the four days' fight at Fredericksburg.

On Thursday evening I received orders to report at headquarters by daylight on Friday morning. This I complied with at once. While there, I was ordered to open a line with the Lacy House, opposite Fredericksburg. I found the wire partially laid, and in one hour's time from leaving General Sumner's headquarters the line was in full communication with general headquarters.

The following are the most important messages that were sent and received during the action, to wit:

General SUMNER:
The advance has started on.

COUCH.

* * * * *

General SUMNER:
I am losing a great many men, being so much exposed. The enemy are covered in their rifle-pits. Send me two rifled batteries immediately; I have none.

COUCH,
General.

General SUMNER:
If you have a good division, send it, if it can be done. It is only necessary now. I have no troops for the purpose.

COUCH,
Major-General.

Maj.-Gen. E. V. SUMNER:

General Burns has moved two brigades across Deep Run, to support General Franklin. Will Cox [you] send the remaining brigade? He requires it. He regrets leaving unguarded the position between Deep Run and Hazel Run.

O. B. WILLCOX,
Major-General.

Sent.

General SUMNER:

The enemy have thrown up new works 60 degrees west of north from Fredericksburg Court-House, I think for artillery.

BROOKS.

General HOOKER:

Loss in one of Humphrey's Brigades about 1,000.

BUTTERFIELD.

LACY HOUSE, SIGNAL STATION.

Captain CUSHING:

General Whipple's Division is now crossing the bridge. The enemy have opened fire upon them, and our batteries are replying.

WILSON.

HEADQUARTERS, SECOND CORPS.

A negro, just in from the enemy's lines, states that those in front fell back last night, and that there are but a few men left; that Jackson went to Port Royal. This negro belongs to Dr. Garland, father of Captain Garland, ambulance corps. The doctor is here, and believes what he says is true. General Kimball gave the alarm.

D. N. COUCH.

There are other miscellaneous dispatches, relating simply to hospital affairs, ambulance corps, etc., which I have considered of minor importance, and have not transcribed.

On Saturday, December 13, I received an order to lay the wire across the river. In less than twenty minutes from the time I received the order the wire was laid and ready for operation at any moment.

On Monday evening, perceiving the troops recrossing, I succeeded, after a great amount of difficulty, in reeling my wire off the pontoon bridge, and am happy to inform you that during the engagement and in reeling up to headquarters I did not lose a foot of wire.

APPENDIX

Messrs. Colton, of the 134th Regiment, Pennsylvania Volunteers, and Creigh, of the 126th, operators, acquitted themselves with great honour, manifesting a spirit of genuine bravery during the engagement.

Messrs. Jones, of the 133rd Regiment, Pennsylvania Volunteers, and Henginer of the 155th line men, though exposed to great danger, performed their part heroically, and deserve much praise for the skillful and acute manner in which they guarded the wire.

In my monthly report I will speak more fully of the working of the instrument.

I have the honour to be, your obedient servant,

DAVID WONDERLY,
Lieutenant and Acting Signal Officer.

Capt. SAMUEL L. CUSHING,
Chief Signal Officer.

H

RIVER RECONNAISSANCE BY A CONFEDERATE ENGINEER.

My special examination of the Rappahannock commenced just below Spottswood Bar, and extended to a point some five miles below Leedstown. Reference is made to the topographical chart of the Coast Survey from Fredericksburg to Port Royal, for the positions reported on between these points, and to the preliminary Coast Survey charts, for positions below Port Royal.

About half a mile above Belvidere there is an old ferry, but this is not protected by any high ground on the north [enemy's] side, nor could [enemy's] gunboats be used advantageously. The banks on both sides are some 40 feet high, and the roads to the ferry cut along their faces.

Nearly one mile below Belvidere, at Mr. Seddon's landing, is the position which I consider the best throughout the whole distance examined for forcing a passage. At A, as marked in pencilling on the chart, is the landing, and almost immediately opposite on the south side of the river is an old ditch bank, flat, solid, and from 8 to 10 feet in width, crossing a small point of marshy land, 80 yards wide, and forming a practicable road for artillery. At the foot of the bank at B is a small muddy ditch 8 feet wide and 2 feet deep which is to be crossed: but the ground is wooded at this point and it could be bridged with little delay. From this point some 200 feet of very light side-hill cutting would be necessary to carry the road to the top of the bank at C, whence the ground is nearly level to the main road. The heights at Snowden are less than 1,000 yards distant from the south bank of the river (at this point 200 yards wide) and they have a command of at least 50 feet over the ground on the south side to the extreme range of artillery. At E the ground is some 20 feet lower than at D, and is out of view until the edge of the bank along C.D is very nearly approached. Gunboats along the bend at F would command a considerable portion of the ground in the rear of C.D.

At Castle's Ferry the position is also very favourable, the north side still commanding, though not with so great an advantage in height as at Seddon's Landing. The details of this position being already known to you, I think it unnecessary to report them here. These two positions I consider among the most important naturally, and they would probably be used in conjunction by the enemy.

At Moss Neck there is a possible crossing, but the advantage of ground is on the south side. Width of river here, about 300 yards.

At the Hop Yard, near the point of Buckner's Neck, there is a road and landing on the north bank, and a landing and practicable way for artillery on the south side, by keeping along the edge of and up the river for some half mile; but after leaving the river the ground is very heavy for nearly a mile.

At a point nearly opposite Berry Plane there is a road and wharf on the north bank, and a landing and practicable way for artillery on the south side, although the ground is heavy for 440 yards. Three quarters of a mile in the rear of this position, and nearly west, the ground rises some 60 feet above the general level of the flat. This height, on which is Mr. Sale's house, commands the river for about half a mile on both sides of the entrance to Buckner's Neck. These last two crossings are the only practicable ones in Skinker's Neck.

At Dickinson's, near Mount Taliaferro, is a possible crossing, but the ground on the left bank, as well as the river, is commanded by high bluffs on the right bank.

On the Hazlewood farm there are two very good positions for crossing—one about 440 yards above, and the other opposite Millbank. The landings are solid on both sides, and a good firm road leads from the landing opposite Millbank to Hazelwood House. Gunboats could be used in covering these positions and sweeping the ground in the rear, which for more than one mile is almost perfectly level. The heights in the rear, along which the Port Royal road runs, are distant more than one and a half miles from either of these crossings. Width of river, 500 yards.

At Port Royal there is no particular advantage of ground, but gunboats could be used very effectively from points above and below. Width of river, 500 yards.

At Camden the crossing is effectually commanded by the ground on the south side, some 100 feet higher, within a few hundred yards of the river.

At Port Micon there are good roads on both sides, the left bank having the advantage in command of some 20 feet: the high ground on the south side is more than two miles distant. Gunboats could be used here. The river here is a mile wide.

Near Calet Point there is a crossing, but with no advanttage of ground. Gunboats could be used. High ground on this (South) side one and a quarter miles from river.

At Layton's there is a crossing, with good roads on each side. High ground on this side 1,500 yards from river.

At Smith's the position is a very strong one. The low ground on the right bank is commanded by high bluffs close to the water on the left bank. The road coming down to the landing on the other side is steep, but practicable for artillery. Gunboats could also be used to some advantage here: river here not more than 440 yards wide.

There is another crossing at Smoot's, about one mile above Smith's, which is also a strong one, as it possesses nearly the same natural advantages, but the river is here nearly half a mile wide.

I

STUART'S EXPEDITION TO DUMFRIES.

Report of Maj.-Gen. J. E. B. Stuart, C. S. Army.

HDQRS. CAVALRY CORPS, ARMY OF NORTHERN VIRGINIA,
February 15, 1864.

COLONEL: I have the honor to submit the following report of an expedition undertaken in the latter part of December, 1862, while our army was at Fredericksburg, in the direction of Dumfries and Occoquan:

The force employed consisted of select detachments from the brigades of Hampton, Fitz. Lee, and W. H. F. Lee, and numbered about 1,800 men and four pieces of the Stuart Horse Artillery. The brigades, after passing up and crossing the Rappahannock at Kelly's Ford, bivouacked in the vicinity of Morrisville, on the night of December 26. I directed General Hampton to move round to the left in the direction of Occoquan, while General Fitz. Lee aimed to strike the Telegraph Road between Dumfries and Acquia, General W. H. F. Lee advancing between the two and by the road running along the right bank of the Quantico directly upon Dumfries, my object being to take possession of the Telegraph Road, to capture all the trains that might be passing. General Fitz. Lee was ordered, after striking the Telegraph Road, to sweep back toward Occoquan, so as to re-enforce the other brigades. Brig.-Gen. W. H. F. Lee proceeded without meeting the enemy until he reached Wheat's Mill, where the Telegraph Road crosses Quantico Creek. Here a picket of 12 of the enemy's infantry was encountered and charged by a squadron of

U

the 9th Virginia Cavalry, the whole being captured. The squadron, supported by two others, immediately pushed across, but on reaching the suburbs of the town they were attacked by two regiments of infantry and compelled to retire. As they moved back, a squadron of the enemy's cavalry advanced, but, being fired upon, retreated. At this stage of affairs I reached the scene of action and ordered up [M. W.] Henry's Battery of horse artillery, which opened with canister upon the enemy's position, and drove them from it. They then brought forward their artillery, and an engagement ensued between their battery and that under Captain Henry.

While this engagement was going on, I ordered Colonel Critcher to move to the left on the Brentsville Road and ascertain whether any force of the enemy was posted on that route. He succeeded in capturing a picket of 11 men, and subsequently some more. The 15th Virginia Cavalry also captured a small picket. The enemy evacuated the town soon after our approach and took position on a commanding ridge overlooking the town—artillery and infantry—in a thicket of pines, and had, from what we could see, a full brigade of infantry and a battery of artillery.

Brig.-Gen. Fitz. Lee had meanwhile passed just outside and on a parallel line to the enemy's pickets, down the right bank of the Chopawamsic, and struck the Telegraph Road at a point about 2 miles south of Dumfries. Here the advance guard from the 5th Virginia Cavalry encountered a patrol of the enemy and captured 2, the remainder escaping toward Dumfries. Proceeding in that direction, the 5th, still in advance, captured six four-horse and three two-horse wagons, laden with sutlers' stores of every description, together with 22 men, who were guarding them.

Brig.-Gen. Fitz. Lee's command having now arrived at Dumfries, the 5th Virginia and the 1st Virginia were ordered to cross the creek, above the town, while detachments from the 2nd and 3rd Virginia moved to cross at the point where the Telegraph Road strikes the Quantico, and below. Rosser (5th) and Drake (1st) were ordered to attack the enemy first, and while their attention was thus called off, the 2nd and 3rd were to dash across the fords and capture the town. This project was subsequently abandoned, as the capture of the place would not have compensated for the loss of life which must have attended the movement, there being evidently no stores in the place, and Brig.-Gen. Fitz. Lee was ordered to engage the enemy with his dismounted skirmishers and artillery, while the rest of the command swung round on the Brentsville Road. Two rifle pieces of Breathed's battery accordingly kept up an effective fire upon the enemy, and the dismounted men on the left continued to skirmish until dark.

In this skirmish, while gallantly leading the dismounted sharpshooters, Captain Bullock, of the 5th Virginia, fell, mortally wounded. Lieutenant [James P.] Bayly succeeded him in command of the dismounted sharpshooters, and gallantly charging across the creek drove the enemy's infantry skirmishers from their ground, captured 11 of them, and maintained his position until dark, when, in obedience to orders, the detachment was withdrawn.

The whole number of prisoners captured by W. H. F. Lee's brigade was 50; his loss, 1 private wounded, 1 non-commissioned officer and 12 privates missing, and 3 horses killed.

While these events were occurring in the vincinity of Dumfries, Brigadier-General Hampton had moved in the direction of Occoquan. At Cole's store he encountered the enemy's picket, and, sending a detachment of 25 men to get behind them, attacked them in front with 20 men. The party sent to the enemy's rear mistook the road, so that the picket when driven in in front were enabled (all but four) to retreat toward Dumfries. Four were captured by Hampton, and the other 11, in endeavouring to reach Dumfries, fell into the hands of Colonel Critcher, who had been sent, as I have already stated, to hold that road.

Having cleared the way, Hampton pushed on toward Occoquan, Colonel Butler with the main body approaching the town in front, while Colonel Martin and Major Delony proceeded by the river road to cut off the enemy's retreat from the town. Before the latter had reached the desired position, Butler drove in the enemy's pickets, dashed into the town, and dispersed several hundred cavalry, who took to flight and escaped in the darkness. Nineteen prisoners and 8 wagons were captured, with a loss upon our part of only 1 man wounded. On this night (December 27) the entire command bivouacked near Cole's store. Two pieces of artillery, whose ammunition was nearly exhausted, and wagons and prisoners which had accumulated up to this time, were sent back under a squadron of the 9th Virginia Cavalry.

On the morning of the 28th I advanced, with Lee's brigade in front, in the direction of the Occoquan. At Greenwood Church I detached Colonel Butler, of Hampton's brigade, with his command, and ordered him to proceed to Bacon Race Church, with a view to cut off a detachment of the enemy which were reported in our front.

At that point he was informed that the rest of Hampton's brigade would join him. Soon after leaving Greenwood Church, I encountered two regiments of the enemy's cavalry drawn up in line of battle near a dense piece of woods. Fitz. Lee's brigade was ordered to charge, and executed the order gallantly, the 1st Virginia leading and advancing in the face of heavy volleys. The enemy did not stand long. They broke, and were pursued 5 or 6 miles, some 8 or 10 being killed and more than 100 taken prisoners.

The pursuit of the enemy was continued to the Occoquan, over which he had fled at Selectman's Ford, and arriving in front of that point, Fitz. Lee discovered that the northern bank of the stream was occupied by the enemy's dismounted sharpshooters in force. Without waiting to exchange shots, they were gallantly charged by file, the 5th Virginia leading across a narrow, rocky, and very difficult ford; but in spite of the heavy volleys directed at our men, they pressed on, crossed the stream, suffered no loss, and captured or dispersed the whole party. Following up this success, Fitz. Lee took possession of the enemy's camps on the north side, which they had abandoned in hot haste, leaving horses, mules, and wagons, with blankets and other stores.

Colonel Butler, of the 2nd South Carolina, rejoined Hampton's brigade just as it reached the northern bank of the Occoquan. He had been sent, as above stated, up the road leading to Bacon Race Church, and when within a mile of that place encountered and drove in the enemy's pickets upon their reserve, consisting of about one squadron. This was charged, put to flight, and pursued by Butler, who suddenly came upon a large force of their cavalry and two pieces of artillery posted not more than 200 yards in his front. They opened a hot fire of canister upon him, which forced him to fall back a short distance. Here he wheeled about to resist the expected charge, but the enemy did not advance upon him. He then moved back about a quarter of a mile on the Brentsville Road, and, after waiting for the enemy for some time, continued to withdraw by the Brentsville Road. In so doing he came upon the enemy, who had occupied the road in his rear, and was compelled to make a circuit of 3 or 4 miles to extricate himself from this perilous position, rejoining the command as the rear was crossing at Selectman's Ford.

His loss was 2 men wounded and several horses shot.

The command he encountered proved to be Geary's division, moving from Fairfax to the support of the troops at Dumfries. Hampton went with a portion of his brigade down toward Accotink, while the main body moved across toward Burke's Station. He encountered the enemy and put them to flight, but did not pursue far on account of the darkness, returning and bringing up the rear of the column. The head of the column reached Burke's Station, on the Orange and Alexandria Railroad, after dark. A party was sent noiselessly to the telegraph office, and took possession without the operators having a chance to give the alarm. Having an operator of my own, I was enabled to detect what preparations had been made for my reception, the alarm of my approach having already reached Washington, and dispatches were passing over the wires between General [S. P.] Heintzelman and the commanding officer at Fairfax Station. I sent some messages to General [M. C.] Meigs, Quartermaster-[General] U. S. Army, in reference to the bad quality of the mules lately furnished, which interfered seriously with our moving the captured wagons. I also detached Fitz. Lee, with Surgeon [J. B.] Fontaine, Lieut. John Lee, and 10 men, to move down the railroad and set fire to the large bridge over the Accotink and rejoin us on the Little River turnpike. This was accomplished, and, striking across toward the Little River turnpike to overtake his command, Fitz. Lee and his party captured a picket, consisting of a lieutenant and 3 men. I had proceeded from Burke's Station toward the Little River turnpike, where, halting the rest of the command, I advanced with Fitz. Lee's brigade toward Fairfax Court-House, with the view of surprising and capturing the place. On approaching, we were saluted with a heavy volley from the enemy's infantry, posted in their breastworks and in the woods near the road. Keeping up the appearance of attack, the rear of the column, turning to the right, continued its march by way of Vienna toward Frying Pan, near which latter point I halted about dawn and fed and rested some hours. Nothing further having occurred, the command proceeded from Frying Pan to Middleburg, from which point Colonel [T. L.] Rosser, with a detachment of 15 men, proceeded by way of Snicker's Gap into the valley, and, capturing the enemy's picket near Leetown, penetrated within their lines and ascertained the strength and positions of the forces in that region, returning by way of Ashby's Gap, without losing a man. From Middleburg the command returned by easy marches via Warrenton to Culpeper Court-House, which place was reached on December 31, and I returned to my headquarters, near Fredericksburg, on January 1, the different brigades resuming their former position.

About December 30, a portion of Sigel's corps crossed the Rappahannock at Ellis' Ford, and returned by the same route to Stafford on the next day without accomplishing any damage to us.

In this expedition my loss was slight in point of numbers. Brig.-Gen. W. H. F. Lee's loss has been stated. General Hampton lost 3 men wounded. Brig.-Gen. Fitz. Lee's was heavier. Captain [J. W.] Bullock was killed, and Colonel Watts and 8 men wounded.

The loss inflicted on the enemy was considerable, but cannot be stated with accuracy. A large number of horses, mules, wagons, saddles, bridles, pistols, and sabres were captured; also over 200 prisoners.

The results in the way of captures on the Telegraph Road were less than had been anticipated, in consequence of the numerous descents upon that road by General Hampton and detachments from his command, which had caused it to be abandoned, except by a few sutlers.

Dumfries, instead of being garrisoned by a few cavalry, as it was when recently taken by General Hampton, was now garrisoned by a full brigade of infantry.

The command returned in good condition from this long march, the benefits of which were three-fold:

1st. The destruction of the telegraph line of communication of the enemy between the Chopawamsic and the Occoquan, being the connecting line between Washington and General Burnside's headquarters; the capture of the enemy's property, and the dispersion of his cavalry on the Occoquan.

2nd. It made necessary the detachment of large bodies of the enemy as a constabulary force for the region of country extending from the Acquia to Vienna.

3rd. In moving toward Middleburg, the impression was created upon the enemy that another invasion of Maryland was contemplated, and drew the main body of their cavalry in that direction, making rapid marches over the difficult roads, thereby crippling his cavalry force in the fruitless effort to thwart me in my real intentions.

Maj. John Pelham, with his horse artillery, performed gallant and exceedingly difficult service during this expedition. Ever up with the cavalry, he crossed the Occoquan at Selectman's Ford, which has always been considered impracticable for vehicles.

I am greatly indebted to my staff for their efficient services.

I have the honour to be, very respectfully, your obedient servant,

J. E. B. STUART,
Major-General.

Col. R. H. CHILTON,
Chief of Staff, Army of Northern Virginia.

J

NOTE ON "HOWISON'S"

Mr. S. G. Howison, of Braehead, near Fredericksburg, who has obligingly looked over my proofs, contributes the following valuable notes:—

"The house you refer to on page 80 as Mr. Howison's is the one in which I am now writing, in which my uncle was at the time living. The writer of the Diary from which you quote (page 72) was my father's sister . . . the view from my house is almost exactly the one from Lee's position of observation during the battle. . . . The reason 'Hamilton's Heights' is not mentioned by Henderson is that there are none such. I don't know how the Federal commanders ever managed to make a 'height' out of a very modest, rising ground which was called Prospect Hill by one of the owners. Lee always speaks of it as Hamilton's Crossing. A county road crossed the railroad at that point. . . . The range of hills in the far background [Stafford Heights] is still crowned with the works thrown up for the guns about 4,000 yards distant. The road along which Franklin's troops marched after crossing lies about 400 or 500 yards from the river and has the same direction. . . . The railroad cutting mentioned on page 140 was finished to grade line, but the rail had not been laid : the 30 pr. Parrott from Lee's Hill commanded it completely at a range of about 1,800 yards. . . . The photographs were taken from an upper window, which is about 30 feet lower than the point of observation from which General Lee overlooked the battlefield. . . . I have read [the proofs] with interest and, I may say, some surprise ; the very graphic style elicits interest, and the remarkable accuracy of detail is a source of surprise : you write as if you had 'tramped' over the ground and taken notes."

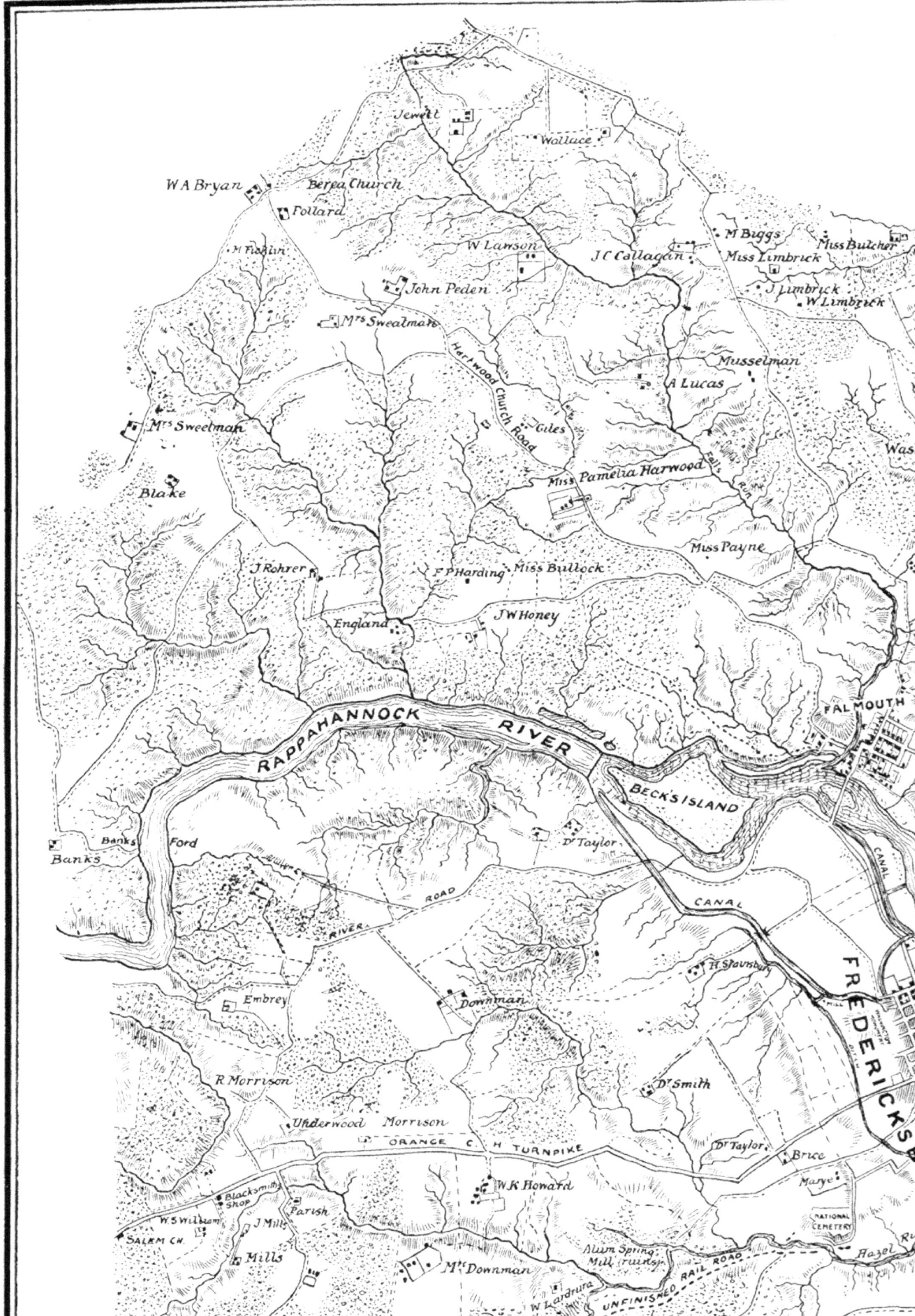

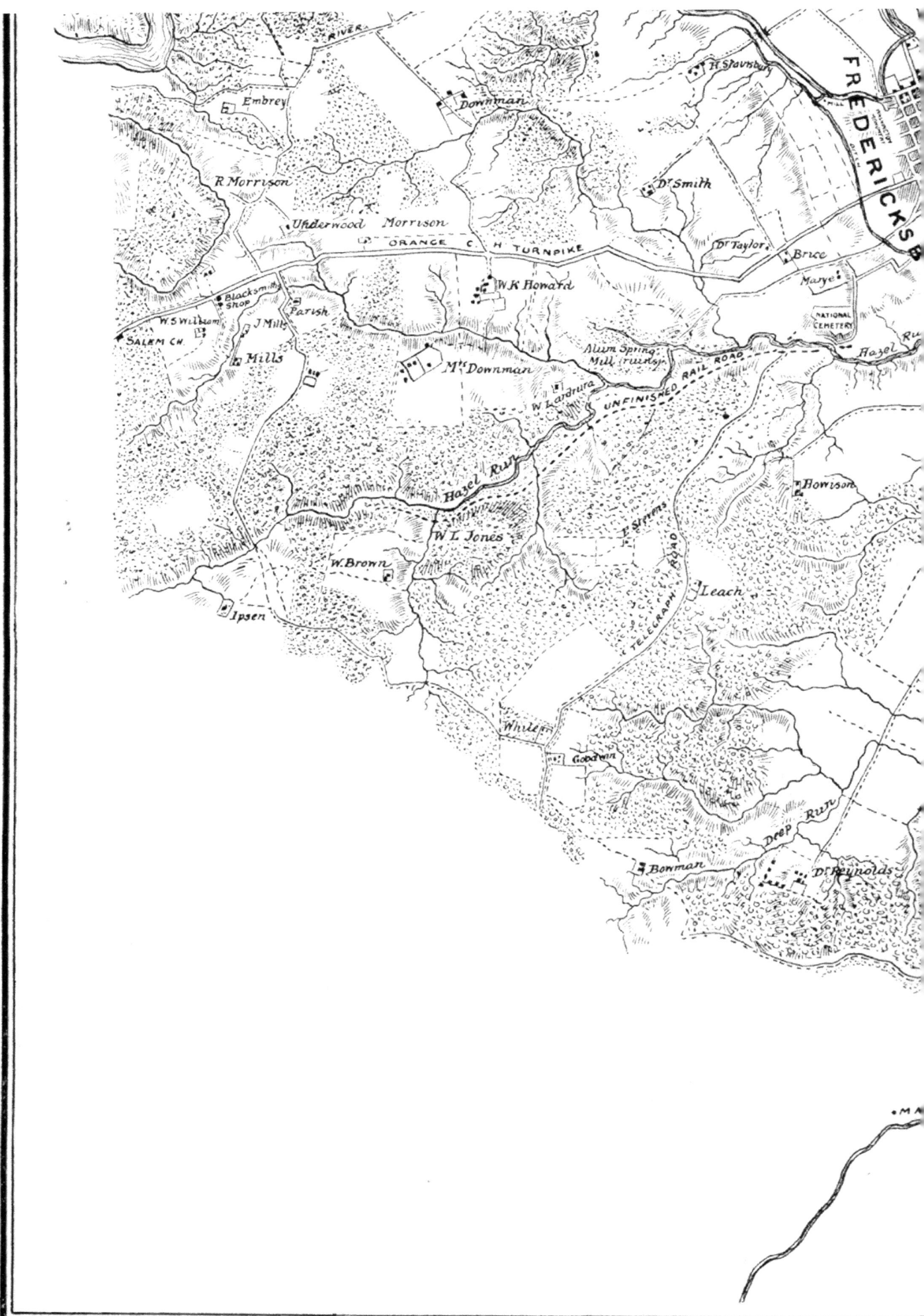

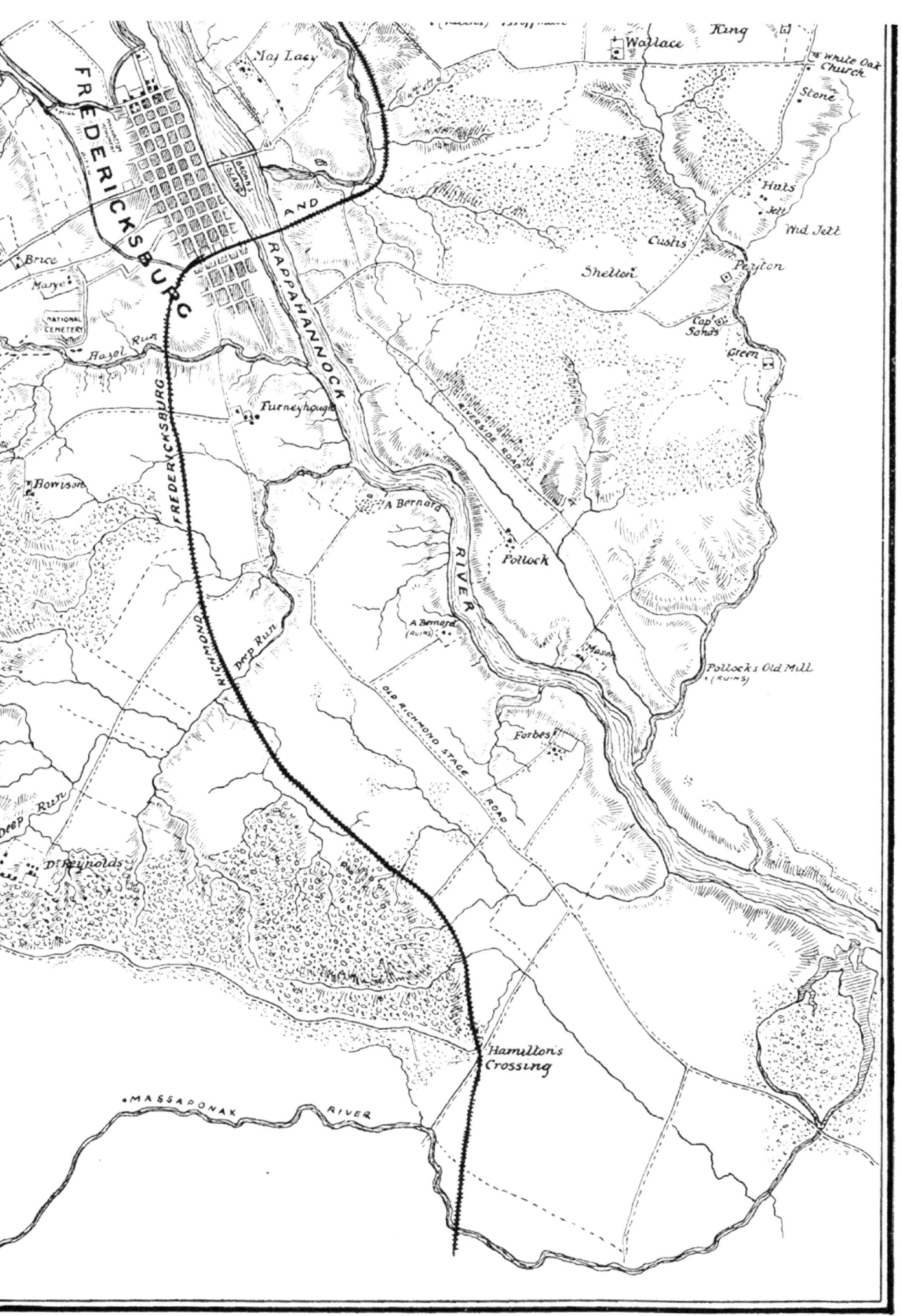

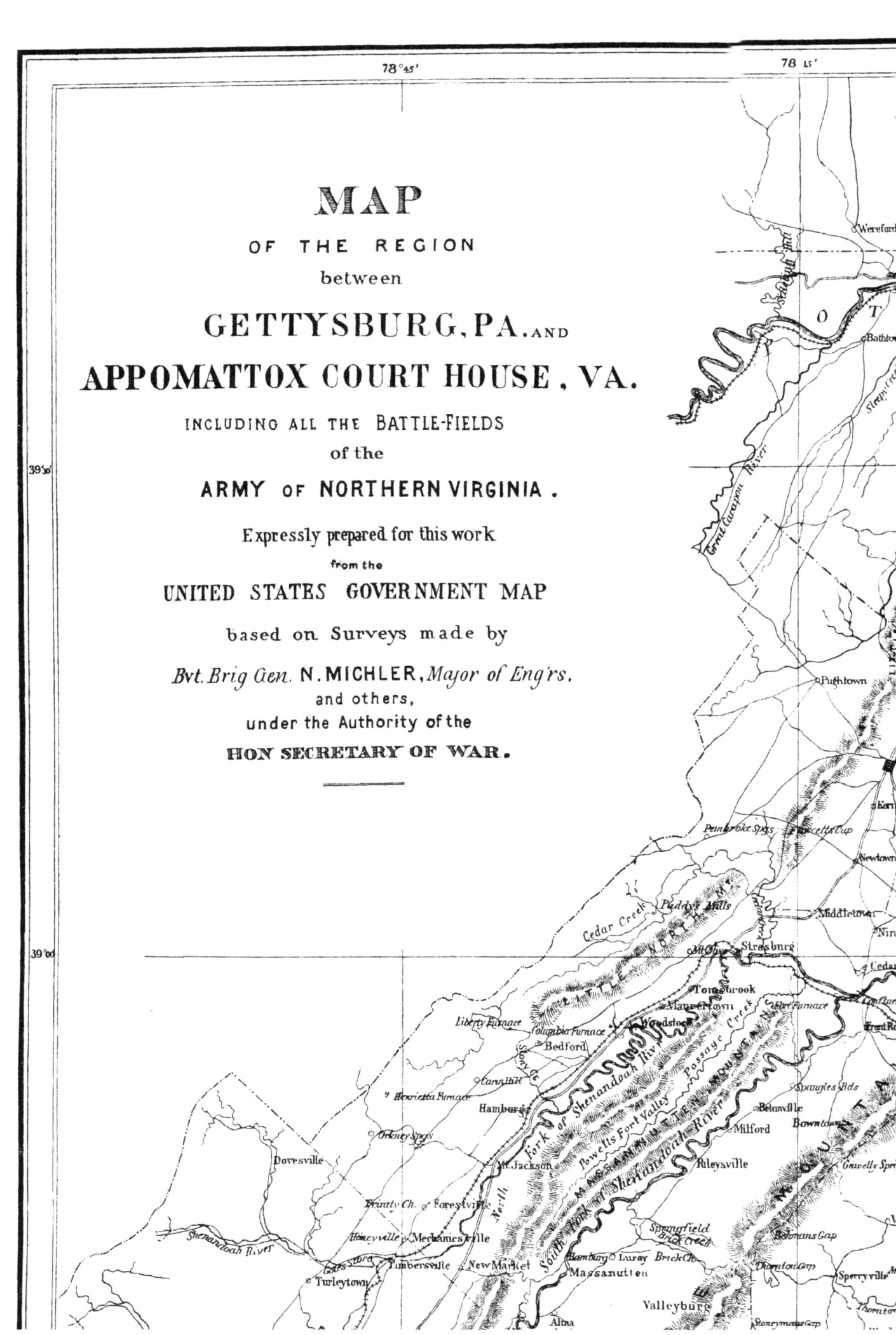

MAP

OF THE REGION
between

GETTYSBURG, PA. AND
APPOMATTOX COURT HOUSE, VA.

INCLUDING ALL THE BATTLE-FIELDS
of the
ARMY OF NORTHERN VIRGINIA.

Expressly prepared for this work

from the

UNITED STATES GOVERNMENT MAP

based on Surveys made by

Bvt. Brig Gen. N. MICHLER, *Major of Eng'rs*,
and others,
under the Authority of the

HON SECRETARY OF WAR.

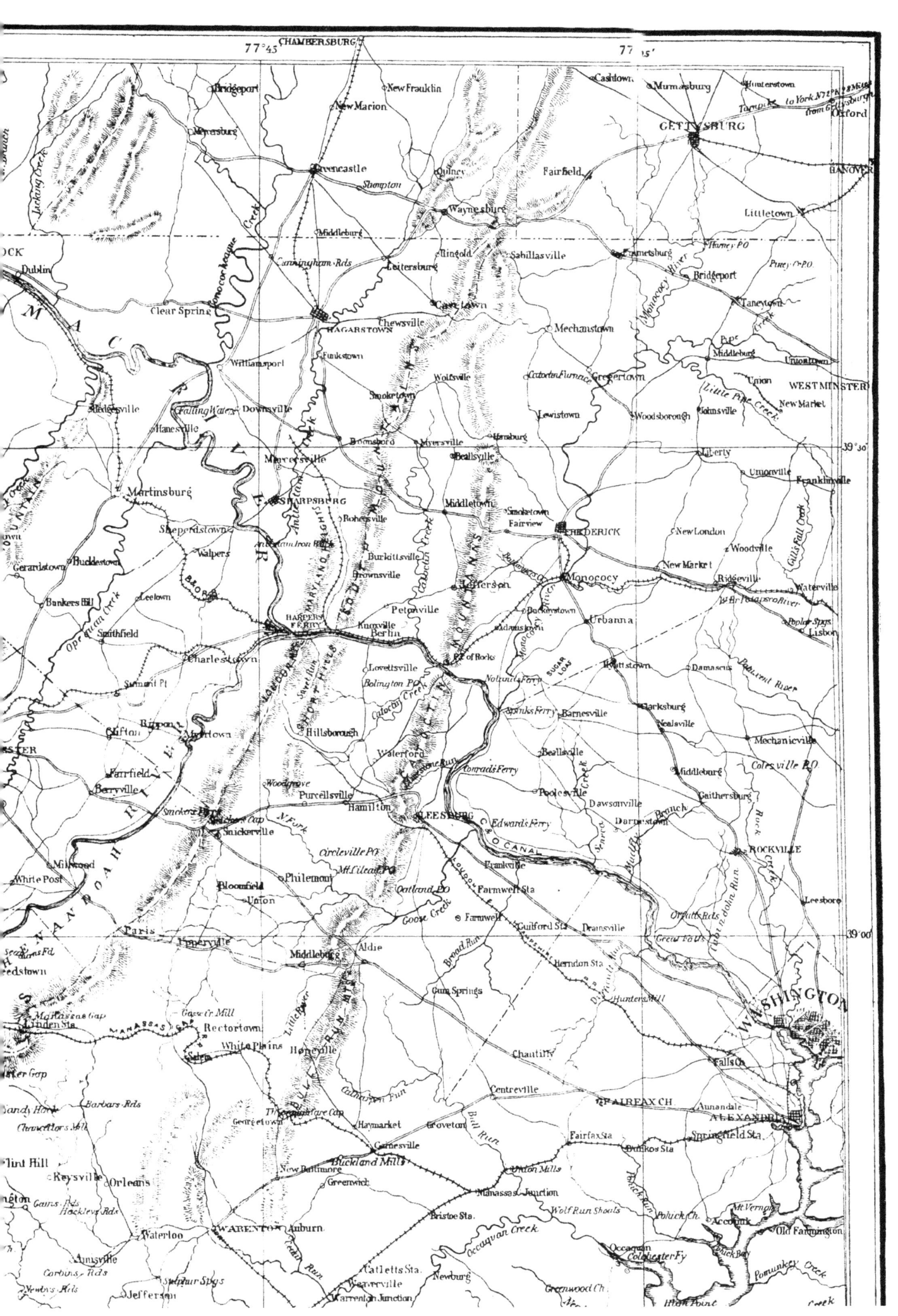

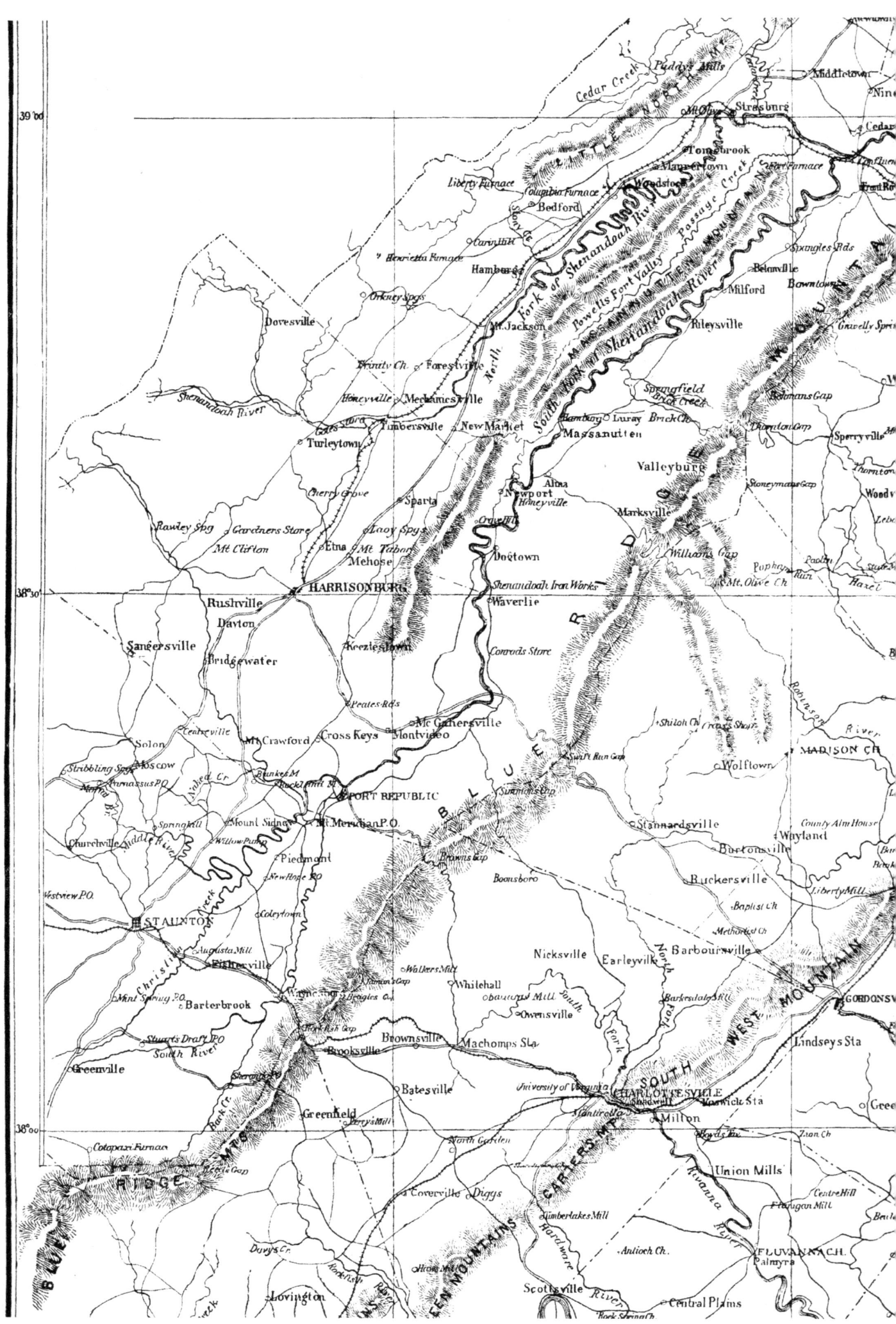

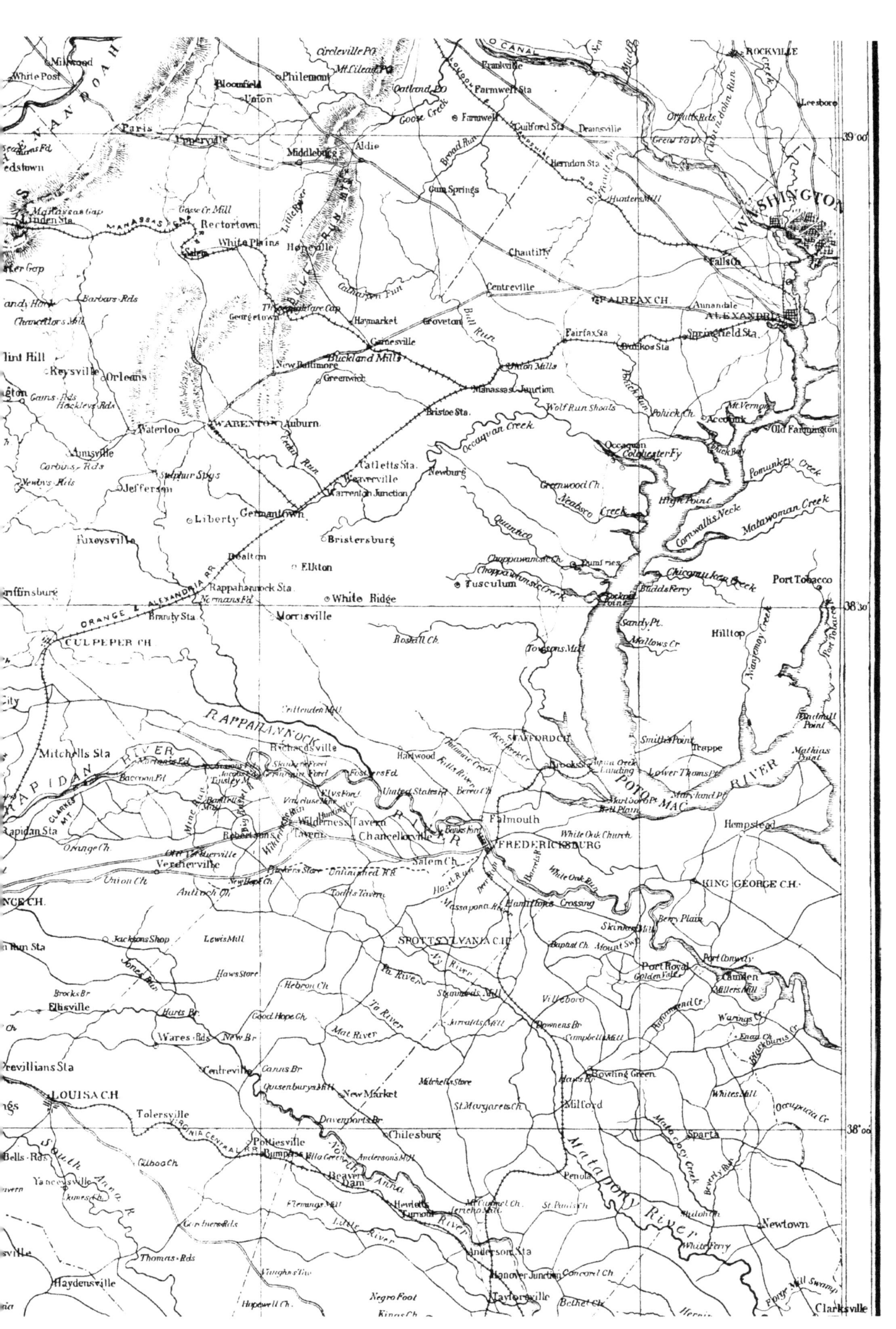

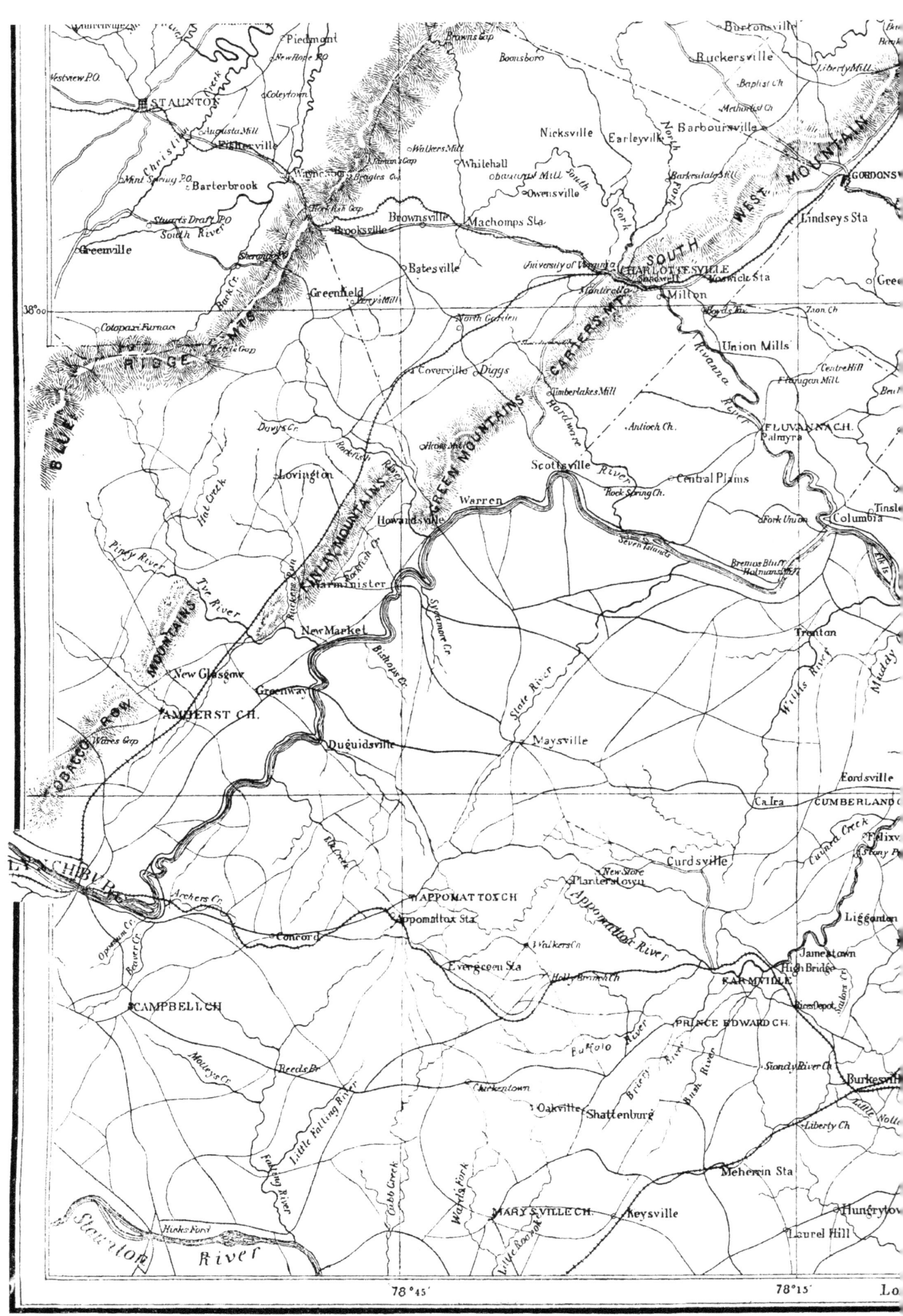

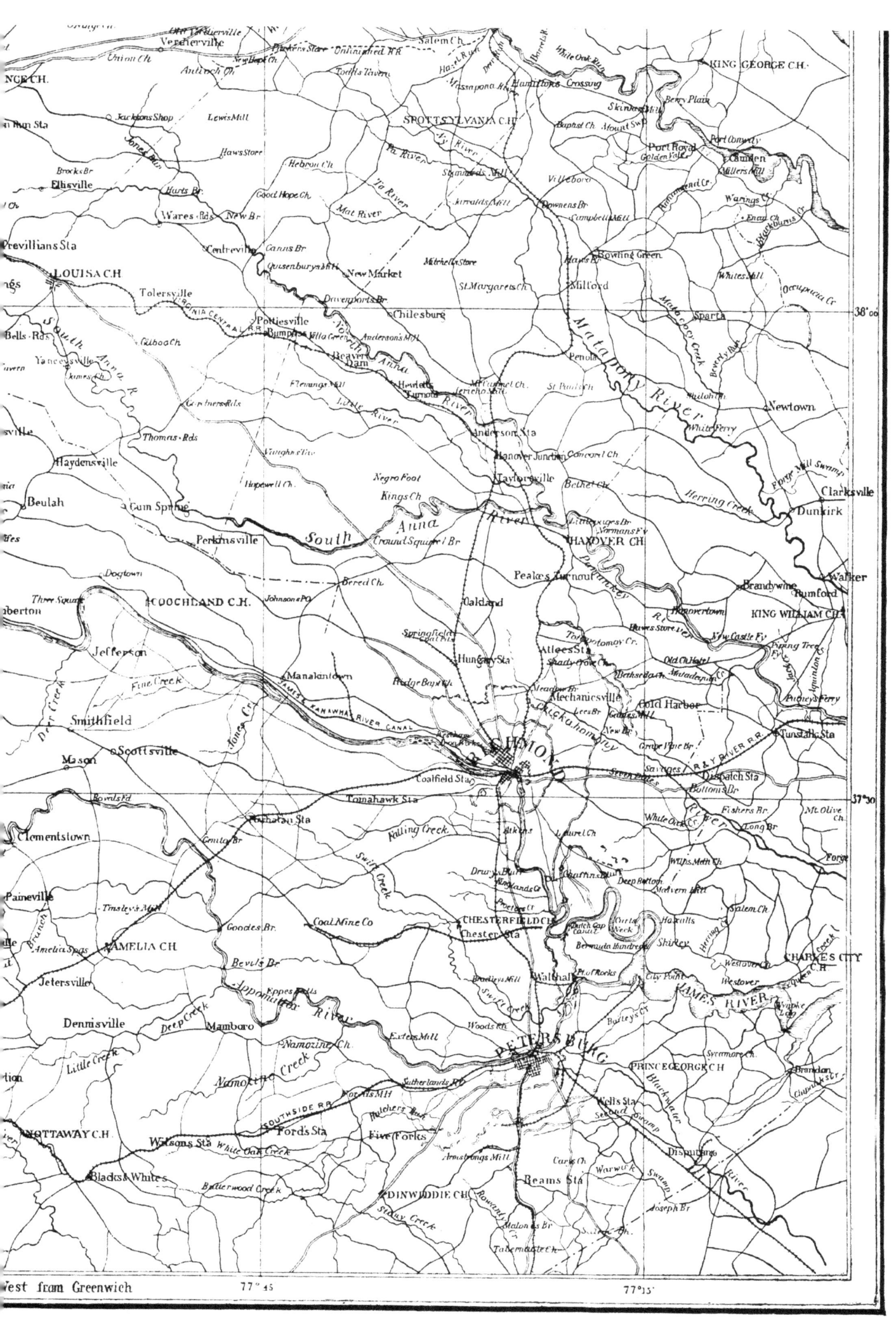

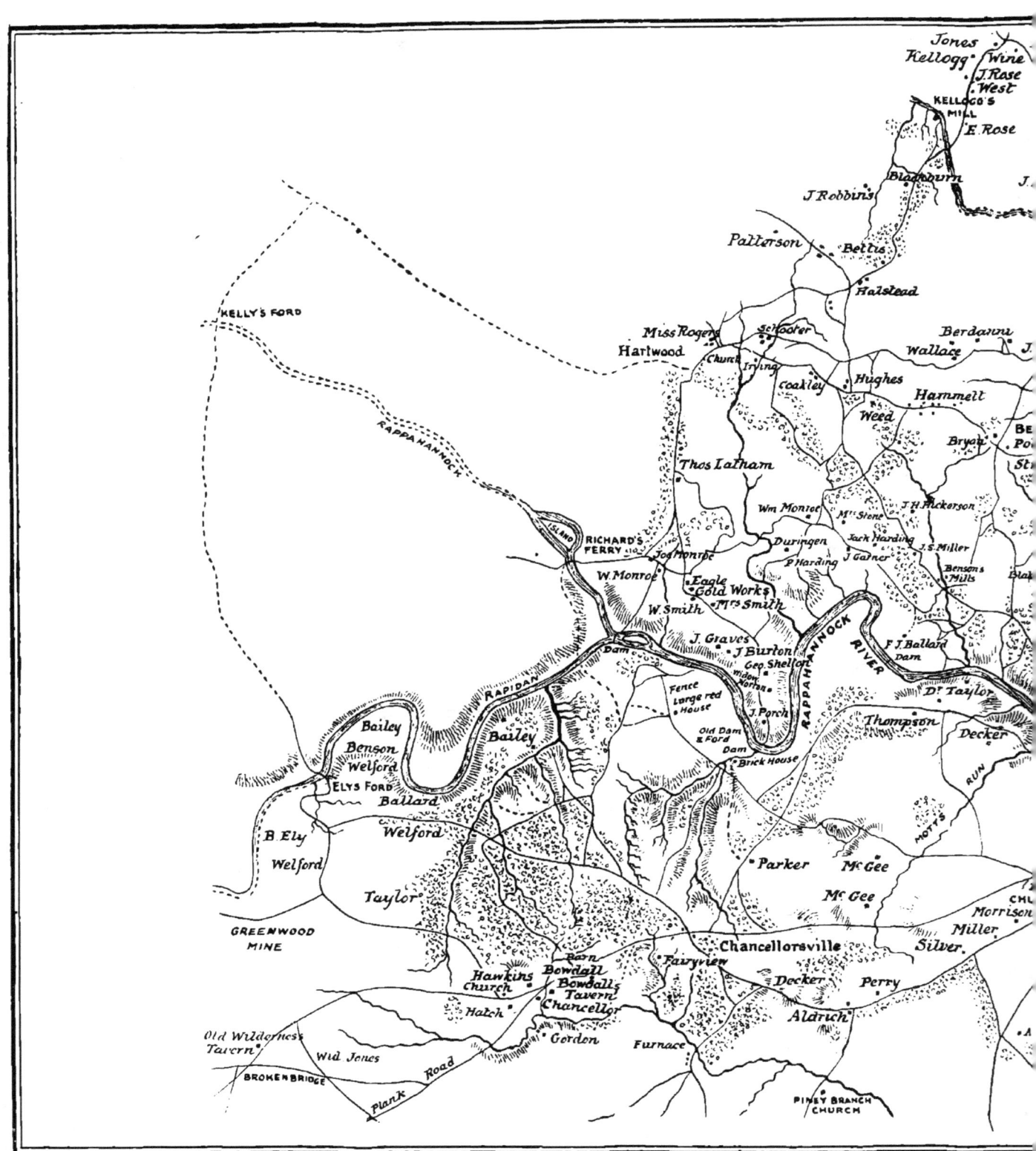

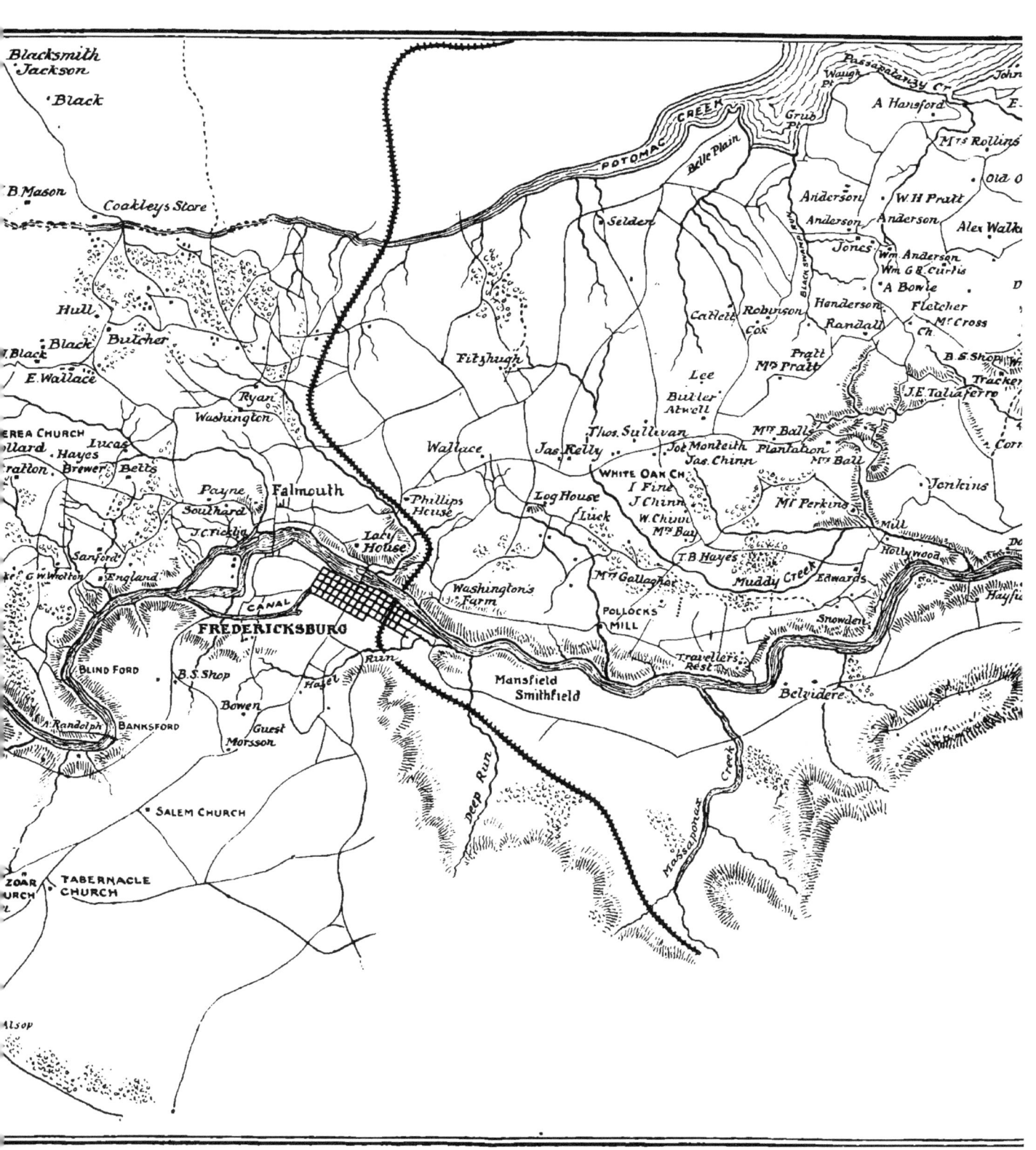

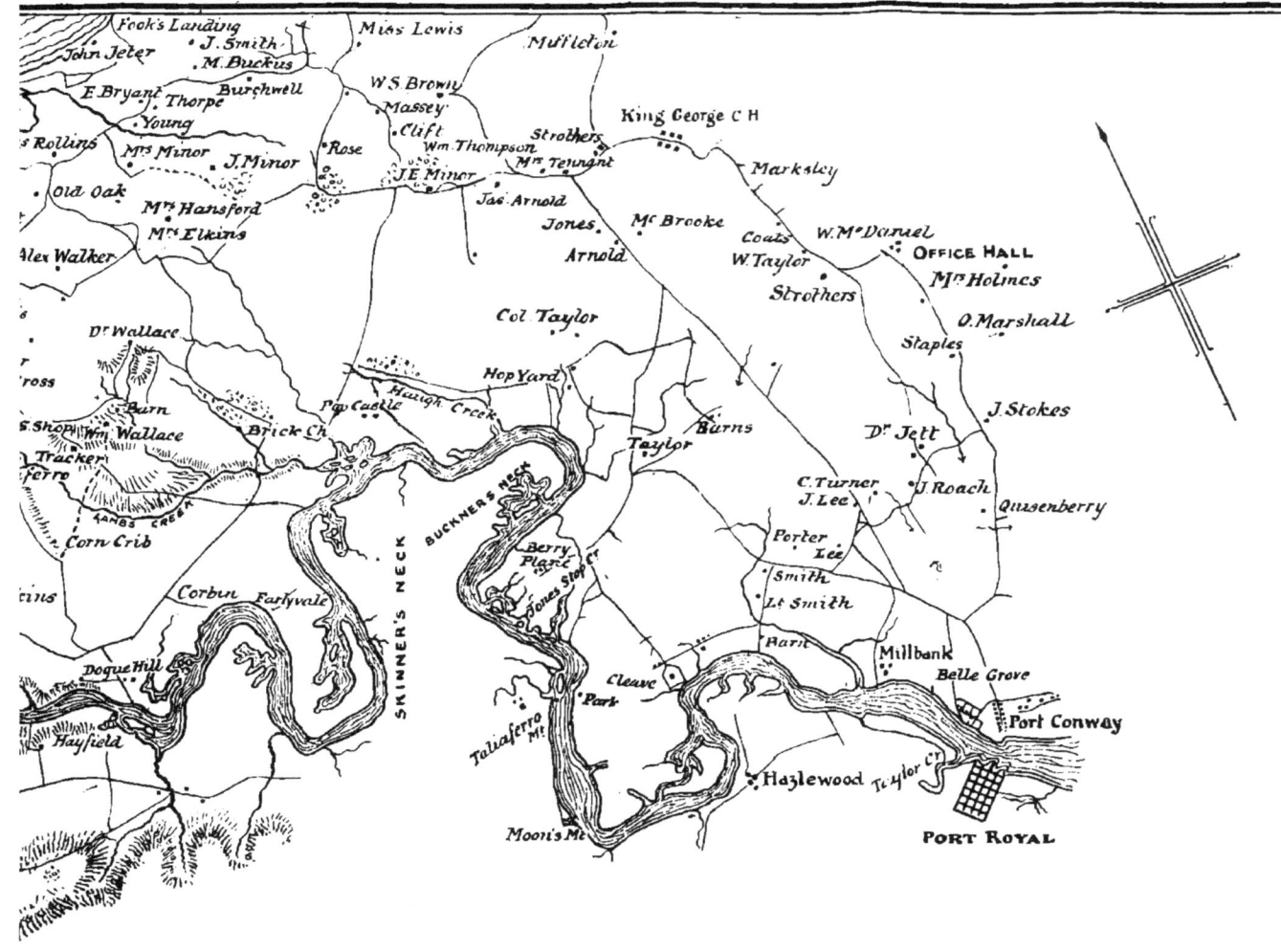

MAP
OF THE
RAPPAHANNOCK RIVER
FROM
PORT ROYAL TO RICHARDS' FERRY.

Scale of Miles

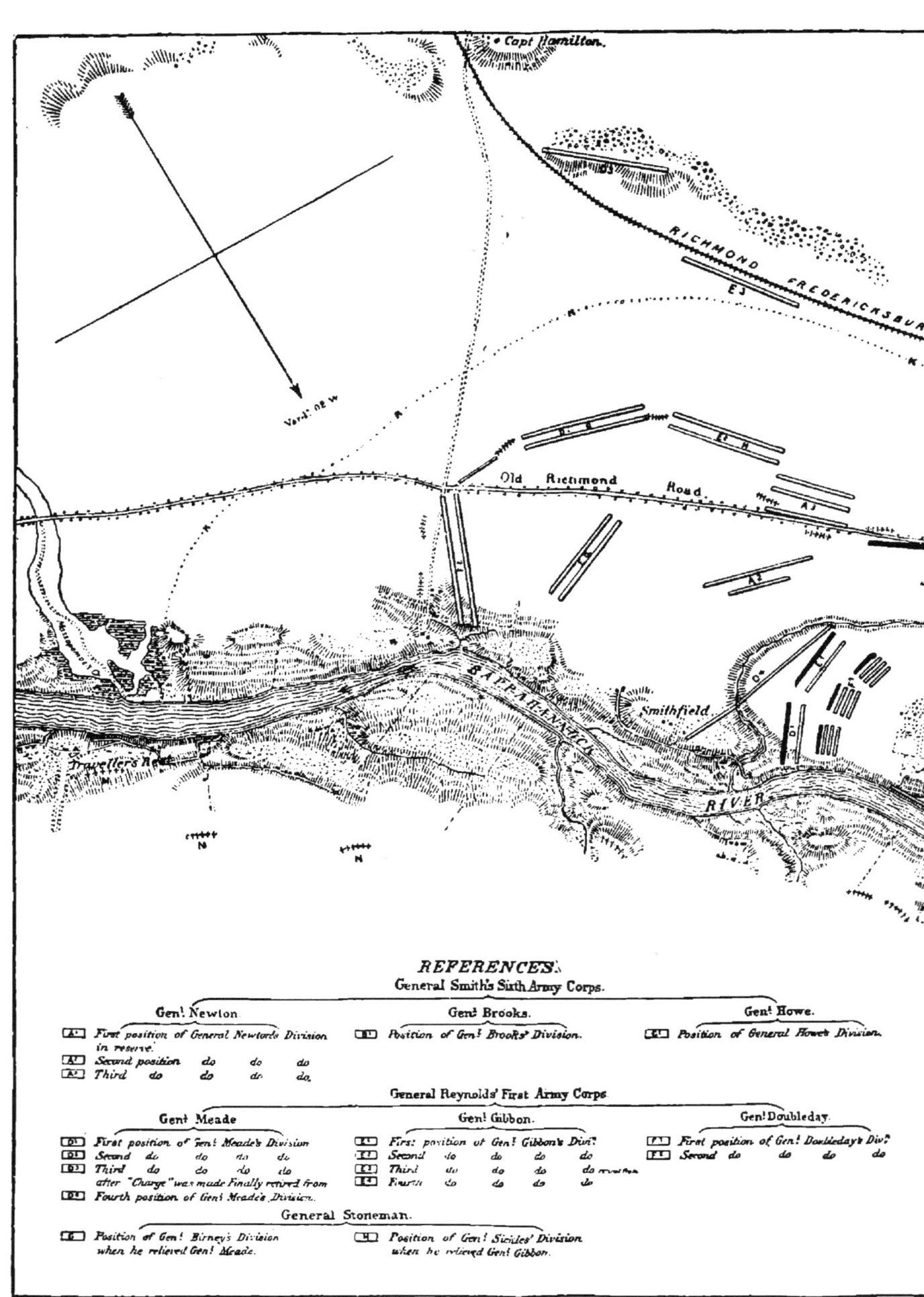

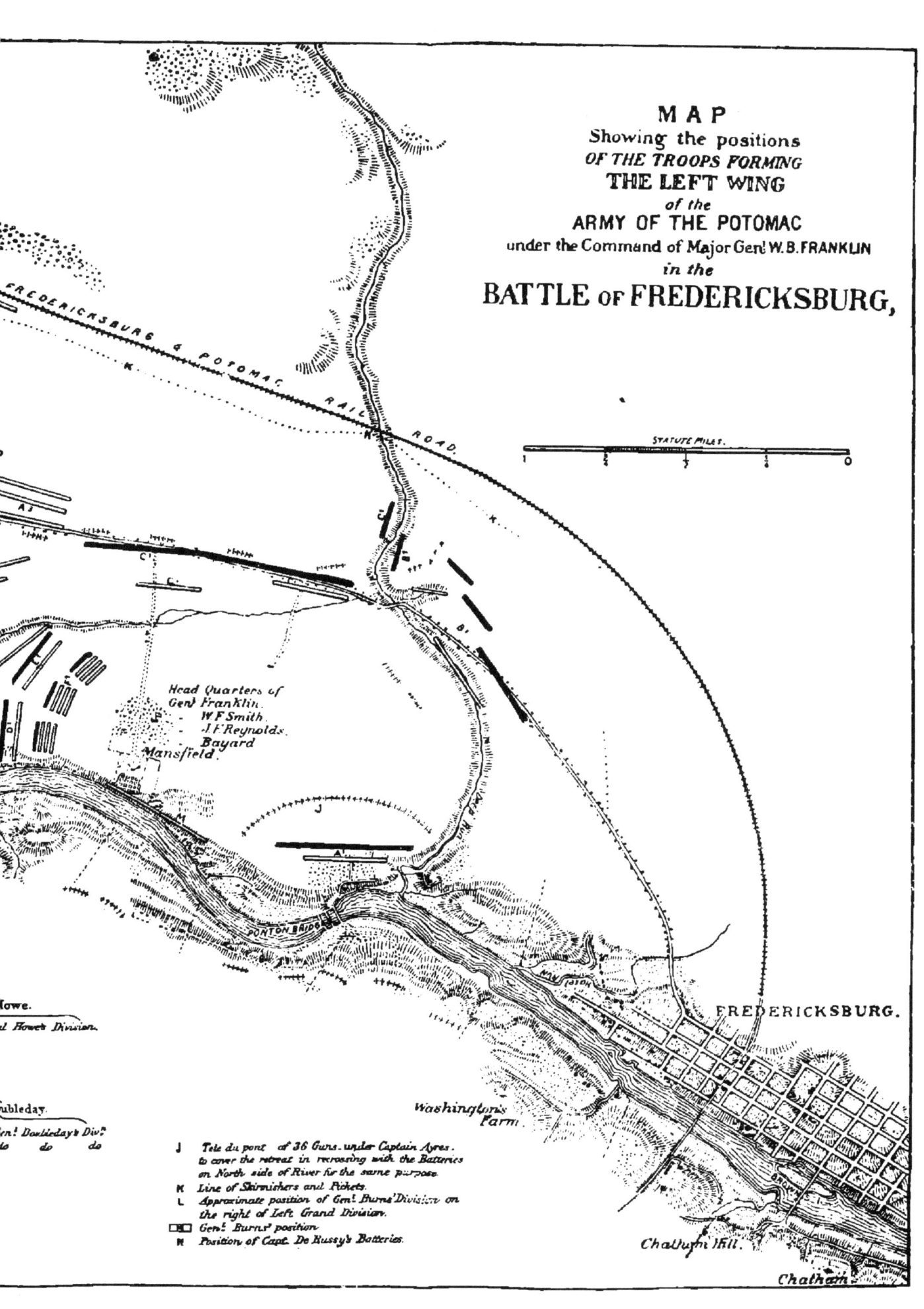

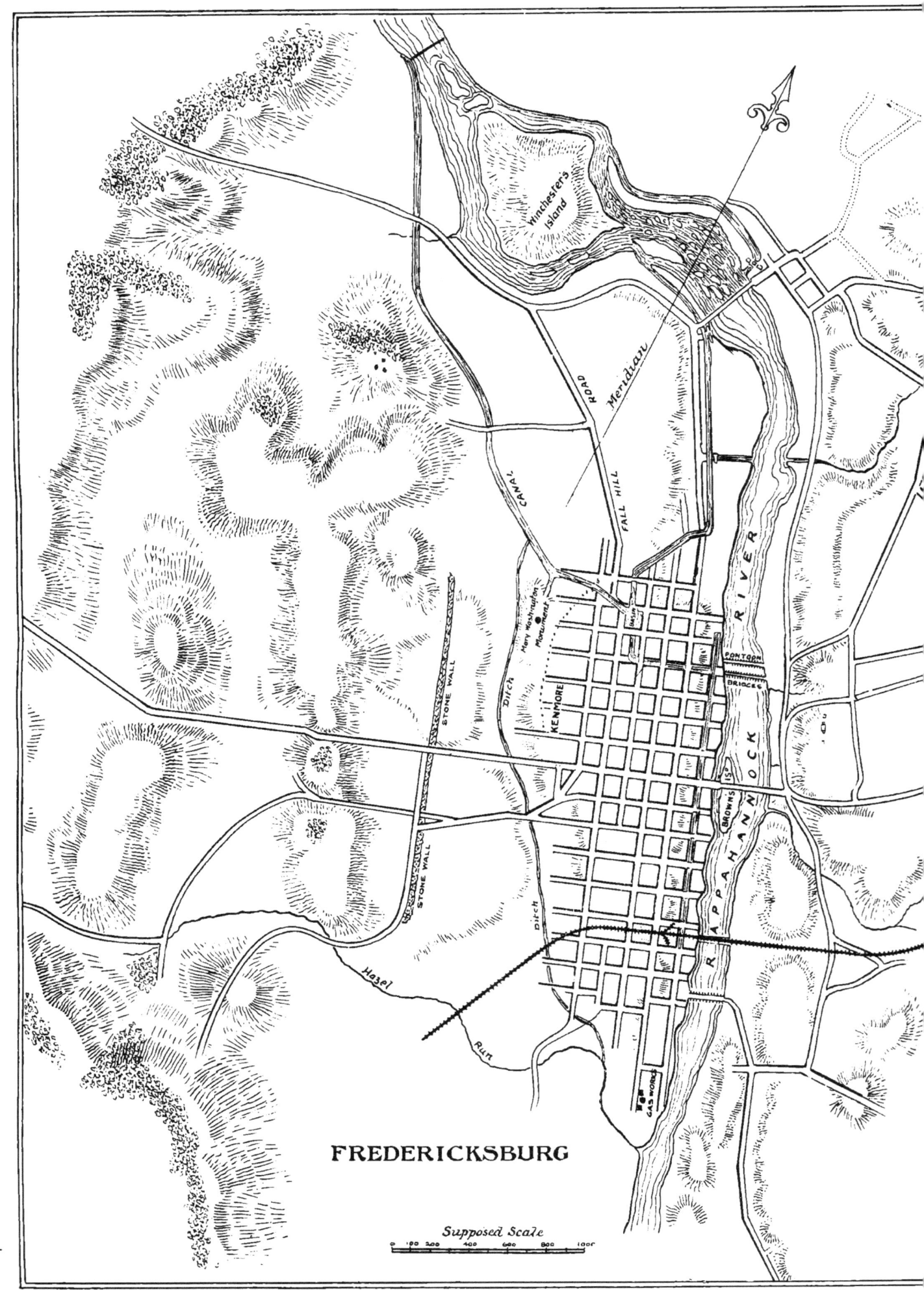

www.ingramcontent.com/pod-product-compliance
Lightning Source LLC
Chambersburg PA
CBHW081518160426
43193CB00015B/2728